ONE RIGHTEOUS MAN

ONE RIGHTEOUS MAN

SAMUEL BATTLE AND THE SHATTERING
OF THE COLOR LINE IN NEW YORK

ARTHUR BROWNE

BEACON PRESS
BOSTON

BEACON PRESS
Boston, Massachusetts
www.beacon.org

Beacon Press books
are published under the auspices of
the Unitarian Universalist Association of Congregations.

18 17 16 15   8 7 6 5 4 3 2 1

This book is printed on acid-free paper that meets the uncoated paper
ANSI/NISO specifications for permanence as revised in 1992.

Text design and composition by Kim Arney

Library of Congress Cataloging-in-Publication Data
Browne, Arthur.
One righteous man : Samuel Battle and the shattering
of the color line in New York / Arthur Browne.
pages cm
Includes bibliographical references and index.
ISBN 978-0-8070-1260-4 (hardcover : alk. paper)
ISBN 978-0-8070-1261-1 (ebook)
1. Battle, Samuel J., 1883-1966. 2. African American
police—New York (State)—New York—Biography. 3. Police—
New York (State)—New York—Biography. 4. New York (N.Y.)
Police Department—Biography. 5. New York (N.Y.)—
Race relations. I. Title.
HV7911.B38B76 2015
363.2092—dc23
[B]
2014043794

CONTENTS

THE HEART OF ONE RIGHTEOUS MAN

AN EARLY READER of this portrait of Samuel Jesse Battle harkened back to the Old Testament, verse three of Psalm 106: "Blessed are they who observe justice, who do righteousness at all times!" The connection was fitting. Battle's enormous courage, seemingly limitless charity, and unfailing insistence on dignity far exceeded his human flaws. He would not be told no when no was unjust. Expecting equal treatment—and occasionally paying dearly for his good faith—he persevered to prevail over some of New York's most closely guarded racial barriers.

The moral bearing that propelled Battle's victories shines most vividly through his own words. In 1949, he hired Langston Hughes to write his autobiography, spent hours speaking with the renowned Harlem Renaissance poet, and provided him with handwritten recollections. The result was a never-published, eighty-thousand-word book titled *Battle of Harlem*. One copy of the manuscript resides among Hughes's papers at Yale University's Beinecke Rare Book and Manuscript Library. Battle's grandson Tony Cherot has custody of a second copy. The two are not identical. After publishers showed no interest, Battle worked with a new partner in hope of making the book more marketable. He also secured a foreword by former First Lady Eleanor Roosevelt.

All to no avail.

Relying on Cherot's copy of the revised manuscript, I set out to bring Battle to life in contexts that stretched from the post–Civil War South through turn-of-the-century New York, through his fight to join the New York Police Department, through the Roaring Twenties and Prohibition, through the glorious rise and tragic fall of Harlem, through the Great Depression and two world wars. From his rambunctious boyhood in 1880s rural North Carolina to his death in Harlem in 1966, Battle was so engaged in his times that his journey illuminates the sagas of the United States and its largest city as oppressively experienced by African American citizens.

To the extent that I have succeeded in capturing the man and his eras, I owe a debt of gratitude to scholars and authors who documented the country's social, cultural, political, economic, sporting, and military evolutions. As but two examples, Gilbert Osofsky's *Harlem: The Making of a Ghetto* was invaluable to understanding how the forces of racial hatred and money shaped the capital of black America, while Jervis Anderson's *This Was Harlem* tells of the people who, against all odds, built a vibrant society there. True to form, the New York Public Library and its Schomburg Center for Research in Black Culture came through as repositories of documents, histories, biographies, journals, and out-of-print memoirs that bolstered Battle's reminiscences. Then there was the *New York Age*, whose crusading zeal and depth of coverage place the weekly in the ranks of America's finest newspapers. Although little remembered even in New York, the *Age*'s seven decades of journalism are foundational to understanding black America from the end of the nineteenth century to the middle of the twentieth.

Arnold Rampersad's monumental two-volume *The Life of Langston Hughes* indispensably illuminated the man, the artist, and his times. Similarly, Cherot's boyhood memories serve as the basis for descriptions of Battle's life in retirement, including his relationship with Hughes.

Battle's own words remain the heart of the matter. They are the wellspring of countless facts, because he turned out to have possessed an astonishingly good memory. As captured by Hughes, his voice breathes personal vitality into passages ranging from brief quotations to sections several hundred words long. I have drawn the vast

majority of these materials from the revised *Battle of Harlem* manuscript (editing lightly for sense or brevity) and present them without
endnote references.

Battle memorialized his life in two additional places: in a 1960
interview with Columbia University's Oral History Collection and in
the written notes he prepared for Hughes. I marked excerpts of these
with references to endnotes.

Words left behind by the remarkable Wesley Augustus Williams
are similarly treated. Inspired by Battle, Williams waged the struggle
to integrate the New York City Fire Department. In retirement, he
recounted his experiences in numerous speeches and in an extended
interview given to the author of a master's thesis. Typescripts of the
speeches and the thesis reside at the Schomburg Center and are the
collective basis for a narrative that intertwines with Battle's.

Reared to be a God-fearing Christian, Battle lived by a simple
moral code. He applied the Golden Rule to others and demanded it
in return, with equally unflagging bravery and optimism, even under
the hardest circumstances. This is one more way of expressing the
thought called from the psalm by my early reader, my friend, the estimable Vince Cosgrove. For Battle was indeed a man who observed
justice and who demonstrated the power that can beat in the heart
of one righteous man.

CHAPTER ONE

QUEST

The arc of the moral universe is long, but it bends towards justice.
—THE REVEREND MARTIN LUTHER KING JR., 1967

WHEN HE SPOKE OF ELEANOR ROOSEVELT, Samuel Jesse Battle often told a story about a glass of water. It was a glass of ice water, poured by the First Lady of the United States. The year was 1943. America was at war against a regime built on racial and religious supremacy, yet America enforced white superiority at home. And here was Mrs. Roosevelt, in Harlem, capital of black America, on stage in a jammed assembly hall. The air grew stifling. A heavyset woman of great dignity was speaking. The heat appeared to be getting the better of her. Mrs. Roosevelt walked to a pitcher of cold water, brought a glassful to the podium, and returned to her seat, her courtesy toward a woman who was "as black as a shoe" indelibly impressing Battle as a symbol of hope.

Now he gathers that memory and many others because one of America's best writers is coming so that they can tell the story of how the son of freed slaves had triumphed in New York, triumphed over New York. He remembers the tour guides who brought people to gawk at the "colored policeman" as if he were a zoo animal. He remembers the death threats and the swinging nightsticks. He remembers the hot night he saved a fallen white officer from a black mob.

After two world wars and the Great Depression, the twentieth century is at its halfway mark. So many of those who had been there are gone. So much is being forgotten. That will change with this book. He walks down the back stairway of the great old town-house, carrying a pad of paper on which he has outlined the story in penciled longhand.

Samuel Battle's step is firm. He is six feet two and 260 pounds, fuller in girth than when he had been in boxing trim but still powerful at the age of sixty-six. No wrinkles etch his deep brown skin; no gray flecks appear in his closely cropped hair. Somewhere along the way he has acquired reading glasses. But nothing else has gone wrong. He proudly attributes his physical condition to clean, moral living.

Florence is in the kitchen with fresh produce. She shops downtown because the markets in Harlem have few fruits and vegetables. It is an hour's subway ride, but she insists on the trip because she keeps the house just so. Home had been Florence's domain from the start. Forty-five years of marriage—Battle smiles to think of her, a sixteen-year-old girl, taking in marriage a young man making his way as a redcap luggage porter at the old Grand Central Depot. He would tell all about the tough, good days of 1905.

Battle studies his wife, noting the personal qualities that are important to the story. She is fair-skinned. She is particular about her appearance, especially her choice of clothing. Her hair is long, black, and straight. She wears this telltale of Cherokee blood in a bun. At the moment, she is getting things right for the famous Langston Hughes, and she is none too pleased by the sound of thumping feet. It's the boy, Tony, their grandson, running, always running. Florence calls up the stairs. The house is not a playground, she says. Take your energy outside, she says.

Battle slips into his study. The walls are crowded with book-shelves. Most of the volumes are histories; in fiction, Hawthorne is still a favorite. Not bad for someone who finished only elementary school, Battle thinks. He places the pad on a desk, the paper listing his milestones: first black cop, first black sergeant, first black lieu-tenant in the New York Police Department.

To get the story right, he would have to tell about all the hard fights, and about all the entertainers, clergymen, journalists, doctors, boxers, athletes, artists, gangsters, and politicians he had known. Many of them had been "firsts" in the way that he had been first.

Through the long era when segregation was not only legal but the norm, when no US president would support even antilynching legislation, when white domination was enforced with unrelenting violence, Battle had lived on the frontier of the American black experience. The men and women of his memory had also blazed trails. Collectively, they had formed the backbone of an American civil rights movement well before America discovered that America had a civil rights movement, well before America recognized that extraordinary men and women were indomitably at work bending the long, moral arc.

Wild and wooly New York would also be a big part of the story. Battle thinks that Hughes will be just the man to tell about the bare-knuckled city because Hughes had known Harlem in its finest glory and because Hughes too had been a path breaker. He seemed to have written about everything there was to write about, but nothing more so than about the lives of black Americans. So, for the considerable sum of $1,500, Battle has hired the poet, playwright, essayist, and novelist to tell the story he wants told.

Young voices bring Battle back from rummaging through history to thinking about the future that was upstairs in his grandchildren: nine-year-old Tony, full name Thornton Cherot, and his sister Yvonne, who was twelve. As he treasured his own country boyhood in the South, he especially values Tony's exuberance on West 138th, a street where kids can play. And Tony plays and plays and plays, stickball, stoopball, catch, and any other game conjured by the imaginations on the block. All the scamps come to the townhouse because Tony and Yvonne have a television that shows *Howdy Doody* in fuzzy black-and-white.

On Friday nights, Tony watches the prize fights with Battle, who instructs the boy in the finer points of boxing and is ready anytime to talk about the Brooklyn Dodgers' box scores. The Dodgers are Tony's team—not the Giants, not the Yankees—because the Dodgers have Jackie Robinson. In front of America, Robinson is answering with grace and superior play the fans and players who would keep him off the field.

Better than anyone, Battle understands, and he wants Tony to understand, too. That's one more reason why he wants his story told. One day, Battle feels proud to know, Tony would look back in awe that his grandfather had made him witness to the creation of the autobiography of Samuel J. Battle as told to Langston Hughes.

It is a short walk for Hughes from his apartment on West 127th to the townhouse on West 138th. Dressed with rumpled style, in a fashion that is casual but hardly careless, his slacks, shirt, and jacket bespeaking both informality and thought, as he comes up the front steps Hughes looks the part of a writer or intellectual. He greets Battle and Florence with easy-smiling courtesy. Battle hands Hughes the lined pad. The heading reads, "My Loving Christian Parents," and the words "God blessed me from birth."[1] Then Battle and Hughes set to work; one reminiscing, the other drawing out the story of how Battle and his contemporaries bent the arc of the universe toward justice.

YOUNG SAM BATTLE had always dreamed of New York. Visions of the big city gripped his mind as he crossed from boyhood into adolescence. He would imagine mighty buildings while he scrubbed the pine board floors of his family's home. He would look at the Atlantic & North Carolina Railroad that came through town, New Bern, North Carolina, and try to see the faraway trains that carried crowds of people on tracks overhead. He would pass among the frame houses allotted to blacks, and he would ache for more than a life that led to a cemetery for dark-skinned people.

Two shining figures had brought the yearning. William and Killis Delamar visited from the North—and not just from the North, but from big, cosmopolitan Brooklyn, which was just across the river from even bigger New York. They traveled down the coast by steamship and train to renew family ties. Battle knew them as his mother Anne's brothers, although William and Killis were likely her cousins. Their arrival in New Bern generated excitement. As of yet, in the 1890s, relatively few Southern blacks had joined America's Great Migration, and a still smaller number had made as good as the Delamars had. They operated horse-drawn trucking businesses, and they seemed to Battle to have conquered the world. He would remember them as proud, good-looking men, who owned "several enormous vans and a number of big beautiful horses" and served "the best families in Brooklyn." He found William's cutaway coat particularly impressive.

Over Anne's heaping meals, the Delamars told of wonders that were a ship's sail away. They had seen the Brooklyn Bridge and sky-scrapers with elevators and streets with electric lights. To Battle, New York became "the center of all the glory, all the wealth, and all the freedom of the world," as poet and novelist Paul Dunbar would describe the magnetism that drew Southern blacks to the city.[2] A half-century later, Battle would tell Hughes, "When I first saw those wonderful relatives of my mother's, I began to long for the day when I might go north to call on them, and to live as they did."

He was, perhaps, fourteen years old. He had left school in the eighth grade rather than take a whipping from a teacher for beating up a classmate. He was so "given to fighting" that neighborhood boys called him "Bully," while prominent black men knew him as a thief for filching their money. Shining shoes and working in the fields were his main sources of legitimate income. And, hard as it would be to bid farewell to his father, Thomas, and his mother, Anne, he was determined to leave the teeming, love-filled little house at 8 Primrose Street, the home of his birth on January 16, 1883, for the North.

OLD AUNT SUSAN had predicted that the baby would arrive by Christmas, like a laughing and crying doll for thirteen-year-old Nannie, and then the weeks had passed. When finally nature took course, Old Aunt Susan laid the baby, round and brown and wet with the residue of birth, at his mother's side. He was his father's twenty-second child and his mother's eleventh. Word spread that he weighed sixteen-and-a-half pounds. The neighbors were sure that they had witnessed the biggest infant ever delivered thereabouts, and Battle carried the fact through life as inspiration. "As a result, I guess I've always wanted to be large, and I have been large," he told an interviewer, looking back after almost seven decades.[3]

By the time Battle reached school age, Anne had given birth to four more children, nursing the babies along with the infants of others.

"I have seen her with a white child at one breast and a black child at the other," he told Hughes. "White people called her 'Sis Annie.' Whenever anyone in the community was sick, hot broth and kindnesses went from her to them."

He recorded that his mother "had no unpleasant memories of slavery so she never spoke with bitterness of the past." He was sure that she was "the best cook in all the world." He loved the feel of her silken hair and "would sit and feast my eyes and soul on her angel face."

Endearingly, Battle would tell Hughes and Hughes would channel Battle's memories to write that Anne began the day with hymns:

Rock of ages, cleft for me
Let me hide myself in thee.

Sometimes with the neighbors joining in from yard to yard—for mother was always up at dawn drinking her cup of black coffee, feeding her children, then early to her washing, boiling the clothes in a big three-pronged iron pot over a wood fire. By sun-up the wash was ready for the line and as she hung the clothes out to dry she sang:

Swing low, sweet chariot.
Coming for to carry me home!

I can see her now, white clothes billowing in the wind as her song rose in the morning air.

My mother received all the children of my father's former marriages as her own. All of these children loved my mother and thought of her as an angel. She cooked and washed for all of us, dosed young and old with castor oil and asafetida when we were ill, gave us sassafras tea to thin our blood in the spring, made biscuits for everybody on Sunday mornings, and prayed for each of us every night by name—Tom and James, Nannie and William, Abigail, John Edward, Mary Elizabeth, Sophia, Lillian, Louise and me. Her prayers are with me, still in my heart.

For so many children there was almost continuous washing and ironing. The big wooden washtubs with staved handles served for both babies and clothes, and the iron pot in the back yard was almost always steaming. All day long my mother was busy; she made her own soap and potash, tended the garden, cleaned and cooked. When I could, I would help her. I did not mind chopping wood for

mother's wash pot or for the big fireplaces which we had throughout the house, masoned by my father. In those fireplaces on autumn
nights we youngsters roasted chestnuts or sweet potatoes while some
studied by firelight. In the winter in the kitchen we held molasses
taffy pulls.

Battle referred to Thomas as "the old man," no doubt because
Thomas was approaching sixty and Anne was nearing forty as Battle reached school age. Thomas never drank or used foul language,
although "on very special occasions he might inhale a cigar." He
would also engage in child-pleasing play.

"At night when he was sitting quietly in his chair, sometimes he
would offer us children two cents for every louse we could find in his
hair," Battle told Hughes. "Of course, we could never find any lice.
Much to the amusement of my mother, he would go to sleep as we
searched through his hair."

Of more lasting significance, Thomas instilled discipline and directed his children out into the world. He infused "a strictly Christian upbringing" enforced by corporal punishment. Battle's father
administered "whippings" as he felt necessary. Anne would slip away
rather than witness the pain. Only once could Battle remember her
laying a hand on him. She struck him "when I was still quite small,"
Battle said, "during a New Year's Eve 'watch-meeting' at St. Peter's
AME Zion Church when the building was rocking with hymns, spir-
ituals and the shouting." He recalled:

At midnight it reached its peak of prayer and song. There had been
many testimonials, rejoicing, and much thanksgiving that the Lord
had carried us all safely through the old year. Suddenly the spirit
entered into my mother and she began to shout. Another woman
nearby began to shout, too.

In her excitement she started to pound her fists on my mother's
shoulders. I thought this intended to hurt my mother, so I leaped on
a bench and started pummeling the woman for all I was worth. My
mother suddenly slapped me, shook me and sat me down on the
bench again. Then, she resumed her shouting.

Early on, Battle proved blessed with intellectual and emotional intelligence. He astutely observed the world and easily mastered reading, writing, and arithmetic, not that he was much interested. Adventurousness propelled him instead to roam the streets, fields, and riverbanks, a head taller and beefier than his peers, blessed with strength and athleticism, and unencumbered by the behavioral expectations of bondage. As a member of his family's first postslavery generation, Battle was freer to be a boy, not a *boy*. He recounted for Hughes, and Hughes sketched, an episode that brought to life the racial strictures of the day and gave a first glimpse at the insistence on dignity that was bred into Battle's spirit.

I passed the home of a prominent white family, the Bryans. On the sidewalk, one of the Bryan boys was playing marbles with others, so I stopped. I was about sure that I could beat any of them and said, "I'd like to shoot marbles. I can beat any of you playing, I'll bet."

I stooped down to play, and they said to me, "We don't want no niggers here." Mr. Bryan's son said that. "We don't want no niggers in here." As he did, I slapped him with my right hand on the side of the face—the left side of his face with my right hand.

The boy screamed because I had a powerful hand—I was a big, strong, husky fellow. There were five or six white boys. The rest of them were afraid to even tackle me. His mother ran out. His mother said, "What is your name, boy? We'll have you arrested." I said, "My name is John Brown," and I walked away.

The Bryan boy's father was a lawyer. It happened that there really was a colored boy in town named John Brown, so the Bryans got a warrant out for him. When the police found him, young Bryan knew Brown was not the lad who had struck him. Brown was practically a runt. It did not take them long to discover that it was Tom Battle's son who had wanted to fight young Bryan.

Since my father was well known to the white people of the town and respected by all of them as a good workman, the warrant was promptly withdrawn. Instead, Mr. Bryan sent word to my father to come to see him and bring me along. We went to the Bryan's back door.

Young Bryan still bore the marks of my hand. When my father saw the youngster's face and learned what I had done—I had struck a white boy—my father offered to let Mr. Bryan or his son whip me.

Before either of them could answer, I said to my father, "I will die first! I will let you whip me, but not anyone else on earth."

No one said a word. So I repeated, "You can whip me, but nobody else."

Seeing that I meant what I said, my father whipped me himself in front of the white boy and his father. I was flogged severely there in the yard. This the white family accepted as satisfactory. I took my father's punishment and did not shed a tear. Nothing in the world could have made me cry. On the way home my father counseled me about butting in where I was not wanted, and that night he prayed that I might learn to get along in this world of Negroes and whites.

WHEN THOMAS WOULD tell his story, he would start with the American Revolution. He believed that his grandfather had fought as a slave shouldering a rifle at the side of a young master in the war that brought forth the new nation. Thomas handed down the lore as a badge of honor that stood as an irrefutable claim to citizenship and spoke of a bloodline whose enduring characteristic was to stand as upright as a person could stand.[4]

New Bern was prosperous as the war for independence had approached. Located at the confluence of the Trent and Neuse rivers, its harbor offered easy access to Pimlico Sound and then the Atlantic. A maritime industry exported goods and brought imports of clothing, shoes, hardware, rum, salt, and other mercantile necessities, including slaves.

Well-to-do whites enjoyed horse-drawn chaises; poor whites earned barely enough to survive. Slaves worked for food, clothing, and shelter. But, comprising roughly a third of the population, blacks had some latitude to live independently. They gathered for recreation and friendship and patronized shops that illicitly catered to them, including with the sale of liquor.

New Bern served as a base for disrupting enemy commerce during the war. With American independence—and ratification of a

Constitution that pointedly failed to outlaw human bondage—came prosperity. Merchants, ship owners, and planters built handsome townhouses and Georgian homes. Eventually, a stately courthouse, complete with a tower for hangings, became a government center.[5]

For a US Census, Thomas reported the year of his birth as 1829. Antislavery agitation was then on the rise. Writing safely in Boston that year, a freed North Carolina slave by the name of David Walker published a pamphlet that came to be known as his *Appeal*. There, he declared, "I tell you Americans! that unless you speedily alter your course you and your country are gone!!!!!" And in neighboring Virginia, Nat Turner would soon lead a slave insurrection that killed fifty-five white men, women, and children.[6]

With fear of bloodshed running rampant, North Carolina's governing institutions clamped the vise even more tightly on bondage. The state supreme court upheld an owner's right to assault a slave—even to shoot and wound a slave—free from penalty, with a chilling turn of phrase: "The power of the master must be absolute to render the submission of the slave perfect."[7]

New laws stripped free blacks of the right to vote, preach in public, carry a weapon without a permit, buy or sell alcohol, or attend public school. The New Bern town commissioners restricted the number of slaves who could offer services for hire to whites. Those engaged in such employment were required to wear badges. All citizens were barred from teaching slaves to read or write.

Regardless, Thomas became devoted to book learning. Even more, while still a slave, he earned a living by laying brick and smoothing plaster for white townsfolk. He also gravitated to the unifying force of religion. Self-educated, he earned the status of minister in the African American Methodist Episcopal Zion Church, a storied denomination that came to be known as the "Freedom Church" in that its members included the giants of early black activism, Frederick Douglass, Sojourner Truth, and Harriet Tubman.

Thomas took on the roles of preacher and Sunday school teacher. By saving his masonry income, eventually, and remarkably, he purchased emancipation. Over the years, he supported relationships with two women, described by Battle as his father's first two wives, and sired with them eleven of his eventual twenty-six children. Why he parted from the women, whether due to death or disagreement or through forced separation, has slipped into the mists.

At the outbreak of the Civil War, at the age of thirty-two, Thomas stood witness to the end of a world. Young whites went off to fight distant battles and New Bern fell to Union troops. Thomas saw whites flee before the assault, and he saw blacks flock to New Bern to escape marauding Confederates. Where the town had counted fewer than three thousand blacks before the war, he saw the number approach fifteen thousand at the conflict's end. And he saw death and fear as yellow fever took at least nine hundred lives.[8]

Still, New Bern stayed largely on the war's periphery, allowing Thomas to persevere as a tradesman and minister. In the only words of his that are known to be extant, he described for John Wesley Cromwell, author of *The Negro in American History*, an episode from his ministry that involved an eight-year-old boy who would grow up to be the Reverend Joseph C. Price, founder of Livingstone College and prominent advocate of black self-help. Thomas recalled:

It was in the year 1862 when I was superintendent of the Sunday School of St. Andrews Chapel that I was led by Providence on a bright Sunday morning to the church door. There I stood for several minutes and while standing there I saw a little black barefooted boy coming stepping along on the railroad track.

When he got opposite the church I halted him and invited him in the Sabbath School. He liked the services so well that he was constrained to come again. At last he joined the Sabbath School and became a punctual scholar.

From his stern, yet pleasant looks, his nice behavior and other virtuous elements that were maintained in him Sunday after Sunday he attracted my attention more than any other scholar. While other scholars would laugh at him because of his boldness of speech and his eagerness to answer the questions that were put forth.

One Sunday in the midst of these abuses which he received, I was compelled to lay my hands on his head and exclaim these words: "The day will come, my dear scholars, when this boy Price will shake

the whole civilized world, and some of you will be glad to get a
chance to black his boots."

Little did I think my prediction would come to pass so exact, but
so it did.[9]

Around the war's end, Thomas took a third wife who was more
girl than woman. Fifteen-year-old Anne Vashti Delamar was the
daughter of a slave mother and a white master. Anne's eyes were blue
and her skin was the color of ivory. Lustrous black hair fell below
her shoulders and completed the impression that she was as white
as any of the women who traveled New Bern's dirt streets in horse-
drawn jitneys.

With the passing of the war, Thomas and Anne shared the jubi-
lation and disorientation of freedom. He supported the family and
gained respect among whites and blacks alike; she tended to their
home. Across the racial divide, whites restarted life in the grand
houses and reasserted their belief in natural superiority. By 1870,
blacks comprised fully two-thirds of New Bern's population. No matter. They were put in their place, if need be at the end of a whip.

As one New Bernian told Whitelaw Reid, a Civil War correspondent who later became editor of the *New York Tribune*, "The
poor, shiftless creatures will never be able to support themselves in
freedom." Reid was left to conclude: "Nothing could overcome this
rooted idea, that the Negro was worthless, except under the lash."[10]

And the lash was officially enforced.

The state legislature passed the Black Code of 1866, a statute
that restricted freedom of movement and barred blacks from carrying unlicensed guns. Worse still, the white power structure responded
to enactment in 1868 of the Fourteenth Amendment, guaranteeing
equal rights to all, and ratification in 1870 of the Fifteenth Amendment, ensuring the right to vote, as if the expressions of the national
will were the decrees of a hostile power.

But Thomas and Anne also witnessed the rise of black churches
and social affairs, saw the federal Freedmen's Bureau open schools
for blacks, and eventually experienced the start of the black franchise. They weathered the good and the evil of the world, while at
home they built a family that was a monument to parental strength,

built on a belief in the goodness of the Lord and reverence for the American ideal.

AS BATTLE TURNED fifteen, Thomas and Anne asked one of his half-brothers to help rear their obstreperous son. James lived sixty miles away in Goldsboro. He had been a teacher and was working as a railway mail clerk, an elevated position for a Southern black. He took Battle in, promising to guide him through high school and instilling the even higher aspirations of going to college and law school. It wasn't to be. After James contracted pneumonia and died, Battle returned to New Bern, brokenhearted at this first death of a loved one and harboring the fantastic notions that not only could he get as fine an education as a white man but he could also become an attorney. He had seen black men of such prominence. They "came repeatedly to our home as if to a shrine" to seek his father's counsel. Many had secured advanced degrees. Never could Battle achieve that in New Bern or in North Carolina or in the South, and a flickering ambition to attain the standing of an educated man now merged with New York's pull.

The attraction was all the stronger because a tide of oppression swept the South as the twentieth century drew near. The US Supreme Court opened the floodgates in 1896 by upholding in *Plessy v. Ferguson* the constitutionality of providing separate and purportedly equal accommodations to blacks. In North Carolina, severe economic dislocations intensified the ruling's corrosive impacts. As plunging cotton prices drove white farmers toward poverty, Democrats flew the banner of white supremacy against a biracial Fusion movement of Republicans and Populists.

In 1898, Battle's hometown newspaper, the *New Bern Journal*, called for renouncing "negro supremacy, indecency, menace to property, destruction of social law and order."[11] An armed white paramilitary rode the countryside to make its Democratic and supremacist preferences plain. Dressed in crimson, they became known as the Red Shirts. After an election, word came from the state capital, Wilmington—like New Bern, a majority black city—that a white mob had deposed the municipal government, driven from town a black newspaper editor who had decried lynching, and killed as many as thirty blacks.

That same year, Battle witnessed the appearance in New Bern of men unlike any he had ever seen: young black men wearing the uniform of US soldiers and preparing for duty in the Spanish-American War. The army had deployed standing regiments, including the all-black Buffalo Soldiers, who had served on the western frontier and who would save Teddy Roosevelt's Rough Riders at the battle of Las Guásimas. When President William McKinley called for volunteers, a soon-to-be ousted North Carolina governor enabled African Americans to enlist in regiments attached to white militia units. On leave, many traveled for recreation to New Bern. To whites, they were arrogant armed men who personified a refusal to accept the lot assigned to blacks; to Battle, they embodied adventure. He dashed to the tracks to watch the soldiers go off by train into places that lived in his dreams.[12]

But he understood that he was not yet ready to follow them. To acquire some of the polish he admired in the Delamars, Battle went to work for Major Graham Davies, whose family lived on grounds large enough for a mansion and a second house. He tended the lawns, gardens, and shrubbery; pumped drinking water from a well; and brought soft water for the laundry from a rain cistern. Indoors, he emptied chamber pots and fanned away flies by pulling a cord that waved paper strips over the dining table.

The household staff included a cook, housemaid, and two coachmen, plus a Miss Dissoway, their demanding leader. Battle wrote letters for them, "as well as the letters for a neighboring white man's concubine who often visited." Eventually, Miss Dissoway allowed Battle to serve as one of the family's mealtime waiters.

"There I learned the proper way of laying a linen cloth and placing silver. As have so many other Negroes, from 'backing chairs' I learned how people of real culture and refinement behave, converse and live," Battle told Hughes, adding, "My period of work with this family of the Old South was a happy one and it was with some regret that I left them. At the age of sixteen, however, feeling myself a man, I decided to pull up stakes and head north to make my way in the world on my own."

There would be no stopping him, nor were Thomas and Anne inclined to thwart their son's ambitions. He had grown past six feet and was on his way to within a ham's weight of 240 pounds, a size that made him several inches taller and more than 50 pounds heavier than the average American male in 1900. He was fit for labor and, thanks to Thomas's tutelage, he had a tradesman's skilled hands. In matters of the mind, he was perfectly literate and had no problem with arithmetical computation. It stood to reason that someone could put Battle to use.

A sister, Nancy, had already headed north to Hartford, Connecticut. The family developed a plan. Battle and Anne would travel together to Brooklyn, where Anne would visit the Delamars. Battle would go on from there to link up with Nancy and make his start in Connecticut. When all was ready, Thomas spoke to his son in typically bracing fashion. Battle told Hughes: "The night before I left home my father, who had always prayed with us and for us, had a long special prayer with me alone. He said, 'Dear Lord, I am now laying my youngest son upon Thy altar.' He prayed that I would learn to curb my temper, quit fighting, and be a good Christian. Then from his knees he arose to give me his blessings and encouragement."

Then the morning of leave-taking arrived, as it would soon come for virtually every black Southern family through the mid-twentieth century, fathers, mothers, brothers, sisters, sons, and daughters atomizing to overcome what they could of the dictates of skin color. In moments that turned out to be the last in which he saw his father alive, Battle left behind the cool rivers and the open fields, the black washerwomen with baskets on their heads and the whites in high carriages, the hiss of hot dirt streets under the spray of a water wagon, and the sweetness of the drink Caleb Bradham had invented in his drugstore, Pepsi-Cola.[13]

Anne and Battle traveled by boat, a ticket on an Old Dominion steamship being less expensive than going by train. The Old Dominion's service to New York from Richmond and Norfolk, Virginia, was then becoming a primary transportation for early black migrants on the Eastern Seaboard. In 1898, the year before Battle and his mother made the voyage, one New York man commented, "Negroes are coming on every boat from southern waters." Another said, "Nobody knows how it happened but on every Old Dominion Steamship that docked there (were) from two to three hundred Negroes landed in New York."[14]

The route took Anne and Battle across Albemarle Sound to Elizabeth City, North Carolina, on a steamer and then by rail to Norfolk. They were a pair who would have drawn glances. Battle towered over his mother, his broad shoulders showing the results of fieldwork, masonry, and the sport of boxing, which had become a favorite. Skin tone distinguished the two as well. Battle's face and eyes were deep brown. By surface appearance, he seemed little related to a woman who had inherited fair skin and blue eyes from her father. In the strange calculus of race, his blood was at least one-quarter white, while hers was at least half Caucasian. Yet for legal, social, and economic purposes, they were equally and totally black—and equally covered by the Jim Crow strictures that greeted them on crossing into Virginia.

The harshness of Jim Crow was a revelation to Battle, because North Carolina was still a year away from introducing fully systematic repression. Battle told Hughes: "In Virginia I saw my first separate waiting rooms, marked WHITE and COLORED. We also experienced segregation on the Old Dominion Line's Norfolk-to-New-York boat. My mother was assigned to a filthy hole with a large number of other colored people."

He would not allow Anne to be so degraded: "It was a long overnight trip, almost twenty-four hours, as I took a part of my money to secure a stateroom for her. Once that was arranged, I spent the night there, too, and nobody bothered me."

FIRST HE SAW the Statue of Liberty—that inspiring monument to promises kept, towering rebuke for promises broken, at the mouth of New York Harbor—and then the full sweep of America's largest city appeared before Battle as the steamer rounded Manhattan's tip. Everything was bigger than Battle had ever seen. More than three hundred buildings stood nine or more stories tall as the invention of the elevator and development of steel skeletal construction allowed for the creation of real estate in the air.[15]

A golden dome sat atop the tower Joseph Pulitzer had built for his newspaper, the *New York World*. At a height of 309 feet, the gilded tip was meant to attract the eye, and it surely drew the look of a small-town Southern teenager with scant possessions. Surrounding Pulitzer's pride were the chest thumpings of America's nineteenth-century capitalist titans: John D. Rockefeller, oil; J. P. Morgan, finance; Andrew Carnegie, steel; James Buchanan Duke, tobacco; Henry Havemeyer, sugar; Jay Gould, railroads. These men had made Lower Manhattan into a landscape of seemingly limitless wealth. They competed and conspired, profited and profiteered, and then they went home to decorous townhouses or fabulous mansions. As recounted by the authors of *Gotham*, an encyclopedic history of New York up to the brink of the twentieth century: "But with outspending one's rivals the only definitive route to preeminence, a steady inflation in extravagance ensued as members of opposing cliques scrambled to convert Wall Street revenue into Fifth Avenue social standing. Dinner parties corkscrewed upward in lavishness—black pearls in oysters, cigars rolled in hundred-dollar bills, lackeys in knee breeches and powdered wigs."[16]

The engorgement of riches grew from America's westward expansion and productivity-improving inventions, such as Edison's light bulb and Bell's telephone. Its scale was certainly beyond Battle's understanding. So, too, the lesser world beneath the skyscrapers' rule, one that was teeming and grimy on land and water.

As the Old Dominion steamer chugged up the Hudson River, Battle and Anne looked out on the traffic of a world metropolis. Barges laden with crops paraded downstream in lines four, six, and eight long. Railroad cars floated improbably on flat boats. Ferryboats traveled back and forth to New Jersey like "the shuttle in the loom," as one contemporary writer put it. After a last slow push, the ship angled cross-flow and eased toward a wharf. Shoreward, the water grew thick with oily refuse. Battle led Anne down timbered planking and onto a street spread with the manure of wagon horses and clogged with "cab drivers and expressmen whose vehicles and manners" seemed even then "to belong to a more primitive age."[17]

He had answered the North's call, and now his summoning dreams met inglorious reality. Turn-of-the-century New York throbbed with the white-faced, strange-tongued poverty of European immigration. Peasants from Ireland, Italy, Germany, and Eastern Europe shared the privations of life in a city that scorned help for the poor. This was the era of the tenement house, four- to six-story buildings with common bathrooms and small, dark living quarters whose windows looked out on shadowy airshafts. Here was where "the other half" lived in the chronicling of journalist Jacob Riis.

As of 1890, Riis estimated that the city's 37,000 tenements were home to 1.2 million New Yorkers. He took his readers into a building on the Lower East Side, a neighborhood that overflowed with more than 700 people per acre, the highest rate of population in the world:

> Be a little careful, please! The hall is dark and you might stumble over the children pitching pennies back there. Not that it would hurt them; kicks and cuffs are their daily diet. . . . All the fresh air that ever enters these stairs comes from the hall-door that is forever slamming, and from the windows of dark bedrooms that in turn receive from the stairs their sole supply of the elements God meant to be free. . . . Here is a door. Listen! That short hacking cough, that tiny, helpless wail—what do they mean? They mean that the soiled bow of white you saw on the door downstairs will have another story to tell—Oh! a sadly familiar story—before the day is at an end. The child is dying with measles. With half a chance it might have lived; but it had none. The dark bedroom killed it.

For blacks, too, New York was anything but the Promised Land.

Commerce with the West Indies had made New York a key player in the slave trade. A market for the sale of humans opened at the foot of Wall Street at the start of the eighteenth century and, finding that forced labor enhanced the quality of life, more than half of the city's households owned slaves by the mid-eighteenth century.

Down through the decades, subjugation produced episodes of horrific violence. In 1712, slaves gathered in an orchard to plot a murderous rebellion. One set fire to a shed. Whites who ran to fight the blaze were met by gunfire and hatchet attacks. Nine died and a half dozen were wounded. Twenty-one slaves were brought to trial and condemned. According to the official report, "Some were burnt, others were hanged, one broke on the wheele and one hung alive in ye towne."[18]

THE UPRISING WAS well remembered twenty-nine years later when nine fires broke out in quick succession, sparking rumors that slaves were conspiring to destroy the city. A white girl reported under pressure that she had overheard blacks planning a massacre. Scores of slaves were arrested and tried without regard to legal or evidentiary standards. Eighteen were hanged and fourteen were burned alive.

After the Revolutionary War, New York confronted the question of abolition, but it was among the last of the northern states to approve even a gradual move toward liberty. Not until 1827 did the legislature grant African Americans the benefit of full emancipation.

In 1860, as the United States approached the Civil War, the census counted just 49,005 blacks among a statewide population of 3.9 million, a total equal to slightly more than 1 percent of all New Yorkers.[19] Still, they were resented by many whites, and all the more so after the outbreak of hostilities.

Two years into the fighting, Congress enacted a draft that did not sit well in a city divided over the merits of forced Southern emancipation. Adding to outrage, the law permitted privileged young men to buy their way out of serving by paying $300 as a bounty to attract less-fortunate cannon fodder.

New York was called upon to deliver two thousand conscripts, their names to be chosen in a public lottery. Before the drawing was finished, hundreds of men marched to the site, set the building ablaze, and ignited four days of violence. Rioters targeted Lincoln's Republicans and other symbols of support for the war. Gangs pummeled blacks, ransacked businesses that blacks owned or patronized, and, yelling, "Burn the niggers' nest," attacked the Colored Orphan Asylum. The 237 children inside were rushed to a police stationhouse as a mob torched the building. When, finally, federal troops restored order, the death toll stood at 191.

For decades after the war, the number of African Americans in the city remained constantly small. Blacks clustered first in the notorious

Five Points section of Lower Manhattan; then they were pushed north into Greenwich Village and then further north into a rough-edged place on Manhattan's West Side called the Tenderloin. By modern standards, it was not a ghetto. The city's black population—counted at 60,666 in the 1900 census, less than 2 percent of the total—still lacked the heft to claim a large area. Instead, blacks lived scattered on a block here and a block there.[20]

As would long be the case, their buildings were the least well-kept and carried the highest rents. As also would be the case, blacks had few employment opportunities. The census put the number of working black men at 20,395, with well more than half holding jobs as servants, waiters, porters, or laborers. In contrast, there were but thirty-two black doctors and twenty-six black lawyers.

An African American pioneer, William L. Bulkley, educated at Claflin, Wesleyan, and Syracuse universities in the United States, as well as at Strasburg University in Germany and the Sorbonne in Paris and soon to be named principal of an elementary school that served the black children of the Tenderloin, described the dynamic:

> The saddest thing that faces me in my work is the small opportunity for a colored boy or girl to find proper employment. A boy comes to my office and asks for his working papers. He may be well up in the school, possibly with graduation only a few months off. I question him somewhat as follows:
>
> "Well, my boy, you want to go to work, do you? What are you going to do?"
>
> "I am going to be a door-boy, sir."
>
> "Well, you will get $2.50 or $3 a week, but after a while that will not be enough; what then?"
>
> After a moment's pause he will reply: "I should like to be an office boy."
>
> "Well, what next?"
>
> A moment's silence, and, "I should try to get a position as bell-boy."
>
> "Well, then, what next?"
>
> A rather contemplative mood, and then, "I should like to climb to the position of head bell-boy."

He has now arrived at the top; further than this he sees no hope.
He must face the bald fact that he must enter business as a boy and
wind up as a boy.[21]

For now, Battle was a country teenager come North with wide
eyes. At Anne's side, he navigated the hustle and muck of the streets
and absorbed the shock of the new. Trains thundered and clanged
overhead. Forerunners of the subways, their steam engines belched
smoke and showered sparks. Where the sun came into view, the sky
was etched with cables strung helter-skelter to carry electricity every
which way.

Crossing Manhattan's busiest north-south thoroughfare, he encountered the New York Police Department for the first time in the
form of the best the department had to offer: the Broadway Squad.
All the men were at least six feet one. They stood resplendent in brass-
buttoned uniforms. Battle was duly impressed. As one writer of the
day said of this elite cadre: "They hold the peace of Broadway in
their arms, and under these broad arms tens of thousands of frightened New Yorkers and strangers pass in safety each day."[22]

Far beyond Battle's view were the darker truths that New York
Police Department was infused with brutality, corruption, and racism. Its ranks, 7,500 strong, were filled largely by ill-educated Irishmen who were given to the liberal use of a club called the "locust,"
so named for the close-grained wood from which it was hewn. They
took orders from the bosses of Tammany Hall, the all-powerful
Democratic Party machine. Many blurred the distinction between
cop and criminal.

Vice was rampant, and nowhere more so than in the Tenderloin.
There, New Yorkers indulged baser appetites away from the scolding
of stiff-necked clergy and the daytime rectitude of proper citizens.
There, sellers of sin shared their bounty with the police, and the police shared the wealth with Tammany chiefs.

The area drew its name from a joyful remark uttered in the last
decade of the nineteenth century by Captain Alexander Williams
on being assigned to the local precinct with all its gushers of graft.
"I've been having chuck steak ever since I've been on the force and
now I'm going to have a bit of tenderloin," chortled Williams, an

immense former ship's carpenter who was renowned as "Clubber" because of his frequent use of the baton.

There were gambling halls. There were nightclubs with curtained rooms for prostitution and galleries for watching sexual "circuses." There were rows of bordellos and brightly lit avenues where prostitutes paraded: white women on the "Ladies Mile" along Sixth Avenue and black women on "African Broadway" along Seventh Avenue.

Battle's trek with Anne took them in front of City Hall to the western landing of the Brooklyn Bridge. He remembered the span as "a wonderful thing in those days," and admitted to a touch of hayseed gullibility: "I heard about selling the Brooklyn Bridge, and I wondered how it was sold, and asked some questions about it."[23]

As much as it was a feat of engineering, the bridge stood also as a symbol of a new urban identity. Only a year before, in 1898, the city of Brooklyn, on the east side of the river, and the city of New York, on the western bank, had been wed, Brooklyn playing the reluctant bride and Manhattan the rakish groom. There was one city now—Greater New York—with a single police force, a single fire department, and a single seat of political power.

What Battle thought on crossing the bridge will never be known. Nor can it be said what transpired after Battle and Anne descended to the Brooklyn shore, there to complete the journey to Anne's dashing relatives, William and Killis Delamar. Battle shared with an interviewer only these slim impressions: "Brooklyn was a great big place. The elevated made so much noise you couldn't hear. There was so much traffic. Of course, I came from a nice quiet little town where everybody spoke to you, but here if I knew somebody and wanted to speak to them they'd think you were fresh or something."[24]

He stayed in Brooklyn for only two days. The parting with his mother came quickly and sadly. Many long years later, pencil in hand, he wrote of Anne: "I admired and idolized my angelic mother, I loved her better than anyone in the world . . . and always said to myself if and when I married I would choose a girl as near like my loving mother as I possibly could."[25]

Likely, Anne embraced her son's big body, the body that had been so large at birth and that was going to carry him forth into the world as a sixteen-year-old claiming manhood. Likely, he spoke of the dream he was setting out to pursue, that of going to college as soon as he could earn the money for tuition and then on to becoming an attorney. Likely, they spoke with earnest optimism of reunions to come. There would be some. They would be few. Mother and son would rarely feel one another's touch again.

AFTER AN OVERNIGHT voyage on a steel-hulled steamer, Battle's sister Nancy and her husband, Alexander Taylor, met Battle at a Connecticut River wharf in Hartford. Taylor had built a painting business. The summer being his busy time, he hired Battle at a salary of $1.50 a day, an amount that seemed princely. When Taylor's trade fell away in the fall, Battle began picaresque travels in search of work. An early excursion took him to the all-white town of East Glastonbury. A German couple owned the local boarding house. They gave Battle dinner and put him up for the night, marking the "first time I had ever been lodged with white persons." In the course of the evening, Battle met the superintendent of the nearby Crosby Woolen Mills. Battle told Hughes:

> He was a dapper little man, friendly and talkative, and after dinner we got into a conversation that lasted quite late into the evening. We discussed every subject under the sun except a job. Finally I got around to that, broaching the subject of possible employment in the mill.
>
> "I would be willing to employ you," he said. "But I don't know how the owners would take it, or the other employees. We have never hired a Negro."
>
> "Why don't you hire one and learn how it would take?" I asked.

Battle wound up with a job in the dye house—at least partly because the dye master jealously guarded his formulas and believed that an African American would lack the intellectual capacity to steal the secrets. In fact, Battle learned the art of fabric dying well enough to run production when the dye master fell ill. A team of mechanics also taught Battle how to operate equipment they had newly installed.

"The result was that when the mill reopened, I was retained in the carding department as a kind of unofficial overseer in charge of the maintenance of the machinery," Battle remembered. "I got more pay than my fellow workers but, since I was colored, the superintendent did not wish them to know this. I received two pay envelopes, one of regular wages at the pay window and the other at a different time."

Despite his accomplishments, Battle's wanderlust took hold. He arranged for his brother John Edward to come North from New Bern to take the job at the mill and moved on, first working on the farm of a prominent judge, who cheated Battle out of pay, and then as a waiter on side-wheelers that ferried the well-to-do on overnight trips between New York City and a rail connection to Boston at Fall River, Massachusetts. He found the job enjoyable, especially summer excursions to watch the 1901 America's Cup sailing competitions between the J. P. Morgan–backed *Columbia* and the *Shamrock* of the Lipton Tea Company's millionaire founder.

Off hours in port, Battle explored New York. The city was still intimidating to a wayfarer barely eighteen years old. Fellow blacks dispensed cautionary advice. There were things that African Americans did in New York at their peril. It was wise to avoid the police; it was foolhardy to cross them. Hard experience taught that New York's cops readily applied the locust, and a police riot that had erupted in the Tenderloin less than a year earlier lived vividly in memory.

At 2 a.m. on a sweltering August night, Officer Robert Thorpe had moved to arrest May Enoch at the corner of Forty-First Street and Eighth Avenue. Enoch was twenty years old and black. Thorpe presumed that she was a prostitute. She was not. Enoch was a young woman waiting to go home with the man she lived with, Arthur Harris. A fresh arrival from Virginia, Harris was trying to beat the heat in McBride's Saloon. He saw Thorpe grab Enoch. Thorpe was in plainclothes, so Harris presumed that Thorpe was assaulting Enoch. The two men fought. Thorpe battered Harris with a nightstick. Harris drew a knife, fatally stabbed Thorpe and fled.

Sixty officers from the local stationhouse gathered at Thorpe's house to pay respects. They were in bad temper. Outside, not far away, a fight broke out between two men—one black, one white. A mob pounced on the black man and, as reported by the *New York Daily Tribune*, the cry went up that a "nigger chase" was on. "Men and women poured by the hundreds from the neighboring tenements. Negroes were set upon wherever they could be found and brutally beaten."[26]

Gangs pulled blacks from streetcars to pummel them. A man threw a clothesline over a lamppost for a lynching. A call went out to hunt down well-known blacks. Cops cheered on the white marauders or joined the attacks until a drenching thunderstorm restored peace.

In the aftermath, there were furious newspaper editorials, protests, and lawsuits. The board of police commissioners assigned a committee to investigate. The panel took testimony, barring lawyers for black complainants from cross-examining police witnesses and crediting the word of officers over their victims. That, officially, was the end of the matter.

The *New York Times* saw "no signs that the citizen of African descent is distrusted or disliked." Quite to the contrary, the paper opined: "He is generally well treated in public, and accorded his legal rights without resentment. His crude melodies and childlike antics are more than tolerated in the music halls of the best class."[27]

BATTLE'S WANDERINGS IN the city passed quickly. Idled by the completion of the America's Cup, he encountered a tout on Forty-Second Street who spoke glowingly of a waiter's position in a hotel a few miles north of the city. Battle went eagerly, but the job was short-lived. In defiance of orders, he took meals in the kitchen rather than in the help's quarters and was fired. Scouting again, he heard about Yale University and headed up the coast to New Haven.

Yale was like nothing Battle had ever seen. The campus was a collection of magnificent buildings, some dating back two centuries, some newly built in celebration of the school's upcoming bicentennial. The new structures included a dining hall whose administrators accepted Battle onto their staff. His place was clear. He was to meet the needs of the best and brightest of white America's sons of privilege. Blacks worked but did not study at Yale; only forty-five were enrolled in the school's undergraduate college in the century that started in 1850.[28]

In the third week of October 1901, a bulletin shocked America: Theodore Roosevelt had dined in the White House with Booker T.

Washington. No president had ever afforded such hospitality to an African American. It seemed impossible to Battle, but it was true. Washington had been a guest in the national residence.

Son of a black cook and a white man, Booker Taliaferro Washington had been born into slavery. Following the Civil War, as a sixteen-year-old, he labored in a saltworks and a coal mine. After two miners talked about a school where blacks could work to pay their way, he made a five-hundred-mile trek to the Hampton Normal and Agricultural Institute in eastern Virginia.

With a mission of training blacks to become teachers, Hampton instilled a Congregationalist work ethic born of a sense that slavery had conditioned its former prisoners to be lazy and hedonistic. Washington excelled, and he discovered his life's work as the creative genius behind the Tuskegee Institute in Alabama.

Relying on student labor, he built the school from almost nothing and became a proponent of providing blacks with an industrial education, essentially training students to be tradesmen, such as carpenters and masons. Washington had no shortage of applicants, but he did have a shortage of money. He became adept at fund-raising, eventually recruiting as patrons Andrew Carnegie, John D. Rockefeller, and J. P. Morgan. America's industrialists were happy to give to the right black man, and Washington fit the bill. In 1895, while Roosevelt was president of New York City's board of police commissioners, Washington introduced the country to his philosophy in a groundbreaking address that essentially offered a racial bargain with four terms:

He accepted the dominant white view that blacks were ill-prepared to participate in American citizenship.

He rejected any insistence on immediate civil and political rights.

He called on whites to bring blacks into the economic mainstream by supporting the kind of skills-based education offered at Tuskegee.

And he took on faith that American society would become welcoming once blacks were productive members of the labor force.

The enduring image drawn by Washington in this "Atlanta Compromise" was that of the races as separate fingers on a united hand. He told his white audience:

> As we have proved our loyalty to you in the past, in nursing your children, watching by the sick-bed of your mothers and fathers, and often following them with tear-dimmed eyes to their graves, so in the future, in our humble way, we shall stand by you with a devotion that no foreigner can approach, ready to lay down our lives, if need be, in defense of yours, interlacing our industrial, commercial, civil, and religious life with yours in a way that shall make the interests of both races one. In all things that are purely social we can be as separate as the fingers, yet one as the hand in all things essential to mutual progress.

Whites heard from Washington the ratification of their superior place in society. Blacks heard the coming of a leader to replace the deceased Frederick Douglass. Praise flowed from seemingly all quarters. President Grover Cleveland sent a congratulatory note: "Your words cannot fail to delight and encourage all who wish well for your race."

The judgments of history have been harsher to a man who came to be known both as the "Wizard of Tuskegee" and as "The Great Accommodator." On the one hand, Washington was a master political tactician and educator; on the other, he avoided antagonizing whites even to the point of remaining silent in the face of lynchings. He can be praised for realism in recognizing the futility of all-out war with a society that tolerated racial murder. And he can be condemned for accepting the unacceptable.

Political leaders courted Washington in pursuit of African American votes. Roosevelt was no exception. Elevated from vice president to president on the assassination of William McKinley, he hosted Washington in the hope that Washington would communicate to America's blacks that they had an ally in the White House. The dinner took place on Roosevelt's thirty-second day in office. At the table were the president, First Lady Edith Roosevelt, a friend of Roosevelt's, and Washington, whose arrival and departure went unnoticed until an Associated Press reporter checked the day's White House guest list. After midnight, the dispatch went out: "Booker T. Washington, of Tuskegee, Alabama, dined with the President last evening."

The South seethed. The *Memphis Scimitar* declared: "The most damnable outrage which has ever been perpetrated by any citizen of the United States was committed yesterday by the President, when he invited a nigger to dine with him at the White House."[29]

A few days later, Yale's administration delivered a second jolt to Battle and his fellow blacks on the dining hall staff as they prepared to serve meals at a celebration of the university's two hundredth birthday: the invited dignitaries included Washington and Roosevelt.

The date, October 23, 1901, proved to be a glorious autumn day. The trees offered reds and yellows as if in fiery congratulations. At the right moment, Battle made his way to a vantage point from which to watch the dignitaries and students in a long procession to Yale's Hyperion Theatre. University presidents joined renowned scholars, government leaders joined military commanders, artists joined writers, lawyers joined bishops, the Secretary of State joined the US Chief Justice, Woodrow Wilson joined Mark Twain, and there was the president of the United States and there was the leader of black America. Battle spotted Washington easily.[30] His lonely skin tone was impossible to miss among the sixty-two white men who were awarded honorary degrees. And there was Roosevelt, with his stout bearing and proud gusto. Battle viewed him as a hero and would count him one for the rest of Battle's life. Soon, he would express his appreciation face-to-face.

NEW HAVEN OFFERED Battle the Yale dining hall and little else. Judging that he would find greater opportunities in New York, he headed down the coast determined "to try my luck there permanently."

It is easy to imagine him, now nineteen years old and feeling himself on the make. Still, it is just as easy to see him as a mark for the hustlers who played the city's angles. Unsurprisingly, his recollections included a bit of a fleecing:

My first experience with politics as a young man came only a few days after I had first set foot in New York. Walking along a midtown street with a friend on a primary election day, we were approached by a white man who asked us, "Would you like to make two dollars?"

Naturally we said, "Yes."

The man handed us two marked ballots and instructed us on how to put them into the ballot box. After we had "voted" we stood down the street a ways from the polls and watched him pay others, Negro and white, to do the same thing. Never having voted before, I had not learned then to take my ballot seriously, and did not realize the import of what I was doing.

Battle's return to New York brought a happy reunion with his younger sister Sophia, who was living with a family in East New York, a countrified area of Brooklyn miles from the commercial center near the bridge. He took lodgings there, set out to find work, and encountered a revelation that would influence the central course of his life. More than a decade earlier, while Brooklyn was still an independent city, seminal African American civil rights leaders and brave blacks had waged a hard struggle to break the color line of its police force. They had succeeded—but only to a point, Battle discovered.

It took gutsy, farsighted vision in the late 1880s to imagine opening the Brooklyn force to African Americans—and Timothy Thomas Fortune, the man who took up the challenge, was nothing if not a gutsy visionary.

Born into slavery in 1856, Fortune was then a generation removed from Irish and Seminole contributions to his blood. After the Civil War, his father, Emmanuel Fortune, supported the family by leather tanning and by farming land he had been given by a white friend. Newly prominent, Emmanuel was elected to the Florida state legislature. Swiftly, though, hopes of freedom died in the horrors of Reconstruction.

The rise of the Ku Klux Klan forged Fortune's youth in blood. His father, a special target, fortified the house so that the family slept in a loft from which Emmanuel could drop through a trap door to return gunfire. Once, Timothy Thomas missed a Sunday-school picnic that became the site of an atrocity.

"All were gathered at the picnic grounds and enjoying to the full their first experience of the kind," he recalled decades later, "when a party of white hoodlums hidden in the surrounding forest, opened a deadly fire with shotguns on the women and children and the very few men in the gathering. . . . The ground was littered with dead and maimed children and grownups."[31]

Emmanuel Fortune moved the family to Jacksonville, Florida, where he continued to serve in the legislature. Having excelled at a Freedmen's Bureau school in Marianna, under the tutelage of two Union soldiers, Timothy Thomas enrolled in a black public school called the Stanton Institute, to be taught by two women from New England.

Again he shone academically, but he stayed only a short time. Instead he embarked on a series of jobs: legislative clerk, postal worker, a newspaper printer's apprentice, railroad mail route agent, and federal customs inspector. Eventually, Fortune's wanderings brought him to reading the law at Howard University at night while working as a compositor for the *People's Advocate*, a black newspaper in Washington. There, he began to write for publication and found the career that led him to New York in 1880 and then to the editorship, between 1881 and 1907, of three successive black-oriented papers, the *Globe*, the *Freeman*, and the *New York Age*. In those positions, he emerged as one of the great United States newspaper editors, but he remains largely unsung because he focused on—and championed—the causes of black America.[32]

Described by a scholar as "a Byronically handsome African-American who once seemed destined to inherit the mantle of the great Frederick Douglass," Fortune was an unparalleled journalistic crusader.[33] His newspapers chronicled the evils of Jim Crow and political developments of special interest to blacks. His uncompromising editorials made the *Age* the country's most influential publication among African Americans. And Fortune did more.

He mentored W. E. B. Du Bois, who was to become the intellectual godfather of the modern civil rights movement, and gave Du Bois his first assignments as a newspaper correspondent. He gave Ida B. Wells a platform in the *Age* to crusade against lynching after vigilantes destroyed her newspaper in Memphis. He founded the National Afro-American League, precursor to the National Association for the Advancement of Colored People (NAACP). He became confidant, collaborator, and critic of Booker T. Washington.[34]

And, as the 1890s approached, Fortune joined three path breakers in devising a strategy to integrate Brooklyn's police force. Philip A. White was the first black to receive a degree from the New York College of Pharmacy. Charles A. Dorsey was one of the few black school principals in Brooklyn. T. McCants Stewart was a minister and lawyer who had been one of the first black students at the University of South Carolina.

First, Fortune's group needed the right men to apply for the job, who were suited to police work, who were capable of achieving a high score on the civil service examination, and who would have the strength to overcome the sure hostility of white cops and citizens. They chose Wiley Grenada Overton to lead the way.

The youngest of at least eight children in a free black family, Overton was born on the eve of the Civil War in Elizabeth City, North Carolina.[35] In the war's ebb, at the age of seven, he began his education at a normal school whose mission was to prepare blacks to become teachers. He graduated at fourteen, taught for two years, and then, still only sixteen, followed a brother north to Brooklyn, the independent city across the river from New York. He resumed his studies, this time at a blacks-only grammar school. After graduating for a second time, Overton went to work for a dry-goods merchant, soon taking charge of the company's sample room. He married, fathered two daughters, and became active in his church. Eventually, he established a successful undertaking business.

Few members of the police force were as well educated as Overton was; fewer still had built successful careers. To Fortune and his colleagues, Overton's willingness to sacrifice his livelihood at the age of thirty-one for the greater good of the race was a godsend. They had no doubt that, with proper study, he would ace the hiring test—and he did. In 1891, Overton's name appeared toward the top of the rank-order appointment list. The commissioner was sure to reach him as he called men for mandatory physicals. Fortune arranged for a doctor to examine Overton in order to prevent the police surgeon from disqualifying him on a pretext. The doctor issued a certificate of good health.

The *Brooklyn Daily Eagle* sent a reporter to plumb the motivations of the black man who had dared to claim a place on the force. So as not to leave readers guessing, its reporter wrote of Overton: "The race which he belongs to is made plain in the most pronounced way by the color of his skin—he is quite dark." The story included this colloquy:

"What induced you to make the effort to secure the position on the police force?"

"Well, I don't really remember. I had been thinking of it for the longest time. I believed that there ought to be some colored policemen, and I was more or less all the time talking about it to my friends. In Philadelphia there are fifty-six colored officers. Boston has eight or ten. In Chicago they are numerous. Trenton, Camden and Newark are not without them, and now that Brooklyn has got into line, there are no cities in the North where my people dwell in respectable numbers, except New York, without black policemen."

Overton also predicted:

I think the treatment I receive will in a great measure depend upon how I carry myself, how I deal with those with whom I come in contact. The worst which I will be made to suffer will be the staring of the curious and probably I'll have to take some guying from the gamins on the streets. The novelty of my appearance, however, will soon wear away and until it does I guess I can stand the staring without blushing too loud, and, as I do not drink and am not hasty in my temper, the street arab will never succeed in making me angry.[36]

Critical of no one and suffused by good will, Overton drew a pleased review from the reporter. He left the interview "impressed with the idea that no city would suffer from having on its police negroes like Officer Overton." Shortly, Commissioner Henry I. Hayden appointed twenty-two police officers. "He passed a good examination," Hayden said, "and as the law makes no distinction in regard to color I do not see why there should be any question as to my duty in the matter."

The following day the *Eagle* declared in a supportive editorial: "There are colored policemen in plenty in states beyond the old Mason and Dixon's line. If the Southerners can stand the admixture why cannot the Northerners?"[37]

And so, on March 6, 1891, Overton left his wife Francis and his daughters, nine-year-old twins Beulah and Mabel, and headed to the stationhouse in Brooklyn's First Precinct, a building a few blocks from the East River anchorage of the Brooklyn Bridge. Outside, Overton looked upon the primitive headquarters of primitive ranks. Waiting inside was Captain James Campbell, who was at an age when his hair and moustache had turned snowy white. Campbell gave orders to lieutenants for execution. Those men in turn relied on roundsmen, today's sergeants, to supervise the precinct's cops. Finally, there was a doorman who ushered officers and visitors into the stationhouse and performed janitorial services. This was the sole job in the building open to blacks.

Inside, Overton met determined silence and discovered that the department had yet to secure a uniform for him and, further, that none of his new colleagues would lend a spare regulation shirt, pants, coat, or hat. As night fell, Overton set out in civilian clothing to patrol until midnight. He walked the gaslit streets of Brooklyn Heights, a neighborhood of townhouses overlooking New York Harbor, home to Brooklyn's wealthiest citizens. The *Eagle* noted that a Sergeant Reeves found that "Overton's carriage was good and that he gave promise of making a first class patrolman."[38]

The work hours were incomprehensibly grueling. A typical schedule called for a police officer to stay on duty for as long as thirty-six hours straight, including time spent in the stationhouse—on reserve—to respond to emergencies. While on reserve, officers slept in dormitories stocked with cotlike beds and thick with men in flannel underwear who smoked pipes and cigars or chewed Virgin Leaf Tobacco. Officers set the legs of their beds in kerosene-filled pans to keep roaches from climbing up from the floor.

Overton clocked in for his first reserve duty at 9:58 p.m. on a Wednesday night. In the stationhouse barracks, he knelt to say prayers beside his assigned bed. Then he lay down, and four men in the room went downstairs to a lounge. They would not sleep in close quarters with an African American.[39] Although commanders ordered the boycott ended, Overton faced still greater hostility. The *Eagle* reported that First Precinct cops had hired career thief William Scheff, described as "a man who breaks stones with his fists in dime museums," to assault Overton "either with his bare fists or with brass knuckles and a pistol . . . to make the colored officer useless for further service on the police force of this city."

Based on the word of a confidential source and on corroborating accounts from Scheff, who said he had been "hired to knock out the nigger," and a police officer, who was quoted by name, The *Eagle*'s headline read: "Hired to Whip Overton. The Remarkable Story of a Police Conspiracy." After the quoted police officer denied the statements attributed to him by the *Eagle*, Hayden dismissed the story as unworthy of belief.[40]

Already, though, Overton's superiors had begun to bring him up on departmental charges. In the first case, Overton discovered that Vaughan's Saloon was doing a roaring business at 10 a.m. on a Sunday morning. A fellow officer was among the carousers. Overton was cited for failing to arrest the proprietor. He explained that he had been specially assigned at the time "to find a mulatto boy . . . who was wanted by the police for stabbing an Italian." He also argued that the first officer on the scene had been responsible for shutting down the saloon. Campbell punished Overton with a reprimand.[41]

Undeterred by the hardships inflicted on Overton, three more African Americans took—and passed—the next hiring exam. Philip W. Hadley worked as a horse-drawn coachman. The *Eagle* reported that he was "a quadroon and a remarkably bright looking young man."[42] John W. Lee served as a stationhouse doorman and hoped to rise above janitorial duties. Moses P. Cobb was a longshoreman who had been born into slavery in Kinston, North Carolina, and who had walked from there to Brooklyn. He was married to Tempy Fumville, a woman of particular note because she was from New Bern and was friends with Battle's parents. The *Eagle* reported that Cobb was "somewhat taller than Overton and he is built on a handier model, for he is raw boned and strong looking while Overton is chunky and has a tendency to run to fat."[43]

In April 1892, the paper quoted a police official as saying, "The appointment of the three colored men whose names are on the eligible list is sure to make trouble unless the commissioner assigns them to do duty as doormen." The following month, Cobb became Brooklyn's second African American officer.[44] The commissioner placed him in a precinct that included a concentration of black residents. Even so, the department restricted Cobb largely to the duties of a doorman rather than place him in uniform on the street. And, increasingly, the department treated its African American officers like a virus needing expulsion.

In June 1892, when Overton failed to signal the stationhouse from a call box at the appointed hour, a roundsman discovered him "in a restaurant much frequented by colored folks." Commissioner Hayden fined Overton ten day's pay, three times the fine he imposed on a white officer who was found drunk on duty and five times the fine he administered to a white cop who went AWOL.[45] In July, Hadley won appointment to the force. The next month, the commissioner fined Cobb two day's pay for sitting down during a tour of duty, but gave a white officer just a reprimand for sitting on a doorstep.

"Colored policemen are not turning out to be the models they were expected by their enthusiastic backers to show themselves," the Eagle opined. "Strange to say, they have the same weaknesses as white men, and to judge from certain recent official utterances, not made in a public way, it will be quite a while before their number is increased."[46]

Hayden again hit Overton with a ten-day fine after a roundsman reported seeing him in civilian clothes while on duty. In November, Hayden fined Overton an additional five day's pay after he was found in a milk depot while on duty. Within a week of this final punishment, twenty months after he was appointed to the force, Overton announced that he was quitting in hope of moving to a position as a United States government clerk. He expressed no recriminations. With a federal job on the line and, perhaps more important, with Cobb and Hadley on the force and Lee climbing the civil service list, he said, "I have no complaint to make of the treatment which I have received. My fellow officers have been very courteous to me, while I have nothing to say of the conduct of my superior officers toward me."[47]

Overton's attempt to resign without generating animosity toward his fellow blacks proved futile. Less than two weeks later, the commissioner fired Hadley on a charge of drunkenness. He had lasted all of four months. At the same time, the commissioner fined two drunken white officers ten day's pay.[48]

Soon, the last of Fortune's candidates dropped plans to become a police officer. On the verge of appointment, Lee asked Commissioner Hayden's permission to remain as a doorman, while collecting a police officer's higher salary. Hayden obliged, prompting the *Eagle* to write that Lee, "about whose race origin there can be no doubt," was "evidently an astute individual and knows pretty well what he is about. As a patrolman he would not have received any too an effusive welcome by his fellow officers. As a doorman he will not interfere with existing conditions, nor in any way offend their more or less refined susceptibilities."[49]

Lee's decision to accept the title of patrolman but perform a doorman's duties set a pattern that held for years to come. Almost a decade later, when African American "patrolman" John Nelson left the force, the *Eagle* would report, "Like all the colored patrolmen on the force Nelson has been doing the work of a doorman."

Stalwart Moses P. Cobb fell into that reduced state. He was still on the force when Battle arrived in Brooklyn in need of accommodations after his wanderings in Connecticut. Battle called on Cobb because his household in the East New York countryside included the friendly faces of Cobb's wife, Tempy Fumville, and Battle's sister Sophia, who was living with the couple's family.

While spending a few days with the young girl he hadn't seen in years, Battle got to know Cobb and something of his work. Battle said both that Cobb had "been a policeman for a number of years" and that Cobb and a handful of others "were patrolmen, but were not in uniform on the beats, but were turnkeys and stationhouse attendants."[50] Denied promotions, they were generally limited to plainclothes so as to spare the white public the sight of a black cop in uniform, Battle said.

Within months after Battle's short visit, Tempy would die, at the age of fifty-five, and her body was returned to New Bern for burial.[51] Sophia stayed with Cobb, matured into a young woman, and at twenty-one, became Cobb's wife for the rest of his life. When Cobb retired from the force—the first black to do so—Cobb and Sophia returned to North Carolina. In 1975, at the age of eighty-five, long after Cobb had died, she told the *New York Times* that her husband had remained a doorman for more than two decades before gaining the rank of a true police officer.[52]

THERE WASN'T MUCH call in New York for a partly educated nineteen-year-old, let alone one who was black. Battle fell back on the skills he had learned as a servant in the finer white homes of New Bern. As so many other young blacks were doing, he started on the path that William L. Bulkley, the pioneering black school principal, had described: he became a "boy."

Battle won a position as a houseboy or, more politely, as a house-man in the home of a retired Spanish banker and his wife, Mr. and Mrs. Norman Gelio Andreini, on West Seventy-Fifth Street, just feet from Central Park. His salary was twenty-five dollars a month plus meals. He remembered Mr. Andreini as "a fine, liberal man" and Mrs. Andreini as a "charitable church woman," although she "was so exacting that she made her household staff work like slaves."

About this time, in 1902, telegrams went out from New Bern with news that Thomas had died. It had been three years since he had sent Battle forth with a prayer, and now the "old man" was gone. Battle felt powerfully called home to stand in honor of his father and to comfort Anne in the loss of her partner of more than four decades, but he chose not to go. Instead, he bought a ticket on the Old Dominion steamship line for his sister Nancy.

"This was one of the saddest times of my life because I was the only child who was not at home," Battle wrote. "I was indeed homesick and lonesome."

He also reckoned with the curtailment of his life's dream. His sister Mary Elizabeth needed tuition for the Slater Industrial School at Winston-Salem, where she was studying to become a teacher, and Anne needed financial support. Battle would no longer be able to afford law school, even as he lived very modestly in a three-dollar-a-month room on West Fifty-Ninth Street, not far from the location today of the 750-foot-tall Time Warner Center. He was north of the Tenderloin, on the edge of another area where blacks concentrated among larger numbers of whites.

Stretching six or seven blocks north from Fifty-Ninth Street on Manhattan's West Side, the neighborhood had strict racial divisions, blacks toward the bottom of a slope, whites toward the top. There was constant racial skirmishing. Inspired by the fighting, the enclave came to be called San Juan Hill after the site in Cuba of Teddy Roosevelt's Spanish-American War victory.

Unsurprisingly, Battle's landlord took a liking to him. James Mayhew served as something of a tutor to Battle, taught him to play the bridgelike card game whist, and gave him a fresh brush with greatness. The players who joined Battle at the card table included a curly-haired man with light cocoa skin—the great Arthur Schomburg.

A decade older than Battle, Schomburg had already embarked on his life's work of collecting the lost histories and overlooked accomplishments of people of color. Perseverance as a bibliophile would make him a seminal figure of modern African American history and place his name on the New York Public Library's Schomburg Center for Research in Black Culture. When he met Battle, he was about thirty years old and working as a law firm clerk.

Battle remembered that Schomburg "took special interest in me" at their twice-weekly card playing. Increasingly focused on fighting for individual and racial dignity, Schomburg believed that blacks needed to stand on the same intellectual level as whites. He impressed upon Battle that learning was imperative. He stressed reading the newspapers. There was Timothy Thomas Fortune's *New York Age* and there were the white newspapers like the *New York Times*, *New York Tribune*, and *New York Evening Post*. He spoke glowingly of books, be they histories, biographies, or fiction. Often in life, he fondly recalled reading Defoe's *Robinson Crusoe* and being enthralled by Alexandre Dumas's *The Three Musketeers*. Battle embarked on voracious reading and, he recalled, "was very much benefited."

Away from the card table, Schomburg moved among talented black men and women. The center of the world became the blocks of West Fifty-Third Street between Sixth and Eighth Avenues. There, Battle witnessed wonders that were unimaginable elsewhere—black people with money, blacks who were prominent entrepreneurs, blacks who were popular actors and musicians, blacks who lived in better-quality housing.

The Marshall Hotel was the place to dine, with a restaurant that featured an orchestra on Sundays, and the hotel's bar was the place to socialize. Here, Battle began to learn from the likes of Harlem Renaissance poet and historian James Weldon Johnson and his brother, composer J. Rosamond Johnson, who collaborated on the music and lyrics of "Lift Every Voice and Sing," the "black national anthem." Here, Battle got to know and be known by the stars of New York's "Negro Bohemia." Bright and affable, he struck up important friendships with Bert Williams and George Walker, the acclaimed musical comedy team of Williams and Walker; with song-and-dance men Charles Avery and Dan Hart; and with rising musician and bandleader James Reese Europe.

The Maceo Hotel was but a half step down in prestige from the Marshall. Weldon Johnson wrote that "the sight offered at these hotels, of crowds of well-dressed colored men and women lounging and chatting in the parlors, loitering over their coffee and cigarettes while they talked or listened to the music, was unprecedented."

So, too, was style on the street. Jervis Anderson, author of the indispensable *This Was Harlem*, recounted that, on Fifty-Third Street, blacks dressed much as Battle had grown used to seeing whites attired on Fifth Avenue: "The men wore frock coats, vests, and wide-bottom trousers. Their shirts, fastened with studs, had detachable stiff collars and cuffs, made of linen, celluloid, cotton, or paper. Heavy watch chains dangled across their vests. Straw hats were commonly worn in summer, and derbies (or 'high dicers') in winter. They carried walking sticks and wore high boots polished with Bixby's Best Blacking. The women were turned out in heavy-bosomed box blouses and full skirts that covered their ankles."[53]

Seemingly wherever Battle went, he encountered African Americans of accomplishment.

On Sixth Avenue near Twenty-Eighth Street, John B. Nail kept a
saloon that catered to upscale black gentlemen. The *New York Sun*
described the establishment in 1903 as "conducted with the quiet-
ness and manners of a high-class Broadway bar and billiard parlor."
Nail told the newspaper: "You must remember that the object of
the wealthy and educated colored man is to be as inconspicuous as
possible, so far as white people are concerned. He doesn't want to
spend his hours in being reminded of the fact that the great mass of
his fellow-citizens despise him on account of his color."[54]

Most clubs were less decorous. Black prizefighters like Joe Walcott
ran joints frequented by fellow boxers and by the black jockeys who
dominated horse racing. Ike Hines's club on West Twenty-Seventh
Street is credited with introducing ragtime music to New York. Ed-
mond's on West Twenty-Eighth Street was "a cabaret over a stable,"
in the words of composer, lyricist, and pianist Eubie Blake.

And, of greatest significance, there was the Little Savoy on West
Thirty-Fifth Street, a nightclub, gambling hall and hotel owned by
Baron Deware Wilkins, king of the sporting life, the realm where
drinks flowed, music hopped, and money changed hands for sex,
drugs, and dreams of beating the odds with a wager or a con.

Born in Portsmouth, Virginia, Baron Wilkins labored as boy in a
US naval yard. After his parents moved to Washington, DC, he hus-
tled as a bellboy in the Willard Hotel and then as the head bellman
of the Grand Union Hotel in Saratoga Springs, New York. Finally,
he moved to the big city, there to meet up with fellow Portsmouth
native John W. Connor, a Spanish-American War naval veteran who
had opened what the *Age* called "the finest cabaret for colored in
New York."[55]

Wilkins followed suit with the Little Savoy. He was as tough as he
was large. He had to be. Competitors were a rough lot, white gangs
were given to extortion, and cops and politicians demanded tribute.
Wilkins paid up to build bonds with the police and Tammany Hall,
and he hired muscle to defend against attacks. Top among Wilkins's
security force was a man who was known as Lamplighter. He stood
post in front of the Little Savoy with a six-shooter.

Perry Bradford was a pianist and songwriter of the era. Recalling the Tenderloin nightclubs, he wrote in a memoir, "Most of these

joints had gals who could pull up their dresses, shake their shimmies and go to town, which the natives liked and tossed them plenty of kale," meaning money. The Little Savoy featured similar fun while blossoming under Wilkins's stewardship into a cultural hothouse.

Rich, famous, and adventurous whites would stream beneath a sign—"No One Enters These Portals, But The True In Heart Sports"—to be wowed by the musicianship of James P. Johnson, Jelly Roll Morton, and Willie "The Lion" Smith, who were bridging ragtime and jazz with the rhythmic style of piano playing known as stride.[56]

"From the stories the boys tell me, Barron Wilkins' place up to about 1908 was the most important spot where Negro musicians got acquainted with the wealthy New York clientele, who became the first patrons of their music," recalled jazz composer Noble Sissle, adding, "It was his fabulous spot that sparked off the renaissance of the Negro musician in New York City."[57]

Up and down the avenues, houses of worship competed with places of entertainment. The black church was on the rise. When blacks were few in number, predominantly white congregations had welcomed them to participate in what were often known as "nigger pews." As the population grew, two trends paralleled: white churches encouraged blacks, to put it politely, to exercise their Christianity elsewhere, and charismatic African American clergy stepped to the fore.

Battle's enduring allegiance, handed down from Thomas, was to the African Methodist Episcopal Zion Church. The Reverend Alexander Walters spoke to Battle's congregation from the pulpit as a seminal civil rights leader. Freed from slavery in Kentucky, Walters was ordained at the age of nineteen and arrived in New York in 1888. Shortly, he joined forces with Fortune. Outraged by enactment of Jim Crow laws and, more urgently, by a rise in lynchings, Fortune published an open letter in 1889 calling for the National Afro-American League's creation. Walter's name appeared as the letter's lead cosigner.

Although the league had petered out, Walters successfully urged Fortune to revive the organization, newly named the Afro-American Council, after the US Supreme Court endorsed the doctrine of separate but equal in *Plessy v. Ferguson*. He served as president for most of the first decade of the twentieth century, the period that led Battle toward integrating the New York Police Department.

African American fraternal organizations were also blooming into a key source of social cohesion.[58] Battle joined the first of many to which he would belong. He chose the most prominent, the Elks, or more precisely the black Elks. The long-established Benevolent and Protective Order of Elks had barred African Americans, prompting two blacks in Cincinnati to form the Improved Benevolent and Protective Order of Elks of the World—and the New York courts enjoined even the use of that name. No matter. The group carried on and Battle mixed with the many leading African Americans who took part. In 1905, he was a grand marshal of a black Elks parade in Brooklyn.

SURROUNDED BY INSPIRING MEN, Battle looked upward, but his vista still was limited to household service. He took advantage of the "recommendation of the head bellman of one of the leading hotels" to leave the Andreinis for a position as a liveried butler in the East Fifty-Ninth Street home of Arthur Holland Forbes, a wealthy man who invested in the daredevil sport of hot-air ballooning. At work, Battle greeted guests and performed household chores in formal attire. Off hours, he slipped into New York's emerging black society, kept up with current events in Fortune's *Age*, and embarked on a determined course of reading. His selections ranged from histories to fiction and included Thomas Hardy's *Tess of the d'Urbervilles* and *The Scarlet Letter*, Hawthorne's classic of sin, guilt, and judgment, which Battle found to be "a revelation."[59]

BATTLE HAD A LIVELY TIME. He had grown into "a well developed young man, healthy, husky, and—so the women said—handsome." But physical appeal was not his only asset. Demographics made New York a guy's paradise. The 1900 census found that black women outnumbered black men in the city by roughly 20 percent. Males like Battle were much in demand. A great observer of the era's black life, Mary White Ovington, wrote: "In their hours of leisure the surplus women are known to play havoc with their neighbors' sons, even with their neighbors' husbands, for since lack of men makes marriage impossible for about a fifth of New York's colored girls, social disorder results."[60]

Battle circulated through casual relationships. Then, at the age of twenty-two, he took up with Florence Carrington, the sixteen-year-old daughter of Henry and Maria Carrington who had come to New York from Newport News, Virginia. With her fair skin and long, black, and straight hair, the couple's parallels with Thomas and Anne were striking, Thomas having wed ivory-skinned, silken-haired Anne when she was but fifteen. Battle squired Florence to the haunts where he had become a regular on West Fifty-Third Street, buying her first alcoholic drink at the Marshall Hotel bar. She was pretty and, in counterpoint to Battle's gregarious personality, reserved. He was smitten, and so was she. The vagabond life of an adventurous young man came to an end.

Six years after Battle left home with dreams of succeeding like the Delamars, he stepped into adulthood under Florence's grounding influence. A butler's income paid for free-form bachelorhood, a bed in a small room, and sums wired home to Anne, but it would hardly support a wife and family. Casting about for new possibilities, Battle heard that blacks his age were pulling down good money as luggage porters at the Grand Central Depot, but the jobs were hard to get. He would have to see the headman, the fearsome Chief James Williams.

In the spring of 1905, Battle headed to the landmark built by Cornelius Vanderbilt for the railroad empire by which he became the world's richest man. Designed to resemble the Louvre, the depot extended along Forty-Second Street for 370 feet and then turned north in an L shape for almost 700 feet. Outside, Battle wove among horse-drawn coaches and streams of arriving and departing passengers. Through the doors, crystal panes atop one-hundred-foot tall trusses overspread a train shed with seventeen tracks. "New York opened its eyes and gasped," the New York Times had said of the depot's opening in 1871.

With more than a little trepidation, Battle made his way to the Chief's cubby of an office. He found a broad-shouldered presence

with deeply set eyes and a bearing that conveyed command and ma-
turity. In fact, James H. Williams was just four years older than Battle.[61] Born in 1879, he had grown up in a household haunted by the
ghosts of slavery. His grandmother Sarah Powell had been taken in
girlhood from West Africa and had been sold into bondage in Virginia. She remembered the white men who had kidnapped her, the
hard ship's voyage, and servitude on the state's Eastern Shore. She
would tell of a plantation owner's son who had taken her as a mistress, who had fathered a baby with her, and who had taught their
son, light-skinned John Wesley Williams, to read and write while
hiding in the woods.[62] John Wesley escaped, reunited with his mother
after the Civil War, started his own family with a woman who also
had escaped slavery, and brought James H. into the world bearing
the gene of his grandfather's fair complexion. Like Battle, James H.
had been born into the South's first postslavery generation of African
Americans. Like Battle, he had an adventurous spirit. Like Battle, he
had left home for the North as a teenager. By 1897, at the age of eighteen, he was living in the Tenderloin, was married to sixteen-year-old
Lucy Metresh of Connecticut, and had found work as a hotel bellman. Lucy gave birth to a son that year. James H. and Lucy named
the boy Wesley Augustus. He was the first of their six children, and
he would grow up to be the most consequential of the brood by far.

Around the turn of the century, James H. took a position with as
unlikely a source of equal opportunity as could be: Charles Thorley's
House of Flowers on Fifth Avenue. To call the House of Flowers a
florist shop would be akin to describing Tiffany's as a corner jew-
eler. Thorley's elaborate floral arrangements were a must-have nicety
among upscale New Yorkers.

Thorley had started in the business at the age of sixteen in 1874.
Enjoying success, he then found even greater wealth as an investor
in the city's booming real estate market. Big money made Thorley a
player in New York. He was a member of a committee dedicated to
making Fifth Avenue the city's grandest boulevard, and he belonged
to the Tammany Hall war council. At the same time, he quietly
helped the disadvantaged. When Thorley died in 1923, two hundred
"down and outers" gathered at a mission on the Bowery to honor the

generosity he had shown them.[63] And many were the black men to whom this rich and powerful white man gave work.

Williams delivered flowers to well-to-do customers and served as the shop's doorman. Thorley's standards were exacting. Meeting his demands steeped Williams in the importance of first-rate customer service, and Thorley was pleased to recommend his protégé for a higher-paying porter's slot at Grand Central. The station had too much work for its twenty-five luggage carriers, only two of whom were black. Williams got the job. Then, recognizing that he could tap a limitless supply of young African Americans for service labor, he presented the railroad with job candidates who met his insistence on reliability, industriousness, and honesty.

One by one, Williams's men proved themselves, and the stationmaster gave him responsibility for hiring porters. In time, the force grew to more than four hundred men, and Williams eventually became Chief Williams to the young black men he helped propel into life, as well as in the minds of the traveling public. Both would revere the Chief for elevating luggage portage into a dignified occupation. Most memorably, Williams outfitted his team with uniforms that included hats topped with red flannel. Thus was born the term by which luggage carriers became widely known—"redcaps."

Brightly visible, they scurried from curbside to trackside, collected a modest paycheck and bigger tips, and served as concierges to the city. Abram Hill, who interviewed Williams as part of the WPA Writers' Project, wrote that the redcaps covered up to ten miles a day as "walking booths of information," each one prepared to answer questions ranging from "the time of departure of the Trans-Atlantic steamers to the time the baseball game begins, and how far is the nearest eating place."[64]

Wearing a red carnation in his lapel over the course of forty-five years, the Chief became well known to Presidents Roosevelt, Taft, Coolidge, and Wilson. He counted as friends New York governor Al Smith, senators Robert Wagner and Herbert Lehman, as well as Archbishop Patrick Cardinal Hayes, spiritual leader of New York's Roman Catholics. Students at Yale and Harvard made sure to send him a ticket to the schools' annual football match.

All of that was still to come for Williams on the day Battle applied for work. As was his practice with every job seeker, he questioned Battle closely about everything he had done over the previous five years.

Battle's brawn was apparent. He would have no trouble hauling luggage. He was also well spoken and schooled in relating to whites. Finally, Williams may well have detected that Battle had the brains to help with the paperwork of managing an expanding work force. He offered Battle a red cap, and Battle eagerly accepted, neither man having any reason to suspect that they and young Wesley Augustus, grown straight and tall at eight years old, were on their way toward grueling fights against racial barriers.

BATTLE BROUGHT FLORENCE the good news. He expected to make the healthy sum of several hundred dollars a month, ten dollars in salary, the remainder in tips. Happily, he left behind a butler's duties, noting with pride, "When I left the service of Mr. Forbes, I never worked in a private home again."

Plunging into twelve-hour shifts, Battle set his mind to building a savings account. To economize, he moved into a hot-bed bunk room, where he was reunited with a brother who had joined the family's dispersal. He remembered:

> I lived for a time with a group of Red Caps and Pullman porters, ten
> or twelve of us sleeping in shifts in a big dormitory basement room
> at 233 West 41st Street at $1.00 a week each. My brother, William
> D., who had come North to work as a Pullman porter, while studying
> for the ministry at Lincoln University, shared my cot, sleeping while
> I was working.
>
> During the summers, a number of young college fellows occupied
> such quarters while employed at the station or running on the rail-
> road as waiters and Pullman porters to earn their college expenses.
> "Making the season," they termed it.

Battle further trimmed spending by joining the redcaps for meals at McBride's Saloon, the establishment where, they all knew, the police riot of 1900 had begun with the mistaken-identity stabbing of white cop Robert Thorpe by black Arthur Harris on a sweltering August night.

"Thanks to McBride's Saloon, no one in our dormitory basement ever went hungry," Battle recalled. "For a dime, a man could get a foaming pail of beer. With the beer, the purchaser was entitled to access to McBride's free lunch corner. I did not drink, but I would put my pennies tighter with those of the other boys and someone would be sent for the beer. While the beer was being drawn he would pick up enough free lunch for all of us."

Then nature disrupted Battle's plans. Florence's frequent queasiness pointed toward pregnancy. Battle brought Florence to the West Fifty-Third Street office of Dr. E. P. Roberts, one of the city's few black physicians.

Born in Louisburg, North Carolina, in 1868, Roberts was raised in a log cabin whose porous roof revealed the stars overhead as he lay in bed. The family had virtually no money. He would laugh to remember that playmates called him "Pillsbury" because his mother had made his underwear out of flour sacks.

By dint of brains and determination, Roberts graduated from Lincoln University in Pennsylvania, where William D. was enrolled (and where Langston Hughes would study), and took medical training at New York's now shuttered Flower and Fifth Avenue Hospital. He was the lone black student and one of just two class members to have completed college.

Roberts's credentials as a physician were overmatched by the color of his skin. Looking back in 1951, still practicing at the age of eighty-three, he remembered being spurned as prospective patients discovered that they had enlisted the services of a doctor who turned out to be black. Whites simply rejected him, while many blacks, conditioned by racial boundaries, refused to trust that a black man was a doctor, let alone a doctor who was as capable as a white doctor.[65]

Roberts's confirmation of the pregnancy propelled Battle and Florence into marriage. Looking back, Battle confessed that Florence fulfilled his hope of marrying a woman "as near like my loving mother as I possibly could." He wrote as he gathered his memories for Hughes: "In this I have been most fortunate in the selection of my mate."

The wedding took place on June 28, 1905, under the auspices of Florence's Baptist pastor, the Reverend George Sims, at Sims's home. A former farmhand and railroad worker, Sims had founded Union Baptist Church in a storefront on West Fifty-Ninth Street. He devoted his ministry to the "very recent residents of this new, disturbing city," was becoming well known for the vigor of his services, and was embarked on building Union Baptist into a major house of worship. Like Battle, Sims had the physique of a heavyweight fighter. "When he talked of Christ from his pulpit, Jesus became alive, a workman, a carpenter who took off his apron and went out to answer the call to preach," wrote Mary White Ovington.[66]

The wedding certificate records that Florence reported her age to be eighteen, rather than sixteen.[67] Never mentioning that Florence was two months pregnant, Battle recalled the day: "My wife was two hours late for her own wedding. We had an appointment with the minister for eight o'clock. I left my work at Grand Central at seven in the evening and was dressed and waiting anxiously at her sister's apartment before eight—but Florence was still out shopping. We were not married until ten at night."

For a short time, Samuel and Florence roomed with her sister in a tenement on the far west end of Sixty-Eighth Street. Then they moved to a place of their own, another tenement, this one "four rooms with a distinguishing brass bed" at 341 West Fifty-Ninth Street. The neighborhood teemed with unemployed and underemployed men, women who went to work as domestics if they were lucky, and poorly clothed children, many of whom were also ill attended.

More than six thousand people were counted as living on a single block just north of the Battles' apartment. Ovington described the tenements there as "human hives, honeycombed with little rooms thick with human beings." "Bedrooms open into air shafts that admit no fresh breezes, only foul air carrying too often the germs of disease," she wrote, adding that, generally, the "people on the hill are known for their rough behavior, their readiness to fight, their coarse talk." She said that vice is "open and cheap," that "boys play at craps," and that "Negro loafers hang about the street corners and largely support the Tenth Avenue saloons."[68]

At the age of twenty-three, Battle had come a long way from Anne, from river-chilled watermelons, from the countryside—from the South, with all its studied courtesy and overt cruelty—only to live among people who had little more space than was allotted to their ancestors on slave ships.

Still worse, the danger of white-on-black violence overshadowed the neighborhood—and the New York Police Department was the most feared threat. Officers operated out of a stationhouse on West Sixty-Eighth Street. They were well known for wielding nightsticks with impunity. Never did they do so more vehemently than during the Siege of San Juan Hill. On a Friday evening in July, about a month after Battle's wedding, a white gang taunted an elderly white peddler on the gang's corner. When a young black man attempted to help the peddler, a police roundsman ordered a black minister, who ran a coal business, to go into his shop. The minister refused.

"You black———, get in there or I will knock your brains out," the roundsman ordered, according to the detailed retelling in Timothy Thomas Fortune's *New York Age*. Inside the store, the roundsman hit the minister. The minister grabbed a gun from a drawer. Police beat the minister senseless. Black residents swarmed the cops when they carried the minister outside.

Across Battle's neighborhood, tensions ran high the next day. The *Age* reported:

> On Saturday Afro-Americans were bullied by the police. Respectable business citizens, if they stood for a minute, were told to get out of the way, and the first man arrested . . . was, according to his statement, beaten after being taken to the 68th Street station. Similar treatment was accorded to every prisoner that evening. On Sunday more needless arrests were made upon frivolous and concocted charges.

On Monday night, a police officer ordered men who were standing in front of a saloon three blocks from Battle's apartment to get off the sidewalk and go inside. A brick thrown from a roof struck the officer's head.

> The police made a rush into the saloon and into the adjacent houses. The back room of the saloon was cleared and a number of shots shattered all the back windows. . . . Later the policemen, firing in all directions swept across the billiard and pool room of Walter Frazier . . . and rushing pell mell into his place of business, where nothing had occurred, and where men were indulging in recreation and sitting around, placed every man under arrest. According to the testimony of Frazier, one policeman said to the other: "Shall we arrest all of these men?" and one of the officers replied: "Yes, arrest every nigger you see."

Dozens were hauled to the stationhouse, where, the *Age* reported, "they found prepared for them a modified form of the Indian torture called 'running the gauntlet.'" One by one they were shoved into a darkened room in which "police officers with clubs proceeded to beat these upon the head and bodies until they were nearly dead."

For weeks after the nightsticks had swirled around Battle and Florence, Fortune trained the *Age*'s editorial firepower on Police Commissioner William McAdoo, writing: "By no one, except Commissioner McAdoo whose enthusiasm over the force too often outruns his judgment, has the behavior of the police in these 'riots' been praised; on the contrary, it has caused blistering denunciation from the most influential members of the metropolitan press, we mean the *Times*, the *World*, the *Evening Post* and the *Evening Mail*."[69]

As 1905 closed, Fortune published an unsigned letter to the editor under a headline that exhorted, "Become Police and Firemen." The author detailed the required physical qualifications. Barred were obesity, "rupture in any form," "fissures, fistulas and external or internal piles," varicose veins, color-blindness, and much more, including "very offensive breath." It was mandatory that heart, brain, kidneys, and genitalia be in good working order.

The author also warned—presciently, as Battle would discover—that an applicant might face medical sabotage after passing the written civil service test: "I am informed that it has been, and is now, the custom when Afro-Americans apply for examination for the examiners to fake up some technical physical defect and thereby reject them, while a white man in similar physical condition would be passed without question."[70]

There was no rush of volunteers. The police department went on as the keeper of an unequal peace and as Tammany Hall's arm of extortion.

FLORENCE'S FIGURE GREW round as fall moved into winter. When finally the time arrived, Dr. Roberts delivered the baby at home, in those four rooms with the distinguishing brass bed. The date was January 23, 1906. The infant was a boy in whom Battle vested his own life's dream, while accepting that, practically speaking, he could not hand down to his son the name Samuel.

He remembered: "Jesse Earl was our first born. We started to name him Samuel Jesse Battle, Jr. But in that day and time, following the era of the 'coon' songs, colored people were becoming very sensitive about names like Rufus and Sambo. Some of our friends persuaded us that Sam was too closely related to Sambo, so we named our son Jesse Earl instead. I had wanted Jesse Earl to be a lawyer—to fulfill a secret ambition of my own."

Around this time, Florence chose the name Jesse as term of endearment for her husband as well. The nickname stuck and would often be used by Battle's closest family and friends for the rest of his life. To them, he would not be Samuel, but Jesse. Battle and Florence had Jesse Earl baptized, and then the redcaps came to a christening party. There were prayers for the baby's spiritual well-being—and, no doubt, for more. There were likely prayers that he would survive to grow up. Infant mortality was epidemic. With sixteen of every one hundred babies dying before the age of one—and with the mortality rate for black infants almost double that for whites—everyone knew mothers and fathers who had lost children. By comparison, the death rate today is more than thirty times lower: five of every thousand infants fail to pass the one-year mark.[71]

After the baptism, the Battles settled into roles they would follow across their six-decade marriage: Florence tended to home and family; Samuel devoted exuberant energy to his work and the social life that flourished around him. He thrived amid Grand Central's pomp and glamour by studying up on the celebrities whose bags he toted. He became as knowledgeable about opera star Ernestine Schumann-Heink as he was about actress Lillian Russell. He read the writing of Richard Harding Davis, who passed through the terminal as he went about becoming America's first celebrity war correspondent. He greeted John D. Rockefeller.

Battle told Hughes, who wrote:

> The famous *20th Century Limited*, the New York Central's eighteen-hour train to and from Chicago, arrived at 9:30 a.m. For every hour it was late, passengers were refunded a dollar of their fare. Many of my customers, when the train was late, would simply hand me their refund slip and tell me to keep the money. Red Caps were never sorry to see the *Century* come in behind time, least of all myself. We were probably the only ones happy when it came in late.
>
> Sometimes Woodrow Wilson, William Howard Taft, Henry Cabot Lodge or Broadway Jones, one of the most popular entertainers of his time, would get off this famous train. I was always particularly glad to see Williams and Walker, the Negro musical comedy stars, or Charles Avery and Dan Hart, the popular comedians, step off the *Century*. They were my friends.
>
> Sometimes, after carrying their bags, I would join them later for a meal at the Hotel Palm on the corner of 53rd Street and Seventh Avenue, the heart of New York's Negro high life. In front of the Palm or Marshall's, one might see the young writer, James Weldon Johnson, or his musical brother, Rosamond, or the poet, Paul Laurence Dunbar, talking with the composer, Will Vodery. I knew many of the Negro show people of the day and appeared in one Broadway show myself.
>
> When the musical comedy *Honeymoon Express*, starring Blanche Ring who sang "Rings on My Fingers, Bells on My Toes" and Irene and Vernon Castle, exotic dancers, was staged, the producers wanted two stalwart Red Caps for the finale. John Mason and I were chosen, both of us being over six feet and about the same shade of brown. As

the final curtain fell we were shown putting the luggage of the cast aboard the "Honeymoon Express" to the rhythm of the finale.

. . .

Enrico Caruso was a genial person, liberal with money and very good-hearted. He sometimes gave me passes to the Metropolitan Opera where I heard my first operas. Because of my admiration for him, I learned to like Italian food and frequently dined at the restaurant that bore his name at Spring and Lafayette Streets. Caruso traveled with quite a retinue. His arrivals and departures were a major event, with crowds of voluble Italians, including some of New York's wealthiest and most prominent citizens, always on hand to see him arrive and depart.

Celebrities who did not tip well were known to all the old-timers among the Red Caps. When such persons entered the station, the senior Red Caps were very hard to find, leaving the younger men to carry their bags. Red Caps often rendered service for nothing to the aged, the infirm, the bewildered, or very poor with no thought of remuneration. In fact, we frequently helped stranded travelers from our own pockets, if the need presented itself. It was only the rich and famous upon whom we looked quietly from behind a remote pillar when they were known to be tight with their purse strings. With people in trouble we sympathized.

. . .

Because of the admiration and high regard in which he was held by Negro veterans of the Spanish-American War and because he had entertained Booker T. Washington at the White House when he was President, Negro citizens had a great deal of affection for Theodore Roosevelt.

One day the Red Caps learned that, having just returned from a hunting trip to Africa, "Teddy" would be boarding the Merchants Limited at Five o'clock for Boston. Quickly a committee was formed. I was chosen as the spokesman for all the Red Caps to express to Mr. Roosevelt our felicitations on his safe return and our gratitude for his interest in American Negro citizens. As he arrived on the platform accompanied by a group of prominent men, a corps of Red Caps stood at attention outside his car. When he approached, I stepped forward.

"What is it, young man?" Roosevelt asked.

I replied with the good wishes of my fellow station workers and gave him our thanks for his interest in the needs of the Negro people. He thanked me, and shook my hand and that of every Red Cap in the group with a firm grasp, squinting his eyes into that characteristic sharp gaze that seemed to look right through a man.

Chief Williams accompanied workplace camaraderie with a family man's advice. He told Battle that San Juan Hill was no place to raise a child—that Florence and Jesse would be much better off where Williams had taken up residence, north in an area called Harlem.[72] It was worth a look, so, with Jesse swaddled in arms, Battle and Florence paid a call on the Chief, his wife, Lucy, and their growing family. The Williamses now had three children. Wesley was nine, Gertrude was six, and Leroy was three. Their apartment was more spacious than those generally available to blacks downtown. The building and those around it were better kept as well. But decent housing came with a drawback. Virtually everyone in the neighborhood was white, and most wanted nothing to do with African Americans. Taking up residence would demand fortitude of Battle, Florence, and, eventually, Jesse, but no more than was already shown by the Chief, Lucy, and their Wesley.

Old enough to feel the sting of racism as nakedly as children can express it, Wesley intrepidly took a desk in a public school whose teachers were white and whose students were white, except for a few highly visible children. He knew much that his classmates would never know because great-grandmother Sarah Powell and grandfather James Wesley would tell of things that were closed to white children. Wesley listened raptly when Sarah Powell told of being kidnapped from West Africa and when James Wesley remembered escaping from slavery able to read and write. Taking to heart that his forebears had prevailed over badness that he could only imagine, Wesley excelled at reading and writing, outran and outplayed his classmates, and learned more about them than they would ever learn of him.

After touring Harlem and finding a landlord willing to rent to African Americans, Battle and Florence settled on a twenty-three-dollar-a-month apartment on West 134th Street, about a block from the Williams family. The first African Americans to live in the building, they became some of the founding citizens of the community that would grow into the capital of black America.

UNIQUE FORCES OF economics and race were coming to bear in the transition of Harlem from a white population to the first place in US history to offer quality housing for the black masses. Seven miles distant from city hall, the area was at one time a rural paradise, complete with farms and marshland that sloped to the Hudson River. The community's character changed with the city's relentless expansion up the spine of Manhattan. By the 1870s, it had grown into an early New York suburb, home to upper-middle-class and wealthier families.

Those families lost their isolation when three elevated train lines reached the area between 1878 and 1881. The next decade brought construction of well-appointed apartment buildings. Many were equipped with elevators; many offered servants' quarters. Townhouses proliferated. Oscar Hammerstein, grandfather of the Broadway musical composer of the same name, opened the Harlem Opera House. Milwaukee beer baron Fred Pabst established the country's largest restaurant, the fourteen-hundred-seat Pabst Harlem, on West 125th Street.

Then success fell prey to mania.

As the century turned, the city fathers announced a plan to extend a subway tunnel from Lower Manhattan to Harlem, where the line would run under Lenox Avenue. This territory became a roaring frontier. Residential buildings went up on every available square inch of land, and speculators borrowed extravagant sums to trade in properties.

John M. Royall, who would emerge as a prominent black real estate man, recalled the frenzy: "The great subway proposition . . . filled the people's minds and permeated the air. Real-estate operations and speculators conjured with imaginings of becoming millionaires bought freely in the west Harlem district, in and about the proposed subway stations. Men bought property on thirty- and sixty-day contracts, and sold their contracts, not their property for they never owned it, and made substantial profits."[73]

When subway construction fell behind schedule, too many property owners owed too much money and had too many vacant apartments. They became desperate to rent. Into the breach stepped Philip A. Payton Jr., a graduate of Livingston College who found work in New York as a handyman, barber, and janitor in a real estate office before striking out on his own at the age of twenty-four to buy, sell, and broker properties. He advertised: "Management of Colored Tenements a Specialty."

Recognizing that fellow blacks would flock to Harlem's decent housing, Payton offered to deliver tenants to landlords in a scheme that was simple, if cynical: he would fill apartments at rents that landlords were accustomed to charging white tenants while collecting from black tenants the higher rents they were used to paying. Landlords took what they could get, while Payton made as much as a 10 percent premium. The formula led him to establish the Afro-American Realty Company, propelling the movement that Battle had joined early on by following the Chief and taking an apartment on the very block where Payton had gone into business. The advantages were plain. "It is no longer necessary for our people to live in small, dingy, stuffy tenements," proclaimed an advertisement in the *Age*, adding, "we have flats of four and five rooms and bath rooms in which there is plenty of God's air and sunshine." And Ovington noted, "Here are homes where it is possible, with sufficient money, to live in privacy, and with the comforts of steam heat and a private bath."[74]

Left unmentioned was the intense animosity that greeted blacks. In December 1905, the *New York Herald* had reported that buildings once "occupied entirely by white folks have been captured for occupancy by a Negro population." The *Herald*'s use of the word "captured" reflected the prevailing tendency to describe arriving blacks as "invaders," an "influx," or a "horde."

The rhetoric was accompanied by antiblack action. First, whites fled, often in panic. The *New York Times* described the scene in 1905 after the owners of two buildings accepted black tenants: "The street was so choked with vehicles Saturday that some of the drivers had to wait with their teams around the corners for an opportunity to get into it. A constant stream of furniture trucks loaded with the household effects of a new colony of colored people who are invading the choice locality is pouring into the streets. Another equally long procession, moving in the other direction, is carrying away the household goods of the whites from their homes of years."[75]

As white departures further depressed real estate values, landlords banded together. Many appended restrictive covenants to their deeds that barred sales or rentals to African Americans. When Battle left for work in the morning and returned at night, he walked by covenanted buildings. When he strolled the neighborhood with Florence and Jesse, he walked by covenanted buildings. He passed them on 129th and 130th streets. He passed them on 131st, 135th, and 136th streets, more than two hundred in all. A typical covenant barred occupancy by "any negro, mulatto, quadroon or octoroon of either sex . . . excepting only that any one family . . . may employ one negress or one female mulatto, or one female quadroon or one female octoroon as a household servant."[76]

The antagonism surrounding the family was more personal and collectively held than any Battle had experienced. By moving uptown, he had crossed one of the invisible boundaries that circumscribed African American life in New York. He was allotted the space where men toted luggage, but he was barred from the territory where men were professionals. He was shunned in the neighborhood where he lived, but he moved enthusiastically in black society, in the Elks, in the Mother AME Zion congregation, among the bright lights of Negro Bohemia.

At home, Florence matured from sixteen to eighteen into a wife and mother beyond her years. Jesse thrived under her care and in his father's big arms. Then, as Jesse approached two years old, Dr. Roberts confirmed that Florence was once again pregnant. Hoping the baby would be a girl, the Battles launched into preparations. Most pressingly, they searched for an apartment better suited to a family of four. At 27 West 136th Street they found a place that accepted blacks and moved in. It was there, on July 8, 1908, that Dr. Roberts delivered Florence D'Angeles Battle, her middle name hailing the baby as sent by the angels. At twenty-five, Battle was the proud father of two.

But joy was short-lived.

At little past three weeks of age, Florence contracted *cholera infantum*, then a terrifying illness likely caused by poor sanitation and now easily treatable by antibiotics. The condition afflicted children with severe diarrhea, violent vomiting, high fevers, and, eventually, dehydration. Often it was fatal. The only available—and ineffective—treatment was Mixture Cholera Infantum, a compound developed by a New York doctor in 1901 and sold today under the brand name Pepto-Bismol.

With Dr. Roberts at her side and Samuel and Florence struggling night and day to ease her agony, little Florence fought for life for more than a week. At the age of one month and one day, she died. Her death certificate set the time of death at 3:30 a.m. on August 9, 1908, and the place of death as "tenement."[77]

After a small funeral, Battle and Florence made a mournful pilgrimage across the East River by ferry and then by wagon into the Queens countryside to an Episcopal Church cemetery. Death had never been so close for Battle, and the toll on Florence was severe. To spare her the pain of confinement where the baby had died, Battle insisted that the family should travel by train to a black Elks convention in Detroit. The redcaps turned out in force to send Battle, Florence, and Jesse off with good cheer, and the Elks families did their best to provide comfort. At the convention's end, Battle took his wife and son for a late summer respite from New York's heat at the seashore in Atlantic City.

THERE WAS BAD news while Battle was in Detroit. Horrific white-on-black racial violence erupted in Springfield, Illinois. The police had arrested two black men for unrelated crimes, one on a charge of slitting a white man's throat after, it was believed, attempting to assault a white girl, the other for allegedly raping a white woman, a claim that was later retracted. A crowd surrounded the jail. Furious that the sheriff had spirited the two men away, the mob trashed black-owned businesses, and killed a barber who tried to defend his shop and hung his body from a tree. Under the watch of as many as twelve thousand people, rioters set ablaze a black neighborhood and cut firefighting hoses.

The intensity of the violence was greater than anyone could remember. The eruption had occurred not in the South but in the North, and not just anywhere in the North, but in the city that had sent Abraham Lincoln to the White House and in which the Great Emancipator was entombed. After visiting Springfield, journalist William English Walling wrote a magazine article headlined "Race War in the North." He concluded with words: "Yet who realizes the seriousness of the situation, and what large and powerful body of citizens is ready to come to their aid?" In New York, Mary White Ovington took the question as a challenge and began gathering allies to meet it.

AT ROUGHLY THIS moment, three African American men gathered with history-changing purpose in Doyle's Saloon on the corner of Lenox Avenue and 136th Street.

J. Frank Wheaton—a friend of Battle's from the Elks—was born in 1866 to a father credited with having been the first black to vote in Maryland after passage of the Fifteenth Amendment. Wheaton graduated from Storer College in West Virginia and studied at Howard University before becoming the first African American to graduate from the University of Minnesota Law School.

A gifted orator, he won election in 1898 to the Minnesota legislature, another first for a black man. He represented a district whose population of forty thousand included only one hundred African Americans. He won passage of a civil rights law that expanded equal access to public places and transportation. In 1905, Wheaton moved to New York, served as an assistant district attorney, opened a law practice, and became "the most loved man in Elkdom."

Bert Williams—a comrade from Battle's nights at the Marshall Hotel—was born in 1876 on the island of Nassau in the Bahamas. His father brought Williams to New York at the age of two and then to Riverside, California, where Williams graduated from the public high school. He let pass an ambition to become a civil engineer to go into show business. He began by playing the banjo in minstrel shows, moved into vaudeville, and teamed with fellow performer George Walker.

The duo, Williams and Walker, introduced New York to a two-stepping dance called the cakewalk. Their rendition, performed with two women, became a craze. In 1902, they made black theatrical history by opening a musical comedy in a Times Square theater. They took the hit to London and were invited to Buckingham Palace to entertain the Prince of Wales on his birthday.

J. C. Thomas was born in Houston on Christmas Day, 1863, and worked as a steamship cabin boy, eventually moving to New York at nineteen. While serving as a steward in private clubs, Thomas took a course in embalming and then opened a funeral parlor for African Americans in the Tenderloin, becoming the dominant funeral director in the region. He also invested in real estate, scoring a windfall when the Pennsylvania Railroad bought up the neighborhood for construction of a majestic Penn Station. His six-foot frame and Van Dyke beard reminded many of a Virginia planter.

Wheaton, Williams, and Thomas each put a hundred dollars on the bar at Doyle's Saloon as a contribution to forming the Equity Congress, an organization dedicated to seeking social equality in practical terms. The proprietor, Doyle, a neighborhood Irishman whose first name is lost to time, also kicked in a hundred dollars, earning a place as the Equity Congress' fourth founding member. Whether Doyle did so out of principle or simply to buy goodwill among a growing black customer base will never be known.

Wheaton, Williams, and Thomas set two goals. The first was to force open to blacks those areas of the civil service that had been closed: the New York City police and fire departments. The second was to persuade New York's legislature and governor to establish a black National Guard regiment that would give the state's African Americans entry into the US military.[78]

IN THE FIRST week of 1909, Mary White Ovington, William English Walling, and social worker Henry Moskowitz began planning to issue a "call" on the one hundredth anniversary of Lincoln's birth.

They recruited white progressives, including Oswald Garrison Villard, publisher of the *New York Evening Post* and grandson of the abolitionist William Lloyd Garrison, and then they enlisted blacks, including W. E. B. Du Bois, the intellectual spirit of the modern civil rights movement, and Battle's pastor, the Reverend Alexander Walters. On February 12, the group issued a manifesto that concluded: "We call upon all believers in democracy to join in a national conference for the discussion of present evils, the voicing of protests, and the renewal of the struggle for civil and political liberty."

Now seen as the founding event of the NAACP, the call was a ray of light for African Americans. Fully twenty years earlier, Reverend Walters had joined Timothy Thomas Fortune to form the National Afro-American League and had renewed the failed dream of founding a national civil rights organization after the US Supreme Court endorsed the concept of separate but equal in *Plessy v. Ferguson*. But now the Lincoln's birthday call of 1909 engendered fresh hope, because committed whites had for the first time joined the cause.

"I did not know personally Oswald Garrison Villard, Mary White Ovington or W. E. B. Du Bois but I rejoiced in their courageous action," Battle told Hughes four decades later.

The call led to conferences in New York in 1909 and 1910, out of which the NAACP emerged. Battle closely followed developments. His readings, his associations with blacks of achievement, and his experiences in the superior and inferior worlds had schooled him in America's racial crimes, from the slavery that had chained his parents to the ingrained prejudices that chartered less for his life and threatened to do the same for Jesse. A young man who was now drawn to action, he joined the nascent NAACP.

"I am a life member," Battle said. "I have been a member since the organization was founded."

AS THE NAACP was germinating, on the morning of March 30, 1909, the *20th Century Limited* rolled into Grand Central carrying America's most cheered and feared black man. Arthur John Johnson—Jack Johnson—was the newly crowned world heavyweight boxing champion, the first African American to win the title. Battle pulled rank for the privilege of carrying his bags.

Johnson was a figure of great fascination to the onetime bullyboy who now sparred in the gymnasium of St. Cyprian's Church on San Juan Hill. The big man from Galveston, Texas—six feet tall, 190 pounds—punched with precision and evaded blows feinting backward. Much more, he had broken America's most jealously guarded color line.

"I will never fight a Negro. I never have and never shall," champion John L. Sullivan had pronounced in 1892, reinforcing a seemingly eternal understanding that blacks were welcome to fight blacks and could match up against whites in lesser bouts—but never for the heavyweight crown.

Those restrictions notwithstanding, boxing was the single professional sport in which African Americans had a shot at making a living. Some excelled, and white society grew wary. In 1895, *New York Sun* editor Charles A. Dana gathered the inchoate fear into words: "The black man is rapidly forging to the front ranks in athletics, especially in the field of fisticuffs. We are in the midst of a black rise against white supremacy."[79]

Johnson embodied Dana's fevered imaginings. He won fight after fight until there was no one left to defeat—except the world champion, if ever the world champion would grant a match. Outside the ring, Johnson reveled in celebrity. Smiling through gold-capped teeth, he favored flashy clothing and drove fast cars. Most combustibly, he kept company with women, many of them white.

In time, Johnson would pay dearly for his "unforgivable blackness," as Du Bois would famously write. Now, though, he had goaded titleholder Tommy Burns into a fight in Australia by branding Burns a coward.

"I'll fight him even though he is a nigger," Burns finally declared, and the *Sydney Truth* blared, "De Big Coon Am A-Comin."

News stories made clear that white America vested combat between men of two skin colors with mythic significance. Something deep in its psyche dictated that the better race, rather than the better man, would win. Blacks, on the other hand, had rooted for a Johnson victory as proof that African Americans would succeed in any field if given the opportunity.

So, Battle had thrilled to read press accounts of the fight: Johnson knocking Burns to the canvas in the first and second rounds, Johnson drawing blood and closing Burns's eye. Johnson taunting, "You punch like a woman, Tommy." Johnson seeming to support Burns round after round so the pummeling could continue. The police entering the ring in the fourteenth to spare Burns further punishment. The referee declaring Johnson the victor. The crowd plunging into mournful silence.

Three months later, Johnson came to New York to entertain at Hammerstein's Victoria Theatre with displays of athleticism and boxing prowess, doing five shows a day and earning $7,000 for a two-week run. When the 20th Century Limited pulled in, cavernous Grand Central was jammed by thousands of people, most of them black.

Red-topped cap on his head, Battle wove a hand truck down the platform. Tenderloin cabaret king Baron Wilkins, who had backed Johnson with money, led a welcoming committee. Well aware of both the man and his nightclub, Battle greeted Wilkins and stood by to serve.

Johnson disembarked into an uproarious swirl. Perhaps the only man there who was larger in height and weight than the champion, Battle pushed through the jostling crowd to collect Johnson's bags and followed the entourage to the street. A dozen large open-topped touring automobiles waited at curbside. Johnson and Wilkins climbed into the lead car while a brass band played "Hail to the Chief." They pulled away for a drive to Wilkins's Little Savoy cabaret, where Johnson was accustomed to staying in a rose-and-gold-hued room. Battle watched them go, thinking about a black man who had upended the world.[80]

SIX MONTHS LATER, in August 1909, while the NAACP was still gelling, Battle saw the drive for national activism merge with rising calls to integrate the New York Police Department. First, in the pulpit of the Bethel AME Church, the Reverend Reverdy Ransom urged the appointment of black police officers in a sermon that illustrates how constricted American racial attitudes were. He declared that African Americans belonged in the NYPD not as a matter of equal opportunity but to better crack down on the misconduct of blacks newly arriving in the city from the rural South. "We who are continuously denouncing the whites should show our honesty, broad-mindedness and sincere desire to see that the laws are not broken by being as equally willing to condemn and seek to bring to justice the disreputable members of the race," Ransom said.[81]

Fortune's *Age* played Ransom's sermon on the front page—only now Timothy Thomas Fortune was gone from the great paper of his founding. He had succumbed to a problem with drink, and there was a new force in the ownership: Booker T. Washington had covertly invested in the *Age* with the aim of countering rising criticism of his leadership in other organs of the black press. Washington installed as editor Frederick Randolph Moore, the son of a slave mother and a white father who had started his career as a US Treasury Department messenger. Moore accompanied the *Age*'s report on Ransom's sermon with an editorial whose thoughts were more apologetic than acidic: "The resentment of the loafing Negroes of 127th street Sunday afternoon against the policeman performing his duty was entirely uncalled for and vicious. The Negro has copied this method of resisting the law from the foreign colonies in New York and it is to be vigorously condemned by every respectable and race-loving Negro."[82]

A week after Ransom's call, congregants packed the pews of Battle's Mother AME Zion Church, now moved from Greenwich Village to a house of worship at the corner of West Eighty-Ninth Street and Columbus Avenue, for an appearance by New York's second-highest elected official. Standing in for a vacationing mayor, Board of Aldermen President Patrick McGowan announced that he supported opening the police force to African Americans. The *Age* reported: "The Acting Mayor declared that he long had been of the opinion that Negro police in certain sections would end the clashes between the police and the blacks and, therefore, favored having Negro police."

Moore's approving editorial was vested with wishful thinking: "The Negro has had a deep and deterring suspicion that politics play the important part in the selection of the policemen. Now to be assured by the city government that the Negro passing the examination will be treated with absolute fairness will doubtless encourage numbers of qualified Negroes to try for the force."[83]

At this point, a new figure stepped to the fore with an appeal to *Age* readers. As a lieutenant of Tammany Hall Democratic boss Richard Croker, Edward E. "Chief" Lee was the city's most powerful African American political operative. Before the turn of the century, Croker had realized that persuading blacks to vote for Democrats rather than for Republicans, still seen as members of the party of Lincoln, could be crucial to gaining an edge. He promised to "place at least one colored man in every department of the city government," and he installed Lee as head of a patronage-dispensing Tammany club called United Colored Democracy.

On September 2, 1909, Moore's front-page headline challenged: "Chief Edward E. Lee Tells *The Age* That Negroes Refuse to Qualify for Positions—September 11, Last Day for Filing Applications."

The story went on: "Chief Lee contends that the absence of negroes from the police force of Greater New York is not due to color prejudice existing in the Police Department, but because in the past members of the race have been backward and unwilling to take the examination. Within the past four years but two Negro applicants have taken the examination and they failed to prove equal to the test."[84]

AMID THIS SURGE of advocacy, Battle decided to be the one. He set his mind on joining the New York Police Department, fortress of a closed white circle guarded by clubs and guns. Decades later, he portrayed his decision as one of routine economics: with a growing family, he saw no chance for advancement as a redcap and no hope of a pension. He also knew that he was smarter, better read, stronger, spoke clearer English, and knew far more about New York and America than many of the Irish cops he encountered on the street. If they could do the job, so could he.

The police department's nightstick racism frightened Florence, but she gave her blessing to a job that, by rights, should have been anyone's to claim. Battle then raised the possibility with a handful of friends. They predicted defeat and counseled against fighting a lost cause. Wary of failure, he retreated into privacy. He chose to be just another applicant and not to stand out as *the* black man who was daring to try for the police department. At all costs, he wanted to avoid having it known that he had washed out. Hundreds of men fell below the hiring mark every time the department replenished the ranks. That was expected. But he would become a black man who wasn't good enough, confirming what so many whites said—that blacks just weren't good enough.

The test was competitive. Ranking toward the top on the hiring list would be crucial. Among the exam topics were the Penal Law, the Code of Criminal Courts Act, the Dance Hall Law, the Civil Rights Law, the Education Law, the General Business Law, general city ordinances, arithmetic, and expertise in getting around the city. A good memory was a big plus.[85]

Would-be police officers typically took classes at the Delehanty Institute, a school that readied candidates for civil service tests. Battle found his way there, only to be barred from admission. Director Michael J. Delehanty would not allow a black man into a course for the police department, nor would his white students. Except for Florence, Battle was on his own.

He told Hughes, who wrote:

I bought a book, "How to Become a Patrolman," purchased from "The Police Chronicle" for fifty cents. My new book indicated other volumes, lists and useful materials which I secured. I used every available moment of free time for study. I carried my books in my pocket while on duty at Grand Central and I spent most of my lunch hour concentrating on them. After I had swept up behind the horses at the cabstand and finished my other cleaning duties, I read while waiting trains. By the time I got home in the evenings it would often be after eight o'clock. As soon as supper was over, I would tackle my studies again. I sometimes fell asleep in my chair after a hard day's work.

My greatest difficulty was in memorizing addresses, streets, place names and locations. For memory training, my wife used to read to me paragraphs from newspapers and, an hour or two later, I would see how much I could repeat to her word for word.

At the age of twenty-six, Battle strode into the test center on the appointed day in 1910. He was alone among 637 white faces. They could not turn him away because blacks were entitled by law to sit for civil service tests. At home afterward, Battle told Florence that he seemed to know the material. They would have to wait to find out whether he had known enough. When the city published the roster of results, Battle found his name at the 199th place—in the top one-third of the pack, easily high enough to be called for the mandatory physical.

He had work to do. Knowing better than to report as just another rookie, Battle turned for advice to the men who knew what it was like to be black in a police department. Wiley Grenada Overton, Philip W. Hadley, John W. Lee, and Moses P. Cobb told Battle that being a good cop would not be good enough. They told him that he would have to be better than the best white cop. And they told him that he would have to weather mistreatment with silent grace, because the department had too many ways to get a man.

While Battle waited to be called for his physical, The Reverend Reverdy Ransom made a fresh push to open the department. A new president of the Board of Aldermen, John Puroy Mitchell, had stepped in as acting chief executive while Mayor William Gaynor recuperated from an attempted assassination. Ransom won an audience with Mitchell.

"We presented a request to him first, to appoint some Negro policemen, not only on regular patrol duty, but also to the city parks," Ransom recalled in a memoir. "Mayor Mitchell throughout the whole interview was both evasive and not committal, and finally disgusted, I said to him, 'Mr. Mayor, it looks like you refuse to appoint Negroes to police duty, even in the parks of the city. Is it because you are afraid they might spit on the grass and kill it?'"[86]

NO SOONER HAD Jack Johnson won the heavyweight crown than the cry had gone up: America needed to knock the black interloper off the throne. Former champion Jim Jeffries became the Great White Hope. The bout was set for San Francisco, July 4, 1910. In the run-up, Jeffries worked out with a fury that returned him to fighting trim after six years spent in retirement on a California alfalfa farm.

Cabaret king Baron Wilkins sent Johnson off to California with a promise to bet big on his friend. Johnson telegraphed on arriving: "Send me seventeen thousand out here as the odds are better. Betting very brisk. Am in tip-top shape and will win sure." The *Age* proudly reported that Wilkins had quickly assembled "Negroes of betting proclivities" into "a pool with a view to making a killing on July 4." They wired $20,000 "with instructions for Johnson to bet the entire amount on himself." Twenty thousand dollars then is the equivalent today of roughly a half-million dollars.[87]

At almost the last minute, the governor of California barred the fight from his state. The promoters hurriedly found a new location in the wilder territory of Reno, Nevada. There, early in the afternoon on America's birthday, with the temperature topping one hundred degrees, Johnson and Jeffries ran through their final warm-ups. In New York, thirty thousand people jammed Times Square to read bulletins posted on three sides of the *Times* building, and thousands more gathered to get the news in Herald Square. Wilkins's best customers milled around a ticker-tape machine specially installed in the Little Savoy's basement gambling hall.

Perry Bradford, the musician, remembered: "In came Lovie Joe, opened his mouth and said that he had that money to bet on Jeffries, Barron called that bet and told Lovie to go back to the syndicate and bring some real money, no more pennies. Lovie came back with twenty thousand dollars more. So Baron covered that bet and asked Lovie Joe if he got any more money."[88]

At 2:46 p.m., the Fight of the Century began disappointingly. Johnson, at 208 pounds, and Jeffries, down to 227, spent the first round shoving and bumping more than punching. In the fourth, Jeffries opened a cut in Johnson's mouth, and whites across the country cheered the telegrapher's news: "First blood for Jeff." Their exultation was short-lived. From the fifth round on, Johnson took increasing command. In the fifteenth, Johnson knocked Jeffries to his haunches with an upper cut and three lefts. Jeffries got to his feet before the count reached ten. Johnson put him down again with a left. Jeffries's seconds reached through the ropes to help him stand. Johnson administered four blows and stood over Jeffries, cocked to put him down if he dared rise. Jeffries's corner threw in the towel.

In shared psychic defeat, the taunts of racial passion cooled into silence, while, twenty-seven hundred miles away in Herald Square, "You could hear a pin drop midst the big crowd which had been screaming every time Jeffries hit Johnson," Bradford remembered. Inside the Little Savoy, Wilkins climbed atop the bar and called out, "Everybody have some champagne on the house." A sporting man named Dude Foster paraded around shaking two bottles of champagne, waving thousand-dollar bills that he'd won wagering on Johnson and proclaiming, "I am God's gift to women. All you beat up gals, and what came with you, if you need any of that little thing called money, see the Dude."[89]

Meanwhile, carrying a purse of $121,000, Johnson headed east by train. Along the way, he got reports that white-on-black rioting had erupted like "prickly heat all over the country," in the *New York Tribune*'s memorable phrase. Racial violence that night in Houston, Washington, Baltimore, New Orleans, Philadelphia, Atlanta, Cincinnati, St. Louis, and numerous other cities and towns would leave as many as twenty-six people dead. In New York, white gangs attacked with such frequency in the blocks around the Little Savoy that wounded blacks arrived at the Tenderloin stationhouse at an average rate of one every fifteen minutes. Whites assaulted blacks on West Fifty-Third Street, where Battle had dined at the Marshall Hotel. On the West Side, a mob of two hundred chased a black man toward Central Park, relenting only when a white doctor held them off with a gun, not far from the home of Battle's former employers, the Andreinis. A short walk from Battle's Mother AME Zion Church, crowds cheered as a band of young toughs known as the Pearl Button Gang set upon blacks. A few blocks from McBride's Saloon, where Battle had eaten lunch with fellow redcaps, someone called for a lynching, someone produced a rope, and "the negro was in a fair way to swing into eternity," when police arrived. On San Juan Hill, near where Battle had set up house with Florence, a white mob set fire to a tenement occupied by blacks and tried to block the doors until firefighters reached the scene. Just down the street and around the corner from Battle's Harlem apartment, whites dragged a black man from a trolley after crying, "Let's lynch the first nigger we meet."[90]

Five days later, Wilkins distributed handbills that read: "To every colored man, woman, and child in Greater New York: Be at the Grand Central Station at 9:30 o'clock Monday morning and let us all shake the glad hand of the stalwart athlete, the greatest of the twentieth century."[91]

Jack Johnson was again coming to New York for a show at Hammerstein's Victoria Theatre. Battle arrived for work early and pulled rank: he would be the redcap who again tended to the champ. The *Washington Post* and *New York Times* pegged the crowd at ten thousand people. They had to wait because a wreck had blocked the tracks. Finally, the *20th Century Limited* pulled in five hours late. Hand truck at the ready, Battle stood near Wilkins as Johnson emerged into jostling that was not to be restrained. He left behind a slender, dark-haired woman, Etta Terry Duryea. She was the daughter of a moneyed family, was divorced from a husband of social standing, was traveling as Johnson's wife, and was white. She remained largely out of view until Johnson and Wilkins had pushed through the jubilance. They had planned a parade to the Little Savoy, but Johnson had arrived just in time for his appearance at the Victoria. Someone in the entourage told Battle that he would be bringing Johnson's luggage all the way to the theater.

A dozen touring cars waited at curbside. Johnson and Wilkins climbed into the first vehicle, and the caravan drove north on Fifth Avenue to Fifty-Eighth Street, down Broadway to greet a crowd outside the Little Savoy, and then on to the theater. Battle loaded Johnson's bags, one containing the blue tights and stars-and-stripes belt the champ would wear on stage, into a horse-drawn hansom cab for the five-block ride to the Victoria, a service for which, Battle would note, Johnson neglected to tip.[92]

BATTLE AND CHIEF Williams brought the story home to Harlem. No one listened more intently to descriptions of the heavyweight champion than the Chief's son, Wesley. Thirteen years of age and approaching his adult physique of five feet nine and 180 pounds, Wesley was bigger, stronger, and faster than even boys who were years older and more developed. He reveled in sports and excelled at all forms of athletics, from basketball and handball to swimming. When he won a roller-skating race against more mature competitors, Wesley caught the eye of C. A. Ramsey, a former wrestling champion who held a black belt in judo. Ramsey was training athletes at an outpost of the Colored Men's Branch of the YMCA. He urged Wesley to come to classes.[93] Happily complying, Wesley soon was more devoted to Ramsey's regimen of pumping iron and self-defense workouts than he was to schoolwork—his sharp mind and powerful body recalling for Battle the bullyboy days of his own youth.

AS BATTLE'S NAME rose toward the top of the hiring list, he was called for the medical exam. Now, whatever anyone may have known about him, there was no hiding his skin color. From head to toe, he was black, and not only that, he was big and strong and black.

And he was stoppable.

The police surgeon diagnosed Battle as suffering from a heart murmur, thus providing a pretext for disqualifying him and proving that the fear of medical sabotage once expressed in the Age had been justified. At first, the doctor's findings mystified Battle. Having carried "tons of baggage miles per week," he was sure that he was fit. Then he was passed over once, and then twice on the list. A friend, Thomas Henry Peyton, warned Battle that a third rejection would doom his chances.

Peyton was a fellow former North Carolinian whose parents had been lured to leave a farm in 1876 by a man with "tales of fortunes, romance and adventures waiting for those daring enough to go" to Africa. The Peytons sent their belongings ahead, sailed for New York on an Old Dominion steamer, and discovered that they had been conned out of all their possessions. The couple returned home, leaving Thomas in Brooklyn, where he had courted one of Battle's sisters and found a place with Moses Cobb in the lower ranks of the police department.[94] Speaking of Peyton, Battle said:

> He had been doing stationhouse duty—they called them "turnkeys."
> One day when I was working in Grand Central, he came up to me
> and said, "Sam, do you know that your name is about to be dropped
> to the bottom of the list, of civil service? The police commissioner
> hasn't appointed you."
>
> I said, "I didn't know, I thought someday they might appoint me."
>
> He said, "No. Don't allow your name to go to the bottom of the
> list. Go and ask for another examination, something of that kind. Do
> something about it."[95]

Thanks to Peyton, Battle realized that he needed help. One man came to mind: Frederick Randolph Moore, editor of the *Age*, the newspaper that had advocated for opening the police department to blacks.

To Moore, Battle's sudden appearance must have seemed like an answer to prayers. Not only had the young man shown the courage to get this far, there was every indication, in mind, body, and character, that he could lead the way for others. Moore summoned surprised allies, among them Edward "Chief" Lee, head of Tammany Hall's United Colored Democracy; Lee's deputy Robert N. Wood; and Charles Anderson, New York's leading black Republican. By appointment of President Roosevelt, Anderson served as commissioner of the Internal Revenue Service in New York, a patronage position of high regard for whites, let alone for blacks. Like Moore, Anderson was loyal to Booker T. Washington.

And, of course, Moore called on J. Frank Wheaton, Bert Williams, and J. C. Thomas, whose missions were to integrate the police and fire departments and to establish a black New York National Guard regiment. Their Equity Congress was by now a thriving organization. The group promised Battle full support.

Moore and Battle also sought the help of Dr. Roberts, but the three men soon agreed that Roberts's medical expertise would be meaningless because he was black. Regretfully but realistically, Roberts referred Battle to an eminent white physician, Dr. James Dowling. Battle recalled to Hughes:

> I arranged an appointment during my lunch period, walking up to his office from the Grand Central. I was given a very complete examination, so painstaking, in fact, that it was mid-afternoon before I got back to work at the station.
>
> When Dr. Dowling finished with me he said, "You are the most perfect physical specimen I have ever examined." I then asked him to check my heart again, because I had to prepare myself for strenuous work, and that was what had given me concern. He rechecked my heart. When he had finished this second examination, he said, "Your heart is in perfect shape. There is nothing wrong at all."
>
> Without informing him of the rejection by the police surgeons, I asked Dr. Dowling for a certificate as to my state of health, again stressing attention to my heart. He sat down and made out a complete report on me. As he was about to sign it, I requested him to put all of his full professional titles down behind his name. With a smile he did so, closing not only with Professor of Diagnosis and Consulting Surgeon, but President of Flower Hospital, one of the leading city hospitals of that day.
>
> When I asked his fee, he said his usual charge for so complete an examination was $150. I must have looked somewhat startled at such a large amount. He no doubt noticed my Red Cap uniform and knew that I did not come from the financial class to which most of his patients belonged. He said that he would charge me only ten percent of that figure, namely his regular office fee of $15. Even this seemed a fairly large sum to me. But I went back to Grand Central that afternoon with my prized certificate.
>
> That evening I took the certificate to Editor Fred Moore. He wrote a letter to Mayor Gaynor enclosing it and stating that I had passed all the oral, written, mental, and character tests required for appointment to the police force, and that the enclosed certificate showed that one of the city's finest physicians found nothing wrong with me physically. He asked, therefore, why my name had been passed over twice when men much farther down the list than I had already received appointments.

Moore's letter to the mayor and Dr. Dowling's clean bill of health brightened the Christmas season of 1910 for Battle and Florence, and for Jesse in the way that a four-year-old, going on five, absorbs parental cheer. Then the weeks dragged without action. In February 1911, Moore wrote again to Gaynor, concluding, "Your general reputation for fairness leads me to believe that you will see that Mr. Battle is given that consideration to which he is entitled and as the police department is under your control I shall hope to see Mr. Battle appointed."

Gaynor responded by tersely telling Moore, "I do not understand that the man you mention is in danger of discrimination whatever. Do you not merely imagine that the contrary is the case?"[96]

While Wheaton pressed Police Commissioner Rhinelander Waldo, Anderson lobbied the mayor, and Moore scathed Waldo in an editorial, Battle could only sit tight.[97] Finally, after more than three months, the department summoned him for a second medical exam.

"A young white man in line just ahead of me fainted dead away as he stood before the doctor," Battle remembered. "When my turn came I said pointedly, 'I'm sure you will find nothing wrong with me, sir—but the color of my skin. No doubt, that young fellow who just fell out in a cold sweat on the floor will pass his examination—because he is white.'"

This time, the doctor said, "I don't find anything wrong with you—or your heart."

And, at last, Commissioner Waldo designated Battle as a candidate for the New York Police Department.

"The next morning headlines announced my appointment," Battle said. "The Negro papers were particularly jubilant, heralding the event and editorializing on it almost as much as they did the year before when Jack Johnson won the heavyweight championship from Jim Jeffries."

Twenty years had passed since Wiley Grenada Overton, Philip W. Hadley, John W. Lee, and Moses P. Cobb had fought to integrate the Brooklyn police force. Twelve had passed since Battle had met Jim Crow as he headed north from New Bern with Anne, whose face and touch had since been memories. Ten years had passed since he had stood in the presence of Theodore Roosevelt and Booker T.

Washington while serving the white students of Yale. Nine years had passed since Arthur Schomburg had schooled him in racial pride and stressed self-education. Six years had passed since he had stopped working as anyone's boy.

He was a husband and a father, and at the age of twenty-eight, he had made history. He was Greater New York's first black cop.

Anderson wrote to Booker T. Washington to assure the great man that he and Moore had been key to a signal victory. Mentioning Battle only offhandedly as "this colored man," Anderson told Washington: "Brother Lee, brother Wood, the Equity Congress and Frank Wheaton are claiming credit for the appointment. I have said nothing, but from the tenor of the Mayor's letter, in which he asks me to 'see that the appointee will be a credit to his race,' it looks as though the Mayor felt that I had something to do with it. As a matter of fact, I think the appointment was largely due to all of us. Moore deserves especial credit, for it was he that interested me in the case."[98]

Then they all moved on, leaving Battle to a solitary fight, as alone as if he were beyond help behind enemy lines.

Because he was.

CHAPTER TWO

STRUGGLE

TONY RISES ON a morning in the summer of 1950 and finds what he needs: T-shirt, shorts, and canvas sneakers, to be complemented by a baseball bat, fishing pole, or homemade frog spear. Leaky comes to Tony's side. He's a mix, resembling a Labrador. He earned his name in the failures of paper training.

The white clapboard cottage is located in New York's first African American vacation community. Known as Greenwood Forest Farms, the enclave comprises several dozen getaways. Prominent blacks purchased the land in 1919, laced it with winding roads, and subdivided it into lots. There's a clubhouse and a lake.

Tony gets going while the going is good, to play before his grandfather can shed the bed covers and run down a list of chores. There were kids to find and, maybe, a catfish to catch or a bullfrog with meaty legs to impale on nails tied to a broomstick, for Florence to fry in an iron skillet.

He is especially hurried because Langston Hughes is sleeping in a guestroom. Hughes and his grandfather are going to spend the day talking, and Hughes is going to write things down. Hughes has come to the townhouse several times to talk and write. Once, Hughes brought a tape recorder with spinning reels that stood tall on the table. His grandfather spoke into a microphone. That is at least interesting. To hear them talk, watch the tape rewind, and hear them talk again is something new. Otherwise, Tony dislikes having

Hughes around. The presence of literary greatness is nothing com-
pared with a youngster's summer joys, and he senses, correctly, that
Hughes has little patience for a boy with a dog who would intrude
on his time.

Hughes is here at the cottage in fulfillment of a commitment
rather than in pursuit of the writing of the great poems, novels,
librettos, and essays that have been his life's work and will be his
legacy. Yes, he sees in Battle's scrapbooks and he hears in Battle's
tales that Battle's life is Harlem's story, and he knows that Harlem's
story is a centerpiece of the rise and persecution of African Americans in the first half of the twentieth century. But, as compelling as
Battle's story is, his biography offers Hughes little hope of producing the next great American work of literature whose characters
would be black folks and whose pages would pulse with universal
humanity. In truth, Hughes had agreed to work with Battle primarily because he had needed a $1,500 check to pay the bills. He has
spent the money, yet he has barely started coming to terms with his
employer's memories.

When he was younger, Hughes had traveled the world, happy to
go it alone in odd jobs, happy to collect a check here and there for
writing that seemed effortless, for language that sounded in the blues
and rose from the African American soul. If the uplift and adulation
of the Harlem Renaissance had meant having but two nickels to rub
together in the 1920s, so be it. Patrons provided support. Publishers
were interested. There was always a way.

Later, when Stalin's Soviet Union invited twenty-two African
Americans to travel to Moscow for what turned out to be a comi-
cally ill-conceived plan for a movie about black Americans, Hughes
turned the project into an often-solitary round-the-world trip. When
the Spanish Civil War erupted, he sent dispatches from the front as
a correspondent for the Baltimore *Afro-American* newspaper. But,
with Hollywood closed to black writers, Hughes has scrambled with
hit-and-miss projects.

At one point, in desperation, he conceived of a plan to write
about whites under a pseudonym. In the depths, he wrote that he
would "withdraw from the business of authoring and try to take up

something less reducing to the body and racking to the soul," adding, "I'll just let ART be a sideline like it used to be in the days when I was a busboy and was at least sure of my meals."[1]

From the same wellspring of despair, he wrote "Genius Child," a poem whose central line was: "Nobody loves a genius child." And whose concluding line was "*Kill him*—and let his soul run wild."

Now, owing Battle his labor and out of excuses for avoiding the project, Hughes submits to the confines of the white-clapboard shanty, rising early and working late, letting Battle talk, and questioning him to elicit facts. Tony runs in and out. Florence serves the two men meals. She is more distant than gracious. Her husband is pouring his heart into a book and a movie that will tell his life story, and she worries that the renowned writer at his side will break it.

THE DAY ARRIVED: June 28, 1911.

Battle dressed in freshly ironed clothing. Florence wanted to be sure he looked his best. She had helped him score well on the exam, and now she stood with Jesse, grown tall at five years old, and sent Battle forth from the apartment with their love.

On the way to the train, he moved among whites who called him an invader and in front of buildings whose owners had covenanted to bar African Americans. Hostility screamed from the *Harlem Home News*: "Heart of Harlem Now to Be Invaded by Negroes."

When a building a short distance from Battle's address rented to blacks, the front page blared: "Black Invaders Capture White Flat in 121st St."[2]

Downtown, the police department's domed headquarters was designed to convey the majesty of the law. Battle strode into a marble-clad reception hall. Forty-four recruits awaited swearing in by Commissioner Waldo. He told the group that "he was glad to have a representative of the black race on the force."[3] Later, the commissioner spoke to Battle more ominously. "You will have some difficulties but I know you will overcome them," Waldo said, implicitly acknowledging that, on the streets and in the stationhouses, Battle would be beyond official protection.[4]

Difficulties. Daunting though the word was, Battle granted Waldo good faith. Putting pencil to lined paper, he noted that Waldo was a North Carolinian transplanted from Beaufort and wrote with characteristic charity, "He was a high class wealthy man who was of sterling character without racial bias."[5]

The department assigned Badge No. 782 to Battle. As he put it, he had become a bluecoat while he was still a redcap. He had a resignation to submit, and he headed uptown. He arrived to find the street in front of Grand Central in full bustle, whites in fine clothing and black men hopping to in hats crowned with red felt. His colleagues of six years had not yet gotten the word. Through all the months of study, he had kept his counsel, and Battle wanted to speak first to Chief Williams, but on this day of all days, the Chief was off on personal business. Battle diverted to give notice to the stationmaster. Uncertain how this first white man to hear the news would respond, Battle was heartened to receive congratulations.

Still, he was compelled to admit that he had no idea how the venture would work out. Rather than quit outright, he asked for a six-month leave, just long enough to cover the probationary period during which the department could wash out any rookie. The stationmaster granted Battle an indefinite leave with an invitation to return at any time.

Word leaped along the platforms, and Battle walked out into a throng. "All the boys, all the Red Caps, stopped carrying the bags," he remembered. "Things were all tied up for a while, to see this first black policeman in Greater New York."

Then Battle headed home to Florence. Again, the news traveled faster than he did. "When I reached my apartment that evening a large group of friends had gathered. And every night thereafter for weeks, people, even complete strangers, kept dropping in to offer congratulations. I received more invitations to address clubs and church groups than I could fill in a year."

Battle and Florence confronted how life had changed. For starters, they would have less money. Battle had earned as much as $300 a month in tips as a redcap; a rookie police officer's salary was $66 a month. To survive, the Battles would draw on money he had banked for just this purpose. Then, too, a police officer worked long hours for days on end. Florence, at the age of twenty-two, would have to care for Jesse largely on her own.

While the police department's terms and conditions were onerous, they applied equally to everyone who joined the ranks. Battle was as prepared as a man could be to take them on, along with a burden unknown to anyone else on the force: that of upholding the black man's honor. Under the benighted standard of the time, he would be judged a credit to his race or he would confirm that African Americans did not have what it took to succeed.

The following morning Battle reported to the police training school. He felt fairly treated among the probationers, but he discovered that the white establishment was hardly approving of his appointment. The *New York Times* captured the sentiment in a condescendingly racist editorial. Conceding that some African Americans "have the requisite size, strength and courage, and some of them have the intelligence necessary" for police service, the paper predicted that "where a white policeman would be resisted once in making arrests, the black policeman would be resisted four or five times."

Still, the *Times* concluded, "New York has in its population enough Negroes to give them a right to claim this sort of 'recognition.'"[6]

The training course extended for thirty days. Battle practiced shooting a gun, drilled on rules and regulations, and met all the physical demands. Along the way, he bought a uniform for twenty-eight dollars at a shop called H. Levy & Son, surprising the proprietor by paying with a fifty-dollar bill rather than on credit, because, Battle told Hughes, "I always tried to pay my way ahead, not behind."

When schooling was completed, the department scattered the new men among the city's eighty stationhouses. Battle's destination was the Twenty-Eighth Precinct on West Sixty-Eighth Street, quarters of the head crackers who patrolled his old neighborhood, San Juan Hill, well known to him as the fortress where cops had forced black men to run a gauntlet of clubs in the siege of 1905. If the higher-ups were out to do Battle in, they chose well. The New York Police Department had no tougher place.

*   *   *

JESSE SLEPT IN the shadows of the small apartment while Florence prepared breakfast. The air of a summer of rains and high heat was heavy, even this early. Battle got "tubbed and scrubbed," and then he put on the uniform that designated authority to enforce the law.

In summer, the department discarded its tailed and high-buttoned coat for a blue blouse cut from light fabric. The year-round constants were trousers seamed with white cord, a belted holster with revolver, and a gray helmet whose shell offered some protection from bricks tossed off tenement roofs, known then as Irish confetti.

Battle kissed his son and his wife, and then he went toward his just due with the confidence that had carried him from childhood, with faith in the goodness of human nature, and undaunted by the *difficulties* that rose with the sun.

From a distance, Battle saw the crowd in front of the stationhouse on the morning when the gawking began. "There's the nigger," some shouted as he drew close. He heard white voices say, "Why, he looks just like Jack Johnson," and, "He's a burly bastard," while some African Americans called out, "Ain't he a fine looking man?"

Battle betrayed no sign that anything unusual was taking place. He needed to appear ordinary so that, in time, he might be accepted as one more cop. The stationhouse door was thickly hewn, as if designed to repulse attack. Inside, an elevated platform—the desk—dominated the central room. From behind its ramparts, a lieutenant oversaw the execution of the laws, as well as compliance with the orders that governed a police officer's life.

The lieutenant pointed Battle to a room where officers congregated before starting patrol. It was here or in a space nearby that blacks had been made to run the gauntlet. Battle offered a greeting that said he expected inclusion: "Good morning."

The group responded with coordinated silence. Soon, a sergeant announced assignments. He gave Battle a post in a well-to-do neighborhood along Riverside Drive between West Seventy-Ninth and West Eighty-Sixth Streets. Then Battle joined a march outside. A superior officer inspected uniforms and equipment. Some in the crowd again referred to him as a "nigger." When the order came to disperse, he set off, trailed by spectators.

The silence of Battle's fellow cops was more than a statement of racial scorn. It was also a weapon. Every man among them had been schooled in policing by his elders. How to make an arrest, how to wield a nightstick, how to avoid the attention of internal affairs "shoo-flies"—stationhouse and street-corner tutorials were critical to survival.

The black man's failure deeply wished for, Battle would have no help as he broke in under a scorching sun. His beat followed Riverside Park, overlooking the Hudson River and passing beneath elegant manses and apartment buildings. Across eight long hours, without a moment for lunch, Battle showed only toleration to the unbelieving who flocked to see a black police officer. Friends from the Marshall Hotel, the musical comedy team of Dan Avery and Charles Hart, "drove by in a red roadster to see if all was well with me," as Battle remembered. Finally, hungry, wet with perspiration, and exhausted, he gave his memo book to a sergeant for signature at 4 p.m. and headed home.

"There he is," a voice cried, as Battle came up out of the subway in Harlem. Fellow blacks swarmed him. He found the apartment filled with friends who wished him well as he ate the dinner he had been waiting for. When finally they were gone, he recounted the day for Florence and Jesse, and, using her nickname of endearment, Florence told her husband, "Jesse, I am proud of you."

THE NEXT DAY and the day after that and the day after that, Battle returned to the silence and the staring. His primary duty involved directing horse-drawn vehicles and early automobiles, while standing on display as if he were a circus performer.

"Everybody came by, and when the street cars would pass, the motormen and conductors would clang the bells, and the conductor would say, 'Look over there at New York's first colored policeman.' When the sightseeing buses would come along, they would announce loudly to the people, 'Here's New York's first colored policeman,'" he remembered.

"Then the colored fellows that drove these open barouches for people on sightseeing tours would bring the people down from the cabarets in different parts of the city, particularly from Harlem and Baron Wilkins' night club, and charge them a dollar each to take them to see this colored policeman."[7]

Battle made his first arrest after a white man failed to stop his horse and wagon in front of a school, as Battle had commanded, and then refused to accept a summons from a black officer, questioning even that Battle was truly a cop. He arrested his first black person at about 2 a.m. one Sunday morning in Central Park.

"I saw what appeared to be a beautiful brown-skin girl in furs and a picture hat. Because it was unusual in that section for women to be out alone at that time of night, I approached and asked her destination," Battle remembered. "A masculine voice answered, 'Just walking.' It was a man in female garb, painted and powdered. Although he begged me not to do so, my duty required that I take him to the station."

Battle felt well treated by the whites he encountered and made interesting friends, among them Felix Adler, founder of the Ethical Culture movement, and Charles Thorley, proprietor of the House of Flowers, who had given Chief Williams a start as his doorman.

"Many a dawn," Battle said, he saw Thorley "galloping by on his saddle horses in the park. He used two horses, changing mounts for the second part of his morning ride. After he got to know me, he always spoke and sometimes stopped for a chat."

Blessed with a sharp eye, Battle took detailed note of his surroundings. And, despite all the *difficulties*, he found much to appreciate. Years later, Hughes would tell the story this way:

> Diamond Jim Brady, at the height of his fame and very much sought after by women, lived in an elaborate house on the north side of 86th Street opposite Central Park. William Randolph Hearst lived at the end of this street facing the Drive. On 72nd Street near Columbus Avenue, adjoining the Dakota Apartments, the Straus family had a large place. At that time many apartment houses in the area, including the Dakota, would not rent to Jewish people, so some of their financiers built the Majestic Hotel which was not restricted, and accommodated large families.

A number of fine houses in the neighborhood were occupied by beautiful young women kept at that time by wealthy men. Most of them lived alone with their maids. And one of the most attractive brownstones facing Central Park was occupied by a Negro woman, the famed Hannah Elias, who had been given a fortune by an aged wealthy paramour. She lived quietly with several servants, including a Japanese butler. I seldom saw her, but when I did she bowed pleasantly.

At the foot of 79th Street, many U.S. Naval vessels docked. Attracted by seamen, this area was a Mecca for dozens of effeminate young men who congregated to welcome the sailors as they came ashore. Some of these effeminate young fellows were professionals, but others were from families of means seeking companions among the seamen. Ladies of the evening, too, gathered here whenever the boats came in.

Everybody liked me. I made wonderful friends. There was a family called the Daltons that lived at the Hotel Majestic on 72d Street, lovely people, very wealthy people. They had a private stable between 67th Street and 68th Street, and their chauffeurs and footmen lived there over the stable. Whenever Madame, the old lady would come out, she would always want to say hello to me, just as though I were a personal friend of theirs.

The children, of course—I didn't get the right treatment from them all the time, and I didn't mind it. Particularly I shall never forget a bunch of white kids, one time, in one particular neighborhood over on the East Side. I'd been over to one of the hospitals on the East Side, on some official business in a police uniform. These kids cried, "There goes the nigger cop, there goes the nigger cop!"

I looked at them and smiled and kept on going. I didn't remonstrate with them, because they didn't know any better. That's all they could think about.

Battle's work chart scheduled his first reserve duty for midnight to 8 a.m. on the Thursday after he started patrol. Finishing a four-to-twelve night shift, he was to sleep in the stationhouse with a platoon on call in the event of an emergency. A dormitory was outfitted with a couple dozen bunks and was draped in the odors of overworked men, discarded shoes, soiled linens, and tobacco smoke.

Fetid air and all, the officers of the Sixty-Eighth Street station-house resolved that this was a whites-only domain. Cops carried a cot upstairs to a room on the second floor, where the precinct stored the American flag, and left the mattress and springs under Old Glory as the black man's accommodations.

Without complaint, Battle went up to the flag loft. Several times, a captain named Thomas Palmer asked Battle how he was faring with fellow officers. Just fine, Battle reported. "I don't expect the men to talk to me and take me in their arms as a brother," he told the captain.

Inevitably, newspaper reporters caught wind that Battle was subjected to silence and isolation. They sought him out, but he held firm to voicing no unhappiness. Interviewed by the *Times* three weeks after he arrived at the stationhouse, Battle made sure to state that no officer had uttered offensive epithets, and he responded, "I have nothing to say about that, Sir," when asked about his fellow officers' refusal to speak with him.

As if to make a much larger point, he shared with the reporter the Battle family lore that had been handed down through bondage and that represented a claim to fully earned United States citizenship: the story of his great-grandfather, a slave, fighting beside a young master in the American Revolution.

"He is a good sensible negro, and his conduct is above reproach," Palmer told the *Times*, adding, "He seems to know what he bargained for in taking a place on the force."[8]

While that was surely true, alone in the flag loft, Battle would still consider the chasm between the ideals of the banner unfurled overhead and the abuse to which he was being subjected:

> Sometimes, lying on my cot on the top floor in the silence, I would wonder how it was that many of the patrolmen in my precinct who did not yet speak English well, had no such difficulties in getting on the police force as I, a Negro American, had experienced.
>
> Some of them had arrived so recently in America that they spoke as though they had marbles in their mouths. Some of them again knew so little about New York City that they could not give an inquiring stranger any helpful directions. Yet, these brand new Americans could become policemen without going through the trials and

tribulations to which I, a native born American, had been subject in achieving my appointment.

My name had been passed over repeatedly. All sorts of discouragements had been placed in my path. And now, after a long wait and a lot of stalling, I had finally been given a trial appointment to their ranks and these men would not speak to me. Native-born and foreign-born whites on the police force all united in looking past me as though I were not a human being. In the loft in the dark, with the Stars and Stripes, I wondered! Why?

True to form, Battle made a blessing of exile. Privacy afforded him the opportunity for self-education. He read, concentrating on police training manuals to start preparing for the promotion exam for sergeant. These men who would not speak with him today as an equal would answer to him tomorrow as a superior. Far from the others, he recited the police department's rules and regulations, and then he relied once more on Florence to test his knowledge.

"When I went home after a night of study, at breakfast my wife would check me to see what progress I had made," he recalled, adding, "Alone in the loft I could kneel quietly at prayer before going to sleep, talking with God for strength to carry on."

On the street, Battle met the demands of pounding a beat, 8 a.m. to 4 a.m., 4 to midnight, midnight to 8, and sometimes 10 p.m. to 6 a.m., perhaps with eight hours off between shifts, perhaps with twenty-four. He offered collegiality but was rejected time and again. "Bright and sunny this morning, isn't it?" he would say on relieving a man on post. There was never a reply.

After midnight, the precinct deployed men in pairs, one posted for two hours at the center of a fixed intersection, one to patrol the neighborhood for two hours and then to switch labors. The man in the intersection was prohibited from approaching the curb.

Battle strove for perfection, even offering help to any white officer who appeared to need assistance, because, he said, "I knew I was on trial, and through me, my race." But scrutiny, ostracism, study, and the standard rigors of policing combined to produce fatigue. After three months on the job, while still on probation, Battle slipped.

"One rainy night, soaked to the skin, having been out of doors during my entire tour of duty, I went home for a brief rest before reporting for reserve. There was no one at home, so I fell asleep in a chair and failed to awaken in time to report at midnight. A complaint was sent in and I had to stand trial at headquarters."

Well aware that the department needed scant excuse to cut him, Battle threw himself on the mercy of the tribunal and was fined two day's pay. His staying power now clear, Battle faced still harder tests as the crucial six-month deadline neared. Death threats arrived in the mail. He hid them from Florence. Then, he found a note pinned over his bed. It was pierced to resemble a bullet hole, and the block-lettered words read: "Nigger, if you don't quit, this is what will happen to you."[9]

Battle told Hughes that he had shrugged off the warning as the work of a coward, "turned back the covers on my bunk, knelt down praying for God's care and turned in for a good night's sleep." Hughes was properly astonished. Facing Battle across the corner of Battle's townhouse desk, one pencil behind his ear, another in his hand scribbling notes on paper held by a clipboard, the tape recorder microphone standing between them with his secretary Nate White at the controls, Hughes exclaimed: "Wheeeeee-ooooooo-eeee! You mean right in the stationhouse this happened?"

Next, Battle's enemies wielded a weapon that had been lethal, often literally, to a black man: the specter of sex with a white woman.

The site of the entrapment was Manhattan Square Park, a bower located on the land today occupied by the Museum of Natural History. Battle was alone on foot patrol. The time was after 2 a.m. A voice called demurely. A well-dressed white woman was sitting on a bench almost entirely obscured from view. Battle approached, but he quickly knew better than to linger.

"When I asked her what she wanted, she began to make coy advances, telling me that she had for some time been attracted to me," he remembered. "I would not allow her near me, and I told her if she didn't get out of the park at that hour of the morning I would arrest her. She left. Some time later, I learned she was quite friendly with other policemen."

Then, ten days before his probationary period was to expire, Battle confronted a trumped-up accusation of malingering. The night watchman of the Ansonia Hotel reported that he had seen "that black cop, Battle," in shirtsleeves, asleep in a restroom.

Hurriedly, the department filed charges and summoned Battle before a second disciplinary tribunal. He would get no slack on a finding of guilt. Recognizing that it would be his word of denial—the word of a black—against the word of a white, he turned for help to the one person who could support his innocence. His future came down to the honor of a white sergeant. For once, he was treated fairly. The sergeant certified that he had given Battle a twenty-minute relief break.

ON DECEMBER 27, 1911, Battle rose from probationary recruit to full-fledged police officer. The newspapers took stock of the historic event, with the *Times* reporting: "Six months ago men thought that Battle would be hazed into resigning, or at least into asking for transfer. Now they know he isn't that sort and he has made himself respected." But, the paper also stated: "The 'silence' that began when Battle entered the Precinct last July is as deep as ever today, not because Battle is a Negro—although that was the reason at first—but because every white policeman is now afraid of what would be said to and about him if he made any attempt to bring the 'silence' to an end."

The *New York Sun* offered an unnamed officer's words about Battle as typical:

> He has never said anything uncivil and he does more than his share of the work. For instance, one day there was a mess of a grocery cart and an automobile on Central Park West. There were three prisoners and all I could tend to under the circumstances were two. Along comes Battle on his way to the stationhouse. Says he: "Want me to take one of them in?" Breakin' my rule about not speakin' to him I says: "I certainly would be obliged." So he takes the prisoner to the house as cheerful as you please; and if you know how the ordinary policeman hates to do anybody else's work, you know what that means. But as for sayin' "Howdydo" to Battle in the station house—not me.

The *Sun* reported that, at the moment, Battle was reading a work by Winston Churchill, had just finished Thomas Hardy's *Tess of the D'Urbervilles*, and that he also favored best-selling author Marie Corelli, whose *Thelma* was a love story set in Norway. The paper noted that Battle had read Gibbon's *Decline and Fall of the Roman Empire* but that he felt it was more important to understand American history about which, the *Sun* concluded, "his memory is accurate."[10]

Never was Battle more alone, and never was he more open to scrutiny by internal affairs shoo-flies who lurked in the dark than when standing fixed post from midnight to morning. Even Inspector Max Schmittberger—the feared Schmittberger—came by personally to check. Once as corrupt as a cop could be, Schmittberger had confessed his crimes before a state senate investigating committee, emerged a hero, and become the scourge of rule breakers. Battle withstood his spying, as well as the unforgiving gaze of William Randolph Hearst, the newspaper publisher, whose windows overlooked Riverside Drive and Eighty-Sixth Street. "We used to look up at Mr. Hearst—he would come and look down on the policemen, and we were afraid not to be there," Battle remembered.[11]

Decades later, putting pencil to paper in the great old townhouse, he revealed the depths of the torment that dogged him:

> With my fellow officers it was a sin to be a Negro, hence the fight of survival and achievement was on. It seemed that all was against me, including God, in whom I had and have a great deal of faith and to whom I prayed fervently and religiously.
>
> The weather was as much as five below or it seemed to me to be even more. I received supervision early and often, but I prayed and carried on, was never given any of the preferred assignments and didn't ask for them.
>
> I had prescribed my medicine and I took it like a brave soldier. Through these my hardest years I went with the prayers of my faithful and devoted mother and wife. Without these I could not have made it alone.[12]

On Sunday afternoons, Battle became a regular at meetings of the Equity Congress in the largest hall of J. C. Thomas's funeral home.

There he associated with the leading figures of the Harlem that was coming to life, activists like Reverdy Ransom, Timothy Thomas Fortune, J. Frank Wheaton, and, when he was not on a stage tour, Bert Williams.[13]

They kept abreast of Battle's progress, while trying to recruit young black men to join him on the force, as well as to find anyone brave enough to try for the fire department. The Equity Congress was also fully engaged in a drive to establish a New York National Guard unit for blacks. This was a long-held dream of men who believed that, by serving in the US military, blacks would prove that they had equal right to the full benefits of American citizenship. As early as 1898, in the run-up to the Spanish-American War, Fortune and Reverend Alexander Walters had pressed New York's governor for permission to raise a regiment. Now, in 1911, Equity Congress members pursued two strategies for creating a unit open to blacks.

They enlisted an assemblyman who represented the changing Harlem to introduce and, hopefully, push through authorizing legislation; and they named lawyer Charles W. Fillmore to lead what was known as a provisional regiment, an unofficial company of volunteers who would apply for mustering into service. Fillmore was a rare example of an African American who had led black troops, the Ninth Ohio Volunteer Infantry Battalion. Now he took lonely command of a unit that lacked for everything—including men. The Equity Congress began calling on African Americans to enlist as a way of proving loyalty to a country that would surely respond with respect. The renowned dancer and entertainer Bert Williams gave star power to the recruitment drive.

By Lincoln's birthday the following year, Fillmore had a large enough troop to parade in whipping snow from Columbus Circle to the Great Emancipator's monument in Union Square for a wreath laying. The display was meant to demonstrate that New York's African Americans were ready to uphold the tradition of the four black regiments that had emerged from Union troops to become the Buffalo Soldiers and that had fought with distinction in the Spanish-American War.

Battle could do little more than wish his friends well. Although many police officers were tied to Tammany Hall, the department barred cops from engaging in political advocacy. There was little doubt that Battle would suffer severe repercussions if he stepped to the fore in seeking a regiment. More, he had his hands full coping both with the rough edges of life in Harlem and on the police force.

On the streets, there was constant danger of racial violence. In one episode in the fall of 1911, a black man accidentally bumped into a white man, provoking whites to pursue him in growing numbers. The black man fired a revolver without hitting anyone and attempted to run.

"Kill the nigger. He's got a gun. Lynch him," the mob yelled.

After running the man to ground, whites kicked their quarry in the head and face until two cops with guns drawn fought through the melee to save him.[14]

At work, the muscle of onetime bullyboy Battle proved indispensable. The law was ruggedly enforced. A bit of clubbing or a liberal pummeling saved the trouble of a court appearance and was surely more effective as a deterring punishment. As Battle explained: "I gradually but regrettably came to believe, along with the other officers, that there was as much law at the end of a nightstick as there was on the statute books."

A man who knew how to handle himself was much valued in the NYPD, all the more so if he also had the courage of his physique. Battle was bigger, stronger, and more athletic than any man in the precinct, and he had honed his fighting skills in the recreational boxing ring. Yet he took what his fellow cops dished out with outward stoicism, never so much as raising his voice or responding with profanity.

And then one day Battle had had enough. As he approached the stationhouse on West Sixty-Eighth Street, white cops who were hanging about uttered the word "nigger" within his hearing one too many times. His patience now gone, Battle delivered a challenge: if they wanted to fight, he would take them on, one or all.

"Any of you men, any man here, or any series of you here, that has anything against me, leave your guns, your billies and your blackjacks upstairs," Battle declared. "I'm going down to the cellar, and I won't have anything but my fists. Come down one by one. If you're not able to go back up, after a certain length of time send another one down. Anything that you have against me, take it out on my black behind."

Battle descended the stairs in front of every available eye, ready for anyone who had the bravery to follow him. None did, and Battle took significant ground in establishing that his stationhouse mates would afford him a minimum of dignity.

Similarly, Battle combined size and strength with courage to command respect in the line of duty. Given the opportunity, he also evened the score of black and white cracked skulls. As transcribed and polished by Hughes, Battle recalled:

> One night when I was sleeping in the flag loft, about two a.m., the call came to go post haste to the aid of the patrolmen of the San Juan Hill district. Since it took some time to hitch up the horse-drawn patrol wagons, ("Black Marias" as they were called) we started out from West 68th Street on foot on the double.
>
> As we passed the firehouse on Amsterdam Avenue, one of the firemen yelled, "There go the reserves—Battle in the lead." I outran the others. We beat the patrol wagons to the scene of the riots. This was my first emergency call, and I was anxious for action.
>
> When we got to the scene of the fighting in the streets, fists were flying, derbies were being smashed, and missiles flying from roof-tops. One man had already been killed and a number injured. The area was in turmoil. Our superior officers immediately gave orders to use our nightsticks to clear the streets, so we swung into the fray.
>
> I was, of course, the only Negro, among the police, therefore doubly open to attack from the angered whites in the mob. The Negro rioters were in the minority. Nevertheless, my fellow policemen managed to club down two or three Negroes for every white. Therefore, to even things up, I began to club down the whites.
>
> When things had finally quieted, I was assigned to the corner of West 62nd and Amsterdam, with orders to allow no one to loiter on the sidewalks. Just before daybreak four young white hoodlums stopped at the corner and refused to move.
>
> "Get along," I said.
>
> They didn't budge. When I repeated my order to move on, one of them made a racially profane insulting remark to me. I placed them

under arrest. They resisted, so physically I was forced to tackle all four. I subdued them before assistance arrived. When help from other officers did come, I refused it and held all four of my prisoners myself until the Black Maria took them away, which gave saloon commentators material for conversation for the rest of the week. This conflict established my ability to hold my own in the district and from then on I was respected.

One night I was assigned to do a special post in Hell's Kitchen where people often seemed to enjoy fighting. But the saloonkeepers and businessmen did not enjoy having their establishments broken up. Just before midnight I was standing in front of a saloon at 52nd Street and 10th Avenue when one of the habitués came out and said to me, "Officer, this is a bad place to stand. You know 'Paddy, the Priest' was killed right on this spot." "Paddy, the Priest" had been a well-known gangster. I replied, "That is just why I am standing here, sir, so if anything happens, I will be in the right place."

Hardly five minutes passed before a free-for-all broke out in a bar just down the block toward 9th Avenue. I went in with my nightstick swinging. In a short time order was restored. Peace reigned and nobody lifted a hand against me, so I was not compelled to make any arrests. By this time I had become well known in the area. Sometimes I needed only to walk into a bar and the fighting would stop.

Eventually, two officers broke the wall of silence.

Jimmy Garvey had joined the force after Battle, so he had not participated in the conspiracy of silence. Still, it took spine for a lone Irish Catholic to stand apart from peers who were so closely knit by nationality and faith that it was accepted practice for a man to skip out while on duty to attend mass. Garvey spoke openly to Battle, man-to-man in a budding friendship, as he proved himself to be a young cop's cop, eager for any duty.

Abraham Stewart was a sergeant who happened to be Jewish. He asked Battle's permission to share the flag loft in order to better prepare for the lieutenant's exam. "I know it'll be quiet, where you are," Stewart explained.

"You don't have to ask me, you're a sergeant, but I'm glad to have you, anyway," Battle responded. "Each time that we afterwards found ourselves together we talked. He was a friendly fellow and sometimes we checked each other in our studies. Stewart made the top of the list in the lieutenants' tests."

With the exception of Garvey and Stewart, the wall of silence remained largely intact when Battle was detailed to election night duty in a precinct headquartered on Manhattan's East Side. After trying to pass the night reading in a chair rather than enter a second-floor bunkroom, he climbed the stairs in the grip of exhaustion. The room was dark. No one could see who he was. He crawled into an empty bunk and heard the conversation turn "to that colored cop."

Surprising Battle, one man said, "I understand he's a pretty good guy."

"Battle's OK," a cop from his precinct answered, further surprising Battle.

He lay without speaking while the officer noted that Battle had never complained and always did more than his share of the work. The officer also said that some of the precinct's cops were starting to regret his silencing.

"I thought, these boys haven't got such a bad heart after all; they're just a little weak-kneed, that's all," Battle concluded with great generosity.

FLORENCE BROUGHT HAPPY NEWS. Once more, she was pregnant. Almost four years after tiny Florence D'Angeles fell prey to *cholera infantum*, Battle looked forward to welcoming a new life into the family. He was twenty-nine, Florence was as yet only twenty-three, Jesse was six.

The baby was due by Christmas. Florence's oldest sister, Elizabeth, came from Virginia to help care for the infant. The holiday passed. Then, finally, while Battle was on duty and with Dr. Roberts at her side, Florence gave birth at home on January 17, 1913, to Charline Elizabeth Battle. Christened at Mother AME Zion Church, she was Battle's pride from the start.

"My daughter, Charline Elizabeth, was such a pretty born child that I bought for her a special rubber-tired baby carriage with an elegant hood," he wrote. "In this I used to push her all over Harlem, accepting for myself compliments paid the child's beauty."

AROUND THIS TIME, a young man by the name of Robert Holmes stepped forward to follow Battle onto the police force. Square-shouldered, stocky, and athletic, Holmes lived with his parents, Henry and Ella, a few blocks from Battle's apartment. Like Battle, he was a member of the black Elks.

Henry and Ella had brought their son north from South Carolina around the turn of the twentieth century.[15] Settling in Harlem with hope, they had taken their places among the whites whose tolerance was growing thin. Now, Henry was forty-four years old and afflicted with deteriorating lungs. Ella, who was forty, was losing her eyesight while eking out a living as a laundress. Fearing for his parents' futures, Holmes was drawn to the police department's pay and benefits.[16] After the Delehanty Institute denied his admission, he studied for the test by correspondence course. Battle happily helped Holmes master the rules, laws, and procedures he would face on the exam. In shared purpose, they became friends, each understanding that this was the way it had to be, one becoming two, two becoming four, accepting the indignities that had to be accepted until they were large enough in number to refuse to accept any more.

Holmes came through with flying colors. So, on August 25, 1913, Battle celebrated Holmes's appointment as the department's second black officer. He was proud to have opened the door and was buoyed in knowing that more young black men appeared to be coming behind him. They sought him out, and he gave all the guidance he could. Then, abruptly, Commissioner Waldo propelled Battle to a new milestone.

To root out the corruption that came with excessive familiarity between cops and the public, Waldo ordered every patrolman, sergeant, and lieutenant transferred from three Manhattan precincts, and he replaced them with freshly promoted superior officers and five hundred newly sworn cops. The West Sixty-Eighth Street stationhouse was among those cleaned out. Waldo dispatched Battle to Harlem.

The shift marked the department's first venture into assigning a black officer to patrol a community with a substantial black population. Waldo's motivations are hidden to history, but there is one indication that African American leaders pressured City Hall to establish a black police presence in Harlem. In a memoir, the Reverend Frederick Asbury Cullen recounted lobbying the mayor and police commissioner to assign Battle to the community. Cullen was the founder of Salem Methodist Episcopal Church and the adoptive father of Countee Cullen, a Harlem Renaissance wunderkind poet like Hughes. The Reverend Cullen recalled that the Reverend Charles Martin, a prominent fellow black church leader, and John B. Nail, the respected black saloonkeeper, joined in the cause. Misspelling Battle's name, Cullen stated: "We succeeded in having the first colored policeman, who was Policeman Samuel Battles, appointed to Harlem."[17]

Battle bid farewell to Abraham Stewart, who had shared the flag loft, and to Jimmy Garvey, who had paid no heed to the conspiracy of silence. Garvey was newly married and was ever more known as a cop who went the extra mile.[18] Battle wished his friend well and promised to stay in touch. His last duty on West Sixty-Eighth Street was to square Holmes away on a lonely inaugural assignment. "Holmes was given my squad and post," Battle wrote. "I gave him my bed and mattress and he occupied the flag loft as I did."[19]

The stationhouse covering Harlem was at West 135th Street and Seventh Avenue, just a few blocks from Battle's apartment. To many longtime white residents he was an "invader," but, with the influx of blacks growing by the day, Battle's fellow officers discovered that he was useful.

"They needed me as much as I needed them and sometimes more because some of them were on posts where there were all Negroes," he remembered. "Then, too, this story had gone out that, 'He's a decent fellow,' and they began to treat me nicely and spoke to me and asked me to join their organizations and things of that kind."

No more an on-duty pariah, Battle took obvious satisfaction both at being treated more like a peer and at watching Holmes surmount isolation in grand style. They shared pride and amazement at an episode in which officers fired their pistols in the cavalier way of the time. Battle remembered for Hughes:

> Holmes first came to the attention of the press on election morning, November 1913. Before dawn that day a herd of short-horn Oregon steers escaped from the New York Stock Company's yards on the North River. Eight of them tore through 59th Street, scattering in different directions as far as Fifth Avenue.
>
> They terrorized the town on both sides of Central Park. A policeman on 59th Street tried to flag some of the steers down. Failing, he and several other cops commandeered two taxies and with drawn revolvers tried to overtake them individually, shooting as they came in range.
>
> What sounded like a gangster's ballet along Fifth Avenue aroused the guests in both the Gotham and the St. Regis Hotels. A waiter at the St. Regis rushed out and was shot in the ankle. A night watchman removing a red lantern from the pavement in 55th Street was hit between the eyes and killed. One steer tried to enter Whitelaw Reid's house, and was shot a few doors away in front of the home of Cardinal Farley.
>
> Meanwhile, along Central Park West, one of the wildest of the animals trampled Patrolman Kiernan, overturned a delivery wagon, and caused panic among early-rising women and children on the streets. Officer Holmes, reporting for eight a.m. duty in the sector, immediately went in fleet-footed pursuit of the beast. He lit in the park.
>
> As the steer turned its head to look at him, Holmes grabbed the animal's nostrils with his right hand, shutting off its wind. Then with a ju-jitsu twist of one of the horns, he threw the beast to the ground and he held him until his feet were tied. This was the only animal returned to the stockyards intact.

The apartment that had brought Battle's old friend Chief Williams from Grand Central to Harlem had grown small. He and Lucy had added a fourth child, and after pumping iron, their oldest son, Wesley, had become a broad-backed, barrel-chested, thick-armed fifteen-year-old. The family needed more room. The chief told Battle that he was moving to the rural expanses of the Bronx, to Williamsbridge, where there was enough wildlife and wooded territory to allow for hunting. Although remote, the area was convenient for the Chief because the New York Central had a rail line to Grand Central. The Battles bid the Williamses farewell.

The chief and his family again rented space in an overwhelmingly white community, and Wesley again took a desk among white children in a public school. Fewer than a dozen African American families lived in the neighborhood. Monthly, they gathered in a clubhouse to discuss how to help their children advance in life. They drummed in that young blacks had only three paths to success: as doctors, lawyers, teachers, or in other professions; as entrepreneurs with independent capital; or in civil service positions. The chief made sure that, just a few years from manhood, Wesley heard the message in the hope that he would act accordingly. But, headstrong and fixated on bodybuilding, Wesley had his own ideas.

WOODROW WILSON WAS inaugurated the twenty-eighth president of the United States on March 4, 1913, with black Americans looking forward to his administration. He was an unlikely vessel for hope. Wilson's heritage was in Virginia. As president of Princeton University, he had discouraged black applicants. As a historian, he had depicted the Ku Klux Klan as an understandable post–Civil War attempt at white self-defense.

W. E. B. Du Bois and Reverend Alexander Walters had met with the candidate during the campaign. After Walters explained that shifting fifty thousand black votes away from the Republicans—the party of Lincoln—to Democrat Wilson could be decisive, Wilson gave Walters a written vow that he had an "earnest wish to see justice done in every matter, and not mere grudging justice, but justice executed with liberality and cordial good feeling." Du Bois then gave Wilson a wholehearted endorsement, helping him to secure unprecedented backing among black voters.

Disappointment came swiftly. While the Equity Congress pressed to open New York's civil service to blacks, Wilson permitted the start of Jim Crow segregation in the federal workforce. Still worse, he spurned pleas to condemn lynching. With Southern Democrats flying the banner of states' rights, Wilson dismissed the killing tide as a matter to be dealt with locally, not federally.

Meanwhile, in Harlem, white residents continued to struggle desperately to bar blacks through restrictive covenants. As the *Age* described the documents: "The property owners bind themselves not to allow any part of their premises to be occupied in whole or in part by any Negro, mulatto, quadroon or octoroon of either sex either as a tenant, guest, boarder, or occupant in any other capacity, way or manner. Tenants of each house or flat may not employ more than 'one male and one female Negro or two Negresses, mulattoes, quadroons or octoroons to perform the duties ordinarily performed by a household servant.'"[20]

The Equity Congress voted to explore whether such a covenant was legal under the law of the day. No one was sure, and frustration was all the more intense because the group had made little progress on its founding goals. It had hoped to open the police department to African Americans—and so far, the black ranks had grown to only two members. Similarly, it had hoped to open the fire department, but no volunteers had stepped forward for the mission. Everyone recognized that firefighters would be even more hostile than cops, because firefighters shared living and eating quarters for days on end. About the only bright spot for the Equity Congress was passage of legislation authorizing a black National Guard regiment.

After two years of lobbying, the group held what the *Age* described as "a big jollification meeting."[21] Charles Fillmore, the once lonely colonel of the provisional regiment, had by now enlisted one thousand men into his unofficial brigade. Many were eager to join a fully sanctioned National Guard unit. They never got the chance. The regiment's champions learned that there was a far distance between authorizing a unit and activating a unit. The governor withheld the activation order in accord with prevailing belief that blacks neither merited the honor of military service nor could be trusted to bear arms.[22]

*   *   *

AS 1913 CLOSED, Battle shepherded a third young African American onto the force. The department assigned Jasper Rhodes to the West Forty-Seventh Street stationhouse in the heart of the wild Tenderloin. "As the first Negro there, he was given a rough road to go for a while," Battle recalled. "Jasper would fight at the drop of a hat, so he soon gained a certain respect after his initial hazing was over."

Battle, Holmes, and Rhodes concentrated both on exceeding all the demands of the job and on asserting simple social equality. Battle became the anchor on the department's tug-of-war team and, with Rhodes, he attended the police summer camp in Brooklyn. Twice, Battle won "the fat man's race," a hundred-yard dash for men over 225 pounds and, he remembered, "Jasper always won the white cops' money at dice."

Clearly, Battle had the most desirable posting. Not only was he respected by Harlem's growing African American population, his fellow officers increasingly appreciated the value of his dark skin.

"I recall one Negro girl refusing to be arrested by Patrolman Anton Strausner, crying, 'I don't want no white police to arrest me. Send for Battle to arrest me.' She appealed to a passerby, 'Don't let this white man arrest me,'" Battle remembered.

> About that time I arrived and Strausner turned her over to me. It was a good thing for a hostile crowd had gathered.
>
> So bitter was Harlem's resentment at having no officers of their own color in the area that, before my transfer there, there had been instances of Negroes taking a prisoner away from a white policeman. When I was sent to Harlem, I inherited not only the ordinary problems that the guardians of the law have everywhere, but the added problems of a racial situation made acute by the American color line. But to Harlemites, even one Negro patrolman seemed better than none.

BRIGHT AS HE WAS, the Chief's son, Wesley, left school at the age of sixteen after finishing the eighth grade. Hours spent sculpting his every muscle group had proven more attractive than homework and had delayed the young man's progress. Years later Wesley would joke: "I was so large that the custodian of the school went to my principal in my last term and said that if I was not graduated he was going to quit his job. He said he was sick and tired of raising my desk and chair so that my legs would fit under the desk. So the principal must have felt that his custodian was more necessary than I to the school. That is how I was graduated."

Still, Wesley remembered his teachers as "true friends" who had "endeavored to guide me correctly," most of all warning "that a criminal record would bar me from a civil service position and to a Negro that is a calamity." Wesley would place one teacher in particular among the people "who played a most important part in my life and fortified me for the battle that was to come." This Mr. Freund "patiently counseled me at a very critical and emotional period of my life," he would recall.

Finished with education and starting what was to become a life's relationship with sixteen-year-old Margaret Ford, Wesley needed a job. Since he was too young to hope for appointment to a government post, New York offered only two options: he could seek the menial employment of a *boy* or he could sign up for dangerous labor with an employer none too concerned about race or age. Choosing the latter, Wesley knocked boldly on the door of a construction company that was digging a subway tunnel under the East River from the foot of Manhattan to Brooklyn.

Flynn and O'Rourke relied on the sweat of newly arrived European immigrants and African Americans. Mary White Ovington wrote: "New York demands strong, unskilled laborers. To some she pays a large wage, and Negroes have gone in numbers into the excavations under the rivers, though a lingering death may prove the end of their two and a half or perhaps six or seven dollar a day job."[23]

Wesley's physique was ideal for working with heavy loads and heavy machinery. A foreman put him on a gang in a dark, dank shaft that smelled of grease, stone dust, and the residue of explosives. Near the Manhattan shore, the tunnel bored through bedrock. Dynamiters set off charges drilled into a stone face. Then, sand hogs, as tunnel workers are still known today, hauled away the chunked rock. Tradition, superstition, or wise practice forbade whistling or singing for fear that musical vibrations could dislodge stone overhead. To minimize the peril, scalers—Wesley among them—poked the newly exposed tunnel top with twenty-foot-long steel rods to break free unstable portions. It took speed to dodge the collapsing rock—more speed than some men proved to have. In that era, roughly forty workers died every year in all forms of accidents while building or tunneling for the subways.[24]

Closer to the Brooklyn shore, the tunnel dome consisted of the riverbed's sandy bottom. Here, construction engineers filled the shaft with compressed air to hold the silt in place and keep river water from draining through. Too little pressure and the sand would collapse; too much pressure and the air would rupture the sand upward, in both cases flooding the tunnel.[25] When such a blowout had occurred in an earlier tunnel, a sandhog named Richard Creegan attempted to plug the fissure with a straw bale that was on hand for such an emergency. The air pressure sucked Creegan up into the hole, shot him through the riverbed and the river, and jettisoned him into the air. Amazingly, Creegan survived. Not so three men who were sucked into a blowout in Wesley's tunnel.[26]

Two weeks after Wesley started work, a New York State Labor Department doctor visited the site. A foreman ordered Wesley to the surface with the warning that the doctor likely wanted to verify that he was of age to work in the tunnel. On the way up, Wesley prepared to lie.

"How old are you?" the doctor demanded.

"Eighteen," Wesley answered, guessing that to be the legal limit.

"Don't you know that you cannot work in the tunnel unless you are twenty-one years of age?" the doctor asked. "Now I am going to repeat the question. How old are you."

"Twenty-one," Wesley responded, and back down into the hole he went.

Soon enough, the grueling work in miserable conditions convinced him to study for a civil service exam. Meanwhile, Chief Williams pressed his independent-minded son to leave the high risk of injury or death he faced every day. Finally, after Wesley turned seventeen, the Chief pulled strings to secure a redcap's job at the Pennsylvania Railroad's magnificent new terminal across town from Grand

Central. There, Wesley found toting luggage "equivalent to a four year college course in humanities." Off hours, he and Margaret fell into young love.

THE WORLD CHANGED on June 28, 1914.

For reasons obscure to Americans, Serbian nationalist Gavrilo Princip assassinated Archduke Franz Ferdinand, heir to the Austrian throne, and his wife. In short order, Europe cascaded into World War I. None of it seemed the business of the United States, and no group felt more remote from the fighting than African Americans. Only in hindsight, is it clear that the war shaped their destiny and American race relations.

The hostilities curbed the European immigration that had provided inexpensive labor to America's expanding industries. Needing bodies at the right price, northern manufacturers trolled the South with the promise of jobs that paid more than plantation labor. The pull proved irresistible and the Great Migration from the South that would eventually number more than six million American blacks gained steam.

New York's black leaders used the war to renew the push for a military regiment. General Nelson Miles, who had served in the Civil, Indian, and Spanish-American wars, offered discouraging counsel to a meeting of the Equity Congress. Calling the conflict "as little called for as any that has ever occurred on the face of the globe," he said African Americans would be foolhardy to participate in a fight that "bid fair to be the most destructive war ever waged."

Miles advised blacks to consider giving up on America entirely, saying "perhaps the intelligence acquired in the past few years by your race may be utilized as a great civilizing force for the great black belt of Africa with its 100,000,000 of inhabitants."[27]

The outcome was even more frustrating when a delegation of black leaders won a White House audience with Wilson in hope of holding the president to his campaign pledges. In a heated dialogue, William Monroe Trotter, editor of the *Boston Guardian*, told Wilson: "Two years ago, you were thought to be a second Abraham

Lincoln. Mr. President, we are here to renew our protest against the segregation of colored employees in the department of our national government."

Wilson tellingly said: "Segregation is not humiliating, but a benefit, and ought to be so regarded by you gentlemen. If your organization goes out and tells the colored people of the country that it is a humiliation, they will so regard it, but if you do not tell them so, and regard it rather as a benefit, they will regard it the same. The only harm that will come will be if you cause them to think it is a humiliation."[28]

Here was the president of the United States saying that black citizens should gratefully accept the lesser stations to which they had been consigned rather than risk the undeterred retributions of white society. Here was the personification of the American promise, a man who had postured as a champion of "cordial" justice, sending a message to Battle that his courage in seeking equal opportunity had been misplaced.

Then, as 1915 dawned, a sensational movie devoted the power of the flickering image to glorifying white-on-black vigilantism. Directed by D. W. Griffith, *The Birth of a Nation* employed compelling new techniques of cinematography to—purportedly—portray Southern history from the Civil War through Reconstruction. Its very essence, Battle knew, was a grotesque lie.

Where Thomas had been forced to buy his freedom, where Thomas and Anne had instilled faith and the work ethic in their children, where Battle had left his parents in a South ruled by Jim Crow, where Anne still suffered the indignities of a lesser citizenship, *The Birth of a Nation* presented the region as dominated by drunken and vengeful blacks, a species whose men lusted for the sexual conquest of white women. The heroes who rode to the rescue were the white-hooded horsemen of the Ku Klux Klan.

Battle watched as *The Birth of a Nation* enjoyed a forty-four-week run on Forty-Second Street and, like African Americans at large, he could only lose hope after Wilson issued a legendary presidential stamp of approval following a White House screening. The movie was "like writing history with lightning," Wilson is reported to have pronounced.

Shortly, violence against blacks began to rise. Editing an NAACP journal called the *Crisis*, Du Bois amassed a count, titled "The Lynching Industry," of extrajudicial killings that had taken place from 1885 through 1914. His tabulations totaled 2,732 murders, with 69 blacks and 5 whites slain in 1914 alone. In 1915, the annual death toll climbed to 94: 80 blacks, 14 whites. Of the blacks, 71 were hanged, 5 were burned at the stake, 3 were shot, and 1 was drowned.[29]

Never a day passed when Battle was not aware that the broad spectrum of white society deemed him inferior. In one episode, orders came down that he and Jasper Rhodes were to report for special training: they had been designated to march—the first blacks ever—in the police department's annual parade.

Appreciating the honor, they reported to a National Guard armory. A captain named Jake Brown called attention. Battle and Rhodes fell into line. Brown's eyes stopped on the two dark-skinned men. He ordered them to stand aside.

"Why are you sending us back?" Rhodes challenged. "Because we are colored?"

On the verge of an insubordination charge, Battle and Rhodes accepted dismissal. Battle long bore a resentful grudge.

"This affected me so deeply that many years later when I was finally invited to participate in the parade, I refused," he remembered. "However, I have since forgiven Captain Brown, and have participated in a number of parades, including the St. Patrick's Day from which, in the old days, Negroes were also barred."

AS WINTER GAVE way to spring in 1915, Florence once more discovered that she was pregnant, and fatherhood again steered Battle's course.

The family's cramped quarters had little enough room for Jesse and Charline; squeezing in a third child was out of the question. Battle needed space, but space was at an increasing premium in the burgeoning new Harlem, the bastion from which whites had fled and the Mecca to which blacks were flocking in ever-larger numbers. Much as he loved "the familiar feeling of being back home in the

Negro section of a Southern town, hearing again the accents of my childhood," it was time to move elsewhere.

He had followed Chief Williams to Harlem, and now, with far-reaching consequences for both families, as well as for New York, he followed the Chief to the Bronx. Renting the top floor of a house owned by a hospitable German woman recalled only as Mrs. Wagner, Battle and Florence joined Williamsbridge's small African American community and renewed neighborhood ties with the Chief, Lucy, and their children.

Wesley was now an imposing eighteen-year-old. Thickly muscled, he had gained a reputation for feats of strength, including a 3,600-pound hip lift, 625-pound one-armed dead lift, and 345-pound overhead press.[30] By taking the civil service test, he had moved on from working as a redcap to a position with the US Post Office. Mail delivery was then changing from horse-drawn wagons to motorized vehicles. Wesley had trained as a driver. Wearing a double-breasted utility coat and a brimmed cap, he negotiated the crowded streets in a rattling, numbered truck with a cargo bed, wooden spoke wheels, and a wooden sign reading "2190 United States Mail."[31]

With the confidence that came with a steady paycheck, Wesley had proposed to Margaret and they had set a date for the fall. Battle offered the young man hearty congratulations and advice. As Arthur Schomburg had done for him, Battle stressed to Wesley the importance of self-education. Wesley followed his counsel. Over the coming decades he would build a fifteen-hundred-book library, and his readings would extend to German philosophers Arthur Schopenhauer and Friedrich Nietzsche and American psychologist and philosopher William James.

On November 9, 1915, Battle and Florence, round with full-term pregnancy, gathered with a small congregation to celebrate the marriage of Wesley Augustus Williams and Margaret Russell Ford. Wesley's sister and brother, Gertrude and Charles, stood witness.[32] The next day, Florence went into labor. Battle was on duty, and Dr. Roberts was miles away in Harlem. She called down to Mrs. Wagner, a woman given to baking pies for Jesse, who was about to turn ten, and for Charline, who was almost three. Mrs. Wagner helped deliver a boy, Carroll Henry, "giving him a slap on the behind and a little gin in his mouth to start him out in life."

The Williams family celebrated the two happy occasions with the Battles; the mothers of the clubhouse group supported Florence through recovery and Carroll Henry was baptized at Mother AME Zion Church. Then life returned to order, Battle at work most of the time, Florence at home nurturing three children, while coping with the fear that shadows the wife of every police officer: Would he come home safely?

THE PERILS WERE real and could be all the more threatening when inflamed by the passions of race. In the summer of 1916, Battle confronted death in the form of an angry white mob.

New York's brute character extended to labor-management relations, and nowhere was the clash between worker and boss harsher than on the city's streetcar lines. A struggle erupted over pay and working conditions, with the Amalgamated Association of Street and Electric Railway and Motor Coach Employees seeking terms that the rail companies deemed to be radical, such as a maximum ten-hour workday.[33]

Strikes began in July and built into September. The line operators readily found strikebreakers among unskilled, unemployed men, while the union fought to enforce its shutdown with violence. Mayor Mitchell deployed two thousand cops to ride the streetcars in hope of maintaining service. Often the cars, and the officers, were bombarded by rocks, bolts, and construction debris.[34] At the corner of Madison Avenue and Eighty-Sixth Street, strikers set upon a streetcar carrying Battle. Rocks crashed through the windows.

Drawing his gun, he leaped from the car. Battle chased two of the attackers, firing, he said, into the air. (Two wounded rioters later alleged that he shot them, but nothing came of the charge.) Battle's quarry darted up a stoop and into a building at the corner of Park Avenue. Battle followed and took the men into custody. Outside, strike sympathizers seethed with hostility.

"Don't let the nigger cop arrest you," the crowd shouted.

Gun in hand atop the stoop, Battle called back, "The first person that tries to stop me, I'll blow your brains out."

No one dared mount the steps. When police reserves arrived, Battle took his prisoners to the stationhouse and would eventually win convictions in court. He looked back on the incident with pride, saying, "In my first real test alone with a crowd of angry whites, I had triumphed as an officer of the law," but at the time he brought home to Florence the dangers that the family shared because of their skin color.

OTHER THREATS WERE nondiscriminatory and grew out of the day's precarious balancing of life and death. In the hot summer of 1916, an invisible killer stalked New York, hunting children like Jesse, Charline, and Carroll the most mercilessly.

Before the turn of the century, New York City's Department of Health revolutionized public health with the realization that poor sanitation bred disease. Drives against fetid water, refuse, and animal excrement helped to eradicate cholera and typhoid at a time when medical science was embarked on combating the germs that carried illnesses. It was an era of important breakthroughs and of at least one tragic consequence.

As sanitation improved, infants and children lost exposure to some microbes critical to developing immunities. Notably, they grew up lacking contact with the poliomyelitis virus. The hidden effect emerged when New York became the epicenter of America's first large-scale polio epidemic.

The city announced the outbreak on June 17, 1916. Health authorities were mystified by the spread of an illness that primarily afflicted children and progressed from fever to crippling paralysis or death. As the toll rose to 8,900 cases, including 2,400 deaths, the health department quarantined stricken children. Those who could not be isolated in crowded tenements were forcibly taken from their families. The city placed placards on the homes of the sick, published names and addresses in the newspapers, and posted warning signs in neighborhoods with multiple cases. A typical one read: "Infantile paralysis is very prevalent in this part of the city. On some streets many children are ill. This is one of the streets. Keep Off This Street."[35]

Battle and Florence plunged into praying against a day that Jesse, Charline, or Carroll might show the feared symptoms. Like hundreds of thousands of parents, they grasped for strategies to keep their children safely isolated, while also accepting that Battle's duties would place him inescapably at the center of frightening throngs.

Many a cop grew fearful after word spread that Jimmy Garvey, the friend who broke the conspiracy of silence against Battle, had brought the disease home to his year-old daughter Helen. Battle could offer only commiseration. Much later in life, Garvey's wife Pauline would point to a steel brace that supported Helen's leg from heel to thigh and say bitterly: "It was in 1916 during the epidemic, while he was still a patrolman. Jim carried a man to an ambulance in his arms and he came home without changing his uniform. The baby ran out and hugged him. Two days later she was stricken."[36]

The scourge passed with the cooler weather of October. The Battles survived the threat unscathed, but it was clear that service on the NYPD demanded an awful lot—and perhaps all.

THAT JUNE, BATTLE passed the milestone of five years on the force. By longevity, he was now eligible to take the promotion exam for sergeant. He applied for test preparation at the Delehanty Institute, and proprietor Michael J. Delehanty slammed the door just as forcefully as before. At the same time, Battle and the Equity Congress crossed a second five-year mark. Their drive to create an African American regiment had gotten nowhere in all that time. Now, though, the drums of war grew louder, even as Wilson ran for reelection with a campaign that boasted he had kept America out of the conflict. Battle, J. Frank Wheaton, Bert Williams, and the rest of the Equity Congress decided the time had arrived to lobby Governor Charles Whitman to activate the black unit that had been authorized by the legislature. Battle's friends expected him to stay on the sidelines because of the department's prohibition on political advocacy. But at a bitter time in a bitter season, ignoring the ban at risk of his career, Battle wrote to

Whitman urging the unit's activation and waited tensely for a reply or retribution.

DURING THE WAIT, there was a lynching in Waco, Texas, that stands as a savage milestone in white-on-black violence. The Fryer family tilled a farm. Jesse Washington was a hired hand. He was black. At seventeen years of age, he had a volatile temper, could neither read nor write, and was, perhaps, mentally retarded. According to a chronicling by Du Bois, who accepted the likelihood that Washington was guilty, the hulking young man raped and murdered Mrs. Fryer while her husband and two children labored in a distant field.

The authorities brought Washington immediately to trial in a courtroom that was built to accommodate five hundred spectators but was crammed by as many as two thousand people. The proceedings lasted just a few hours before the jury returned a guilty verdict. An investigator sent to the scene by Du Bois reported what happened next:

> The mob ripped the boy's clothes off, cut them in bits and even cut the boy. Someone cut his ear off; someone else unsexed him. . . . While a fire was being prepared of boxes, the naked boy was stabbed and the chain put over the tree. He tried to get away, but could not. He reached up to grab the chain and they cut off his fingers. The big man struck the boy on the back of the neck with a knife just as they were pulling him up on the tree. . . . He was lowered into the fire several times by means of the chain around his neck.

Du Bois left nothing of "The Waco Horror" to the imagination by publishing graphic photographs of the lynching, including a picture of Washington's charred and dismembered body hanging by a chain from a tree.[37]

THE MEN WHO hoped to serve in the military admired Battle's courage in writing to the governor. They were relieved when the letter passed without harm, and they were forever grateful when Whitman signed a regimental establishing order on June 16, 1916.[38] They would one day refer to Battle as "godfather" of the regiment.

While the timing was right, cause and effect were, at best, attenuated. Instead, the regiment had an unlikely champion. William Hayward was a white Nebraskan whose father had represented that state in the US Senate. He was trained as a lawyer, served as a captain in the Spanish-American War, and appeared on the cover of the *Saturday Evening Post* as the handsome, rock-jawed image of the ideal soldier. After his service, Hayward's career took him to working as Whitman's gubernatorial counsel.

Military command was an important credential for social or political advancement, but openings for officers were few. Hayward saw his opportunity in leading the black regiment. Although lacking cachet, the position was his to seize. More, Hayward had come home from the Cuban expedition with a deep respect for the soldiering of his black comrades. Whitman named him colonel of the regiment, with one condition: that Hayward bar blacks from the ranks of superior officers.[39]

Battle, Wheaton, and Bert Williams celebrated a great victory—a largely unqualified one because Hayward disregarded Whitman's restriction. While he built a command structure of socially prominent whites for this new Fifteenth Regiment, he gave the rank of captain to Charles W. Fillmore, the rare black commanding officer who had built the provisional unit from nothing, and bestowed the same standing on the extraordinary figure of Napoleon Bonaparte Marshall.

Born into a well-to-do Washington, DC, family, Marshall had attended Phillips Andover Preparatory School in Massachusetts before joining the handful of African Americans who had been admitted over the years to Harvard. He graduated from Harvard Law School and served as counsel to a US Senate investigation that introduced Marshall both to the honor of black soldiers and to racially driven injustice at the highest levels of American government. In the worst racial blot on his presidency, Teddy Roosevelt had ordered 167 African American soldiers discharged without honor and without hearing after a shooting spree outside Fort Brown in Brownsville, Texas. Marshall took the case apart, but realized in the end that Washington would hold the troops guilty no matter how devastatingly he undermined the evidence against them. After three years, he helped win reinstatement of only fourteen men, and the so-called Brownsville Raid entered white America's consciousness as proof that blacks could not be trusted as soldiers in arms.

Marshall came to New York, married into a prominent black family, and fell in with a small fraternity of black lawyers. After a German U-boat sank the ocean liner *Lusitania*, killing 1,198, including 128 Americans, he wrote to President Wilson "offering my services in the recruiting of a volunteer Negro regiment of infantry," he recalled in a memoir, adding, "This I believe constituted the first offer of services in the World War of any colored citizen in the United States." He would tell young men who jeered at volunteering that "any man who was not willing to fight for his country was not worthy to be one of its citizens."[40]

Within six weeks of Whitman's activation, the regiment had drawn more than five hundred recruits. But manpower was not matched by money or equipment. As he tried to bring cohesion to the raw corps, Hayward raised funds among well-off whites and found unconventional routes of supply. He leased a vacant Harlem cigar store to serve as a headquarters and took occupancy of a dance hall on the second story of a building a block away that became known as the "armory."

Enlistees assembled for drills in front of the nearby Lafayette Theatre. Battle stopped by to cheer the men as they marched in raggedy uniforms, if they had uniforms, and bore broomsticks in the absence of rifles. The unit was a source of pride to many in Harlem and was cause for ridicule to others. The *Age* predicted that "the Fifteenth will be the crack regiment of New York," while another newspaper story recounted that onlookers laughed at "these darkies playing soldiers."[41]

Opinion was also sharply divided on the question of whether black men should risk life and limb by joining the military at a time when Jim Crow America appeared to be marching toward an unfathomable war. "The Germans ain't done nothing to me. And if they have, I forgive 'em," James Weldon Johnson heard a man say in a Harlem barbershop.[42]

While Bahamian-born Bert Williams was excluded from formal service because he was not an American citizen, he backed the regiment with celebrity. Another of Battle's friends from the bar of the Marshall Hotel gave the regiment additional star power. James Reese Europe was a leading black band director. Trained as a classical violinist, he made his way from Washington, DC, to New York in hope of earning a living as a performer. At the Marshall, he met a wealthy white man seeking a quartet to play the jazzier rhythms associated with black musicians at a social event. Europe got the gig—he is believed to have coined the word—and came into high demand at white society functions. He took over the band that played for Vernon and Irene Castle, white dancers who were wildly popular for introducing whites to then-black dances like the fox-trot.

On September 19, 1916, at the age of thirty-five, at a time when he had a dozen tuxedo-clad bands playing New York venues, Europe joined the Fifteenth Regiment. He was inspired in part by Vernon Castle, who was English and who had abandoned his career to join the Royal Air Corps. More fundamentally, Europe had fought to improve the lot of black performers, and he believed deeply that Harlem needed strong institutions to help shape the lives of the poorly educated African Americans who were flocking there.[43]

Hayward was delighted to have Europe's company as well as that of Europe's protégé Noble Sissle, a young bandleader and baritone. Cleverly, Hayward gave Europe free rein to assemble a regimental band that could play Sousa marches with the best and leap into ragtime at the drop of a baton. The ranks grew as Wilson campaigned for reelection as the war-avoiding president, won the White House, and promptly led the United States into a declaration of war on April 6, 1917. By then, the regimental roster included men from every walk of life, from poet to criminal, from farmer to Negro League baseball star. One showed up on Battle's doorstep.

Needham Roberts was born in 1898 to a North Carolina family that was intertwined enough with the sprawl of Battle's kin for Battle to count Roberts as a cousin. His parents, Norman and Emma, had migrated north to Trenton, New Jersey, where Norman earned a living as a porter in a bank and served as pastor of an AME Zion church. Needham dropped out of a segregated high school to work as a hotel bellhop and drugstore clerk. In 1916, he tried twice to enlist in the navy but was rejected for being underage. After the United States declared war, he ran away to New York with money his father had given him to pay the poll tax and headed to the regiment's recruiting office in the old cigar store. "Readily they signed me up," he remembered, adding, "In a few hours afterwards I was in the New York National Guard."[44]

ON THE SUNNY morning of Sunday, May 13, 1917, the Fifteenth's ragtag troops set off for formal training. They assembled near Grand Central Station and marched behind the rousing play of Europe's band. He greeted spectators with a brassy "Onward Christian Soldiers." At the New York Central freight yard abutting San Juan Hill, the men boarded trains for a trip up the Hudson River to Camp Peekskill. There, intense drilling produced a regiment that capably assembled and disassembled weapons and qualified in deliberate and rapid fire. They returned to New York on Memorial Day as a disciplined unit.[45]

Six days later, America suffered an eruption of white-on-black violence whose fury was unprecedented, even in the era of lynching. The forces of racism and economics flowing from the northward migration of blacks came virulently together in East St. Louis, Illinois, to produce a massacre that Marcus Garvey summarized with the words: "The mob and the entire white population of East St. Louis had a Roman holiday. They feasted on the blood of the Negro."[46]

Located across the Mississippi River from St. Louis, Missouri, East St. Louis was an industrial and meatpacking city of seventy-five thousand people. The accelerating exodus of blacks from the South brought some five thousand African Americans there between the start of 1916 and the summer of 1917. Most came seeking factory jobs in answer to advertisements. Many wound up living in riverbank shanties and signed on as strikebreakers. Whites resented being displaced, and their anger grew deadly on trumpeted reports of African American criminality.

On July 1, white men drove through a neighborhood called Black Valley, shooting into houses. Blacks carrying weapons came out into the street. When another carload of whites approached, the blacks opened fire, killing two of the men in the vehicle. They were police officers. Whites by the thousands rampaged the next day. Often encouraged by police and National Guard troops, they shot, stabbed, beat, burned, and hanged blacks over three days. Thousands of African Americans fled as rioters doused shacks with gasoline and set them ablaze. The official death toll was thirty-nine but scores more are believed to have been murdered, their bodies burned or thrown into the river.[47]

While Battle was struggling one man at a time to integrate the police force, and while so many of his friends were pleading to place their lives at risk in service of their country, America's racial hostility had produced mass bloodshed. Then, just as the violence subsided in East St. Louis, a New York police officer assigned to the West Sixty-Eighth Street station encountered two dozen men from the Fifteenth on a San Juan Hill corner. The officer, a white man named Hansen, ordered the troops to move. As they started to disperse, Private Lawrence Joaquin objected, saying that Hansen failed to respect the uniform of a US military man. Hansen arrested Joaquin, only to have a crowd of African Americans attempt to free the soldier. Hansen backed Joaquin into a hallway, fending off the prisoner's would-be saviors with his nightstick. Neighborhood whites swarmed into the conflict. Soon, the *Times* reported, police reinforcements found "two-thousand persons gathered around the corner and most of them fighting, with knives and clubs swinging and bricks flying through the air."[48]

Frederick Randolph Moore of the *Age* and the Reverend George Sims, the pastor of Union Baptist Church, who had married Battle and Florence, protested. "So far as we can ascertain, the men of the Fifteenth were entirely within their rights in standing on the corner. They were in uniform, were perfectly quiet and orderly, and were not interfering with traffic," Moore said, adding, "The Fifteenth is a picked regiment, composed of the very best, self-respecting, law-abiding negroes in New York. There never has been any complaint against the men of the regiment before and if they are being unjustly treated because of their race we propose to find out about it."[49]

Of course, nothing would come of it.

A FEW WEEKS LATER, Battle witnessed a parade of, by, and for African Americans, a parade unlike any he or America had ever seen. Six thousand—some said ten thousand—black men, women, and children walked silently down Fifth Avenue on the steamy Saturday afternoon of July 28, 1917. Led by youngsters dressed in white, they moved to the cadence of muffled drums and carried banners that had been inspired by the killings in East St. Louis, the lynching in Waco, and other white-on-black violence.

One banner read, "We Are Maligned and Murdered Where we Work." Another asked, "Mother, Do Lynchers Go to Heaven?" A third was addressed to Woodrow Wilson: "Give Me a Chance to Live, Mr. President. Why Not Make America Safe for Democracy?" Black Boy Scouts distributed leaflets that explained "Why We March." They answered most pithily: "We march because we want to make impossible a repetition of Waco, Memphis, and East St. Louis, by arousing the conscience of the country, and to bring the murderers of our brothers and sisters, and innocent children to justice."

Where Battle had been barred from the department's annual celebratory march, he now stood sentinel at the Silent Protest Parade, America's first mass civil rights demonstration.

THE HOT SUMMER moved on, long days of police work giving way to equally long nights of foot patrol. At 11:45 p.m. on August 6, 1917, Battle got ready to stand post from midnight to morning at the corner of West 139th Street and Lenox Avenue. He was due there in fifteen minutes to relieve Robert Holmes, who was finishing night duty. Holmes had transferred into the precinct. It felt good to have him there, and Battle looked forward to chatting with Holmes as they changed the guard.

Just then the noise of a burglar opening a window awakened Garfield Rose in a first-floor apartment. Rose rushed to the window and struggled with the intruder. The burglar fired four shots and fled. Holmes ran toward the gunfire and gave chase on Lenox Avenue. The man darted into a building, snuffed a gaslight, and waited in the dark. Holmes dashed in and was felled by two shots to the head.

Battle was left to look at Holmes's blood on the floor, red blood like that of any man, yet not the blood of a man who could walk in the police department parade or earn a choice assignment as reward for exemplary performance. To New York, Holmes had not been a policeman, but a Negro policeman.

News traveled from building to building, apartment to apartment, that Holmes had been killed. Thousands rushed into the street. A superior officer brought the fact of their son's death to Henry and Ella, whose declining health led the newspapers to describe Henry as elderly at the age of forty-nine and Ella as now blind. The police commissioner—Arthur Woods had assumed the office—said: "In Patrolman Holmes' death the force loses a faithful and courageous officer, who died as he had lived—a fearless and loyal servant of the public, doing his best to the last to protect the lives of others placed in his charge." And then, cognizant of Holmes's race, Woods added: "His work was successful in a neighborhood where there were a great many colored people and he had never had any complaint for his work with white people."

The department accorded Holmes a full-dress funeral. He was buried in Queens and was followed to the cemetery by Henry, who died of pneumonia and pleurisy in March 1918, and by Ella, who succumbed to postoperative shock when treated for a uterine tumor in September of that year.

"The bullet that killed Holmes made another wound which took their lives within fourteen months," Battle remembered.[50]

ON AUGUST 26, 1917, Florence gave birth to the last of the Battle children. They named the boy Theodore in honor of Teddy Roosevelt. Battle wrote to the hero he had seen at Yale and had met at Grand Central, and he "received a very pleasant letter in reply."

*　*　*

WHILE THE ARMY scattered the men of the Fifteenth to guard New York State posts against sabotage, orders came down dispatching a storied unit composed largely of Irish Americans, including the Fighting Sixty-Ninth, to a training camp at Spartanburg, South Carolina, last stop before France.

The city scheduled a parade to send the contingent off as part of a Rainbow Division melding troops from twenty-six states. Hayward asked permission for the Fifteenth to march in recognition that they, too, were about to join the fight. Permission was denied. Black was not a color of the rainbow, he was told.[51] Raising a hand before his men, Hayward pledged: "Even if they won't let us parade with them in going away, that we will have a parade when we come home that will be the greatest parade . . . that New York has ever seen."

He had the Fifteenth swear in unison "that whichever may be in survival as commanding officer of this regiment when we get back to New York, that we see to it that the glory and the honor of the Negro race in America may be served by having our welcome home parade celebrated." One witness recalled, "And to that pledge and prophecy, all present clasped hands—and said:—'Amen!'"[52]

THE REGIMENT'S HOPES dimmed with fresh racial violence, this time disastrously involving black troops who were successors to the Buffalo Soldiers. The War Department deployed members of the Twenty-Fourth Infantry to Camp Logan outside Houston. Anticipating the arrival of African American servicemen, a newspaper advertisement warned Houstonians to "Remember Brownsville," site of the trumped-up shooting that lived on as a rallying cry against arming blacks.

The soldiers of the Twenty-Fourth were experienced men and accustomed to respect. They refused to sit in the blacks-only section of movie theaters or to ride at the back of streetcars. Whites chafed at their seeming insolence. Then, on August 23, a black soldier named Edwards happened upon a group of white police officers manhandling a black woman. When Edwards tried to intervene, the police pistol-whipped and arrested him. A short time later, a black MP, Corporal Charles Baltimore, protested Edwards's treatment at the stationhouse. He was assaulted and fled under gunfire. A rumor spread that the police had killed Baltimore. Soldiers broke into the weapons storage and, with one yelling, "To hell with going to France, get to work right here," more than one hundred troops did battle with white cops and armed white civilians. The death toll was sixteen whites, including five police officers, and four blacks. With rapid efficiency and Woodrow Wilson's approval, the army soon hanged nineteen soldiers.

The Houston riot "left a bitter taste in the mouth," Battle remembered. For the men of the Fifteenth, it also raised fears that the War Department would sideline the unit entirely. But, under Hayward's pressure, the War Department put the regiment on notice of a deployment to Camp Wadsworth in Spartanburg, South Carolina. The mayor there told the *Times*: "I am sorry to learn that the fifteenth Regiment has been ordered here, for, with their northern ideas about racial equality, they will probably expect to be treated like white men. I can say right here they will not be treated as anything except Negroes."[53]

On arriving, Hayward appealed to the regiment not to meet "the white citizens of Spartanburg on the undignified plane of prejudice and brutality," and he urged that "if violence occurs, if blows are struck, that all of the violence and all of the blows are on one side and that side is not our side."[54]

Napoleon Marshall complied when he was ordered off a trolley after paying his fare. When two whites threw a company member into a gutter, the Fifteenth stood down while white soldiers from New York, in a rare show of solidarity, pummeled the assailants. Noble Sissle took a kicking from the manager of a hotel who had knocked his hat off. When white soldiers in the lobby rose up to retaliate, James Reese Europe issued a booming order for calm.[55]

Finally, because of Hayward's relentless persistence, the order arrived: the two thousand men of the Fifteenth would sail for France. On November 8, the regiment assembled on Central Park's Sheep Meadow for its only farewell parade. Battle's kin, the Reverend Norman Roberts and his wife, Emma, came for last moments with their son Needham, a runaway transformed into disciplined soldier. And there was Napoleon Marshall's wife, Harriet Gibbs, the first black graduate of the Oberlin Conservatory of Music, preparing to part from a man who, well past draft age, was going to make a point. And there were all the others who esteemed Battle as the unit's godfather.

James Reese Europe conducted his band of renowned musicians in a program that included "Auld Lang Syne," "Religioso March," "a kind of half-syncopated arrangement of 'Onward Christian Soldiers,'" "Come Ye Disconsolate," and, finally, George M. Cohan's swinging, patriotic anthem "Over There."[56]

WITH THE REGIMENT'S departure, Battle raised his aspirations yet again. He had subscribed to the Equity Congress's three goals: establishing a black regiment, breaking the color line of the New York Police Department, and integrating the New York Fire Department. The first two were now achieved. Accomplishing the third would require finding the ideal man to seek admission to a firehouse. Battle focused on Chief Williams's son, Wesley.

Approaching the age of twenty-one, Wesley was the father of two sons. He supported Margaret and the boys—James, who was approaching two, and Charles, who was a newborn—on the steady, if modest, salary of a postal truck driver. While the job could carry a black man through a career and into a pension, its opportunities for advancement were slim and its duties were purely humdrum. By all rights, an adventurous young guy like Wesley would find greater fulfillment as a firefighter; and the fire department would be lucky to attract a job candidate who had Wesley's combination of brains, strength, and athleticism. But he would have to force open a barred door and then conquer brutal resistance. Battle judged Wesley to possess the emotional resilience to weather the unceasing hostility of white men in close quarters. Just as important, he also had no doubt that Wesley could whip just about anyone if necessary. Finally, the Chief's powerful friends could be invaluable.

Battle broached the idea of joining the fire department with Wesley. Fully aware of the *difficulties* that had beset Battle, Wesley bought in. His great-grandmother had come through slavery and his grandparents had escaped from bondage. Now, Wesley could endure the worst that white firefighters dished out in order to prove that a black man could excel in the job. Because Wesley knew that he would excel. So did the Chief and Margaret, who was as frightened as Florence had been in Battle's early days.

THE NEWSPAPERS OF May 1918 brought Battle up short. Almost six months had passed with scant news of the Fifteenth, but now a headline declared:

Two N.Y. Negroes
Whip 24 Germans
Win War Crosses
City's Colored Men in First
Fight, Decorated for
Gallantry

Then, with mounting joy, Battle read a war correspondent's astonishing words: "Our own 'cullud folks'—negro infantrymen mainly from the State and City of New York—have met the Germans and worsted them." And there, just below, was a tale of "dusky warriors" and "the glorious exploit of Privates Henry Johnson and Needham Roberts."[57]

All across the United States, Battle's cousin Roberts and Johnson, a redcap from Albany, were a heroic sensation. Honored as few blacks had ever been honored, they delighted Battle and his colleagues at the Equity Congress for proving in extraordinary measure the American fiber of the black soldier. The path from the Sheep Meadow to valor had been long and hard.

At the beginning of 1918, the Fifteenth had landed in Brest and boarded boxcars for transport to Saint-Nazaire, where the troops were pressed into laying railroad tracks and building docks, a hospital, and a dam. The Saint-Nazaire camp was "a racial war zone" in the description of Gail Buckley, whose *American Patriots* is an impressively researched history of African Americans in the US military. Interviewed by Buckley, one aged veteran recounted that white Marines "began killing black soldiers one by one," prompting blacks to retaliate by killing whites.[58]

The men pressed Hayward for a transfer into combat. Hayward appealed to General "Black Jack" Pershing without success, but a desperate French army offered to take the troops to the front under its command. With Pershing's approval, the Fifteenth then became the first American regiment to serve entirely beneath a foreign flag. The French dubbed the men *les enfants perdu*, the forgotten orphans.

Redesignated as the 369th Infantry, the regiment went to the front as the first of the thirty-seven thousand American black troops who were allowed into combat, while more than four times as many were limited to logistical duties.[59] The men plunged into the horrors of trench warfare amid exhausted Frenchmen and heavy German attack. The trenches were muddy and ran with blood. Beyond barbed wire, rotting corpses littered no man's land. Artillery shells, laden with explosives and shrapnel or poison gas, dropped random death to earth.

Spread on a four-kilometer line that ran from the ruins of Ville-sur-Tourbe to the Aisne River, the orphans took to the fight—with the exception of Jim Europe's band. On orders, he led a goodwill tour that introduced the demoralized French to swing music unlike any they had ever heard. Every performance was a rousing success. In Aix-les-Bains, the audience "rose en masse" with word that the band was heading to the front and carried the men to a troop train.

The regiment built forward ambuscades to guard against night-time stealth attacks. Post 29 was isolated near a bridge over the Aisne. There, Battle read in the newspaper, Needham Roberts peered into the blackness after two-thirty in the morning. His partner on guard, five-foot, four-inch Henry Johnson, was about forty feet away. Roberts heard a sound, perhaps the click of wire cutters. When Roberts and Johnson heard the sound again, they fired an illuminating rocket and shouted "Corporal of the Guard" in alert.

A raiding party opened fire and hurled hand grenades. Roberts and Johnson were wounded and knocked down. Propped against a door of the dugout, Roberts threw grenades toward where the Germans had been. Johnson got to his feet. A German loomed out of the darkness. Johnson fired, taking the man down but emptying his magazine. A second German rushed forward with a pistol. Johnson cracked the man's skull with the butt of his rifle.

Two of the enemy had hold of Roberts and were dragging him off. Johnson fell under gunfire, struggled to his feet, unsheathed a bolo knife, and plunged the eight-inch blade into the skull of a German who had Roberts by the shoulders. He turned the knife on the second of Robert's captors. The attacker who had fallen under the blow of Johnson's rifle butt fired a Luger. Wounded again, Johnson disemboweled the man. As American sentries arrived, Johnson threw grenades after retreating Germans. Then he slumped, wounded in both legs and both feet.[60]

Major Arthur Little, a white veteran who had enlisted in the Fifteenth because no white regiment would take him at the age of forty-three, tracked the German retreat "by pools of blood" and enough abandoned equipment to indicate that the raiding party had included as many as twenty-four men. That morning, three New York war correspondents happened to visit the regiment and sent home the story read by Battle and all of America.

And, eight years after starting the fight to create an African American National Guard regiment, the Equity Congress sent a dispatch to the "Officers and Men of the 15th Regiment of New York; with the American Expeditionary Forces in France." It read: "Colored people of New York and America in general, join the Equity Congress (your association) in congratulating you upon your splendid victory; especially Privates Henry Johnson and Needham Roberts."

The war to end all wars was over for Johnson and Roberts. They were hospitalized for long recuperations, while the report of their exploits prompted the French, for the first time, to award the *Croix de Guerre* to Americans. In recognition of Johnson's hand-to-hand fight, they bestowed on him the still-higher honor of the *Croix de Guerre avec Palme*. Both men sailed from France without the slightest official American recognition, not even a Purple Heart.

ANTICIPATING MIGHTY RESISTANCE, Battle strategized with Wesley and Chief Williams to maximize Wesley's chances of winning appointment to the fire department. Wesley would have to pass a written examination and a medical evaluation. Additionally, the department required applicants to undergo a physical test that assessed strength and speed and to submit written attestations of good character. With no shot at enrolling in the Delehanty Institute, Wesley embarked on intense self-study. Publications available for review at the municipal reference library covered subjects including fire department duties and rules, technical descriptions of steam pumpers, fire prevention techniques, the safety obligations of theaters, and the structure of city government—plus memory and arithmetic drills.

After Wesley registered for the civil service exam, his honey-colored skin was a notice to the department that its twenty-seven hundred applicants included a black man. Called for the physical test, Wesley assembled with several hundred of the men against whom he was competing. There was a distance run. Wesley far outpaced his heat with one of the fastest times ever recorded by the department. Loaded down with gear and weights, he raced up and down ladders and climbed over and under obstacles with similar ease. He proved to be the sole applicant—and only the second in the department's history—to achieve a 100 percent score. Then, he was almost as proficient on the written exam.

The marks ranked Wesley in the thirteenth spot on the hiring list, guaranteeing that the commissioner would reach his name. Battle celebrated with Wesley and the Chief and insisted that Wesley undergo a physical by a white doctor to be ready with indisputable evidence of good health. The doctor pronounced him in excellent condition.

The Chief, meanwhile, secured letters of recommendation from some of the prominent men with whom he had become friendly as head of the redcaps. To Battle's delight, Teddy Roosevelt gave Wesley an endorsement. The chief also stopped by to see Charles Thorley in the hope that the politically connected proprietor of the House of Flowers would back Wesley if need be. Thorley committed to providing whatever help he could.

It was widely believed that the fire department had never admitted a black man. In fact, in 1898, William Nicholson of Brooklyn had passed all the tests required for appointment, but he was relegated to working as a groom for wagon horses. In 1914, John Woodson, a former mail messenger, quietly joined the department and kept a low profile in a Brooklyn firehouse. Neither Battle nor Wesley nor anyone in the Equity Congress knew of Woodson, nor was he aware of them.

Now, word spread that an African American would be assigned to a firehouse. Woodson got the news when the black-oriented *Chicago Defender* published a story. He wrote to Wesley with advice that was remarkably similar to Battle's: "Do your work and do it as near perfect as you can" and "do everything the commanding officers tell you to do, no matter what it might be, do it." Woodson also counseled: "If they speak of our race before you, in your presence, as niggers, pay no attention—go and do something or take a newspaper and read."

While Battle and Wesley accepted Woodson's words as wise counsel, they also took for granted that Wesley would need more than forbearance: they expected that he would have to use his fists. Wesley had learned self-defense at the Colored Men's Branch of the YMCA under the training regimen of wrestler and judo black belt C. A. Ramsey. He and Battle would also run through boxing workouts there. They were in excellent company because two of the greatest heavyweights of the day trained at the Y. Sam Langford had come up through the ranks known as the "Boston Tar Baby," had lost to Jack Johnson early in his career, and had spent years seeking a rematch that was never to come. Jeremiah "Joe" Jeanette had fought Johnson seven times before Johnson claimed the world title and then was denied a further bout. Both fighters had held the colored world championship. They happily ran Wesley through sandbag and punching bag drills and sparred with him.

"Look, you better stay in shape, Sonny," they warned, "'cause when you get downtown with them Irishmen—you are going to have to defend yourself."

IN FRANCE, THE regiment fought on through the bloody concluding thrusts of the war and was the first to reach the Rhine. Never having fought under the American flag, the men who had been ridiculed as "darkies playing soldiers" were now the renowned "Hellfighters of Harlem." They had spent 191 days at the front, longer than any other company, had never surrendered a foot of ground, and had never lost a man to capture. Two hundred had given their lives in combat and eight hundred had been wounded.[61]

A little more than a month after the armistice, on December 13, 1918, the French pinned the *Croix de Guerre* on the regimental colors of the 369th in recognition of the unit's courage and sacrifices. The men then returned to the indignities that came with serving under American command. At the port of Brest, a military policeman clubbed a private for the affront of interrupting the MP's conversation to ask for directions to a latrine. Orders barred MPs from saluting officers of the 369th, white or black, because, Major Little was told, the "niggers" were "feeling their oats."

WESLEY'S APPOINTMENT TO the New York City Fire Department came through on January 10, 1919. He was assigned to Engine Company 55 in Lower Manhattan, a neighborhood renowned as Hell's Hundred Acres. The buildings were of two kinds: tenements whose wooden construction was akin to kindling, and factory lofts filled with flammable materials and supported by cast-iron columns that were prone to melting and collapse in a fire. By New York Central and subway, the firehouse was two hours from Williamsbridge. The long commute seemed the department's way of telling Wesley that he was not wanted. Firefighters tended to work close to home, and dozens of firehouses were closer to Williamsbridge.

Concerned that the brass had begun a campaign of harassment, Chief Williams took advantage of Thorley's Tammany Hall connections to get word to the fire commissioner that Wesley was in the department to stay. The commissioner responded that the door was open, but once through, Wesley would be on his own. With that sure understanding and with last words of love and support from his parents, Margaret, and Battle, Wesley set off to face what came. He could see his destination from far down the street. Opened in 1899, the firehouse was among dozens that had been ornately designed in a burst of construction. Its three stories had a brick and limestone façade and a copper-tiled mansard roof. A tower rose an additional eight feet and was fitted with hooks that allowed for hanging hoses down through the firehouse to dry after use. A single arched doorway that had been built to accommodate horse-drawn equipment dominated the front and was topped by a carved stone banner, "55 ENGINE 55."

The company's sixteen men anticipated Wesley's arrival. Some were on the street. He greeted them. They said nothing. He walked into a long, rectangular, vaulted chamber and reported for duty to a captain named Doyle. The entire company had been alerted to watch. Doyle ostentatiously stormed into retirement. The men expressed their feelings with mute hard glares. Wesley asked about equipment and accommodations. Responding to the most limited extent possible, the men pointed him to a second-floor bunkroom. They had removed a bed from the standard arrangement and had set it aside by the toilet. This was where he would sleep during a workweek that entailed staying on duty for five straight days, with four hours of free time each day. Wesley took the bunk without complaint.

Deprived as Battle had been of man-to-man workplace instruction, Wesley absorbed rules and routines by observation, as a campaign of harassment unfolded. When he went upstairs to the second floor, the men went downstairs, and vice versa. After his first meal at the company's communal table, a firefighter broke the plate and drinking glass that Wesley had used, setting a standard practice of throwing out any kitchen utensil that touched a black man's lips. A lieutenant assigned Wesley to stationhouse cleanup, as was customary for a rookie. The work included emptying spittoons—and, for Wesley, extended to finding them filled with urine. Every firefighter filed for reassignment, most writing on transfer requests that they refused to work with "a nigger." The commissioner barred transfers for a year.[62]

Depending how close a firefighter lived to the station, he could go home once, twice, or three times a day to eat and relax on his four hours of free time. Not Wesley. He could barely get to Williamsbridge and back in four hours. So he stayed confined to a building that was only twenty-four feet wide and one hundred feet from front to back. He felt that he had been sentenced to prison.

THE FIFTEENTH, NOW redesignated as the 369th Regiment, sailed into New York Harbor in February 1919. Battle met changed men. In the beginning, they had been given to excessively saluting superiors; now they were confident figures who looked others in the eye. Many showed the toll of the war in uneven gaits and the wheeze of damaged lungs. Napoleon Marshall, age forty-three when he landed in France, was upright and mobile only with the help of "a special steel corsage to support my back." Despite the severity of his injuries, the military classified Marshall as only 29 percent disabled, less than the 30 percent needed to qualify for benefits. Still, he was as ebullient as ever. He wrote:

> Even after all I have suffered from my adventure in patriotism—for adventure it was, since I was beyond the age of conscription—I have never had any misgivings or felt any remorse, finding cheer and comfort always in the immortal lines of the beloved Edward Everett Hale:

> *Breathes there a man with soul so dead*
> *Who never to himself has said,*
> *This is my own, my native land?*[63]

Hayward had promised the regiment "the greatest parade . . . that New York has ever seen." They would not be invited to the Victory Parade in July, but New York on February 17, 1919, scheduled a celebration in honor of the only American regiment to bear a state's name. That Monday morning, as "godfather" to the regiment, Battle joined the line of march. Led by the music of James Reese Europe's band, with Noble Sissle out front as drum major, the returned heroes stepped off in solid, square phalanxes, thirty-five feet on a side. Battle strode with Needham Roberts beside a car bearing a flower-draped Henry Johnson, for whom walking had become a struggle.[64] One shinbone had been replaced by a steel tube; most of the bones in one foot had been lost, so that Johnson moved "in a manner that might be described as 'slap-foot.'" His discharge papers would state that Johnson had been "severely" wounded, but they would also rate that he had zero percent disability, disqualifying him, too, for benefits.[65]

The formation stepped up Fifth Avenue from Twenty-Third Street, in front of a reviewing stand on which sat dignitaries including Governor Al Smith, former governor Whitman, William Randolph Hearst, and Secretary of State Francis Hugo. Hundreds of thousands of New Yorkers, white and black, cheered along the seven-mile route that culminated in tumultuous Harlem. In the outpouring, it was possible to believe that heroic service had finally won full United States citizenship for blacks, as had been hoped for in the story of Battle's ancestor in the American Revolution, as Frederick Douglass had envisioned in the Civil War, as African Americans had dreamed in the Spanish-American War, and as Battle and the Equity Congress had sought in fighting for a regiment whose accomplishments had far exceeded expectations.

THE GREAT MIGRATION had accelerated through the war years, so that, by the armistice, an ascendant black majority dominated Harlem. At the same time, the proud bearing of the regimental marchers exemplified a sense that the United States had reached a racial milestone with the rise of the New Negro, a people prepared to demand the equal treatment that had always been owed. Du Bois trumpeted the spirit in "Returning Soldiers," an essay in the *Crisis* that concluded:

> We return.
> We return from fighting.
> We return fighting.
>
> Make way for Democracy! We saved it in France, and by the Great Jehovah, we will save it in the United States of America, or know the reason why.[66]

The rallying optimism of the moment proved ephemeral. In 1918, the war's last year, the country recorded seventy-eight black lynchings, including those of a husband and wife, Haynes and Mary Turner. A white mob in Georgia shot Haynes dead in random retaliation for the murder of a white man. After Mary, who was eight months pregnant, protested her husband's murder, a mob hung her by the ankles, doused her with gasoline, and set her ablaze. A man cut open her belly. Turner's near-term baby fell to the ground, uttered a cry, and was stomped to death.

Bitterly, Battle noted that the story of the Turner murders appeared in the newspapers on the same day as the first reports that Johnson and Roberts had killed twenty-four Germans. He followed closely as one abomination after another plunged America into the country's worst period of racial violence, culminating in the Red Summer of 1919.

On April 13 in Carswell Grove, Georgia, Joe Ruffin, a black farmer, attempted to bail out a friend who was handcuffed in the back of a police car. The ensuing events climaxed when a white mob set a church ablaze and threw two of Ruffin's sons into the fire. On May 10 in Charleston, South Carolina, white sailors erupted into rioting when they concluded that a black bootlegger had cheated them out of money. A mob beat four blacks with clubs, iron pipe, and hammers, one fatally. On June 9 in Ellisville, Mississippi, a white woman reported that a black man named John Hatfield had raped her. After a posse shot Hatfield, as many as ten thousand people watched a lynching party hang Hatfield, cut off his fingers, and burn his body.

The bloody tide had profound impacts. Du Bois's militant march toward democracy became for African Americans a girding in an immediate fight to survive. The more powerfully that blacks claimed equality, it seemed to Battle, the more virulently that whites fought back.

SOMEONE STOLE WESLEY'S BADGE. Someone sliced his rubber coat into ribbons. He found his boots filled with excrement. Then came the alarm for Wesley's first big fire. Whipping on his gear, he clambered aboard a rig. The cellar of a building on the Bowery had gone up in flames. Announcing that he wanted to see just how brave Wesley was, a lieutenant ordered Wesley to take the hose and lead a crew into the smoky darkness. Wesley grabbed the nozzle and led a line of men who were to pull the hose and watch his back. The lieutenant was at his shoulder. Suddenly, fireballs rolled overhead. Standing his ground, Wesley trained water on the ceiling until the flames had died. Only then did he discover that the lieutenant and crew had abandoned him.

The episode established that Wesley had the courage to do the job, while also warning that he could not have faith in his fellows. Worse, he heard "veiled threats that they would throw me off the

roof at some fire or push me into a burning cellar if I did not resign."
Wesley spoke with the company's new captain, John J. Brennan, a
man who had committed to treat Wesley fairly, while leaving him to
overcome man-to-man bigotry. With Brennan's permission, Wesley
faced the entire company with a threat of his own: "I announced at
roll call what I had heard and if that was attempted I would try to
grab the nearest man to me and we would both go down. So that
kept everyone far away from me on the roofs."

Wesley detected a slight change in attitude even as the company
kept its distance. "White men respect courage," he would say years
later, echoing a thought often stated by Battle. A sign of the shift
emerged when a lieutenant told Wesley that the men would speak
with him if he agreed to sleep in the basement.

"I don't care whether anyone speaks to me or not," he responded.

A firefighter named John O'Toole became an arch-antagonist.
The brother of a fire captain, O'Toole had transferred into the department after working as a cop. He would boast in front of Wesley
about having beaten blacks while serving as a cop. O'Toole's brother,
the captain, visited the firehouse for the express purpose of making
his feelings clear. With Wesley listening, he said that "the fire department was a white man's job and not meant for niggers," and he told
Brennan: "What are you doing with that nigger? Why, I would work
him so hard that he would quit in two weeks. Why, if he was in my
company he would never last. I would keep him going night and day.
He would have to quit."

Wesley stared at O'Toole and thought, "A hundred men like him
could not make me quit."

THE RED SUMMER continued to peak. On July 18 in Washington,
DC, a nineteen-year-old white woman married to a Naval Aviation
Corps employee reported that two black men had tried to steal her
umbrella. Rumors transformed the incident into a serious assault.
White mobs began a four-day antiblack rampage that provoked
black warfare in response. The dean of Howard University saw a
mob hoist a black man "as one would a beef for slaughter" and
shoot him. On July 27 in Chicago, black teenagers drifted on a raft

toward a whites-only Lake Michigan beach. A white man threw rocks, striking one teen in the head and causing him to drown. After police refused to arrest the alleged rock thrower, a black mob converged on the beach. A black man shot at police. A black police officer returned fire, killing the shooter. Wild stories led to four days of white–black warfare. Men, women, and children—white and black—were hunted, beaten, stabbed, and shot. Buildings were burned. Streetcars were pulled from the tracks. Trapped in his apartment, a black cop held off a mob with an automatic rifle. The toll: 38 dead and 537 injured.

The trajectory of the violence troubled Battle. It had moved north, first to Washington, then to Chicago, a fully northern city. Could New York be next? In Harlem, the police department was the target of intensifying anger. Often harsh, if not brutal, the department had long since expended good will, and now many saw police as working against, not for, blacks. Battle suffered guilt by association. He was a cop, and cops had stood by while white mobs rampaged. He was a cop, and cops had freely swept up blacks in the disturbances. He was a cop, and cops had refused to arrest even the white man who threw the fatal rock in Chicago. More than ever, Battle felt the sting of a perception that would haunt many black cops for decades—that of being viewed as on the other side.

"This was one of the problems inherited by the Negro policeman in New York City at that time," he remembered. "His duty was to uphold the law—but Negro citizens looked at the law across a bitter color bar."

In September, New York reached the brink of a riot, with Battle singlehandedly at the center of the action. The events started innocently enough with a man's straw hat, a style that was fashionable in summer but became the object of youthful sport as the season faded. He remembered:

> There was a custom then all over Manhattan of bashing the straw hats of men bold enough or forgetful enough to wear such headgear after September 15th when the season for straws ended. Crowds of young men would pounce upon a straw-hat wearer, snatch the hat from his head and send it rolling down the street, or bash it over his ears.

This custom was tolerated and generally considered amusing—
to everyone except the owner of the hat. The law did not take such
a pastime seriously. For example, The *Evening World* reported hu-
morously on an irate citizen who had brought a teenager before the
Men's Night Court. The citizen stated, "Your Honor, I was sitting
in Seward Park when a gang came up laughing at my hat. The de-
fendant took it from my head and smashed it." The court declared,
"Straw hats have been called in. You're late, step down." And the
case was dismissed.

After midnight on September 15, Corporal Amanda Hayes
changed into street clothes in the locker room of the Harlem stationhouse. He left the building for the walk to a subway entrance with
a straw hat atop his head and a revolver in his holster. The night
was warm; people seeking relief from the heat filled the sidewalks. A
group of young blacks found amusement lying in wait for men who,
that very morning, had passed the straw-hat deadline. Along came
Hayes, looking very much the ordinary white civilian.

In high spirits, the teenagers reached for Hayes's hat. Hayes identified himself as a cop. Backed against a building, he ordered the
teenagers to move away. They complied. Hayes then chased the pur-
ported ringleader into a billiard parlor and placed him under arrest.
When Hayes returned to the sidewalk, prisoner in tow, the teens set
upon him again. They broke his hat and freed their friend.

"In a twinkling," the *New York Times* reported, "Hayes was the
center of a mob, battling for his life. He was felled by a blow that
broke his jaw and continued to be the target for kicks and blows."[67]
Struggling to his feet, Hayes fired his gun, mortally wounding a black
man named Ephram Gethers.

On duty not far away, Battle raced toward the gunfire. By the
time he reached the scene, Hayes was amid a kicking throng. Liberally wielding his nightstick—"striking right and left," in the description of the *New York Globe*—Battle pushed through the mob to
stand over the helpless Hayes with his gun drawn.

"This man is a policeman," he shouted, waving the club to widen
the circle of attackers.

"We'll lynch him anyway!" came voices in answer.

As Gethers's life ebbed, hundreds of people flocked angrily to the street on hearing that a white cop had killed a black man. Police reserves poured from the stationhouse. They found Battle standing his ground as Hayes's protector. Showered by bottles and chairs thrown from above, they launched into a club-swinging drive to restore order. Reinforcements from other precincts sealed the area through the night and the coming day. They all heard the story: the black cop had saved the white cop from rioting blacks.

Finally, in those moments of danger and bravery, Battle had done enough to win the gratitude of the department's white rank-and-file. They gave him in return a toehold on equal footing. Some knew that Battle hoped to become a sergeant but had been denied admission to the Delehanty Institute. A test preparation course was getting underway. The class voted unanimously to grant him entry—for the first time conceding that a black man, this black man, was fit to command whites.

CHAPTER THREE

BETRAYED

TONY HEARS HIS grandparents talking about Langston Hughes. He will be coming to the cottage again for a couple of weeks. A year has gone by since he last came to Greenwood Forest Farms, and Battle and Florence are frustrated that Hughes has made far less progress on the book than he should have. Florence is especially impatient. The one-time Southern girl who left school well before the age of sixteen had devoted her life to home and family rather than to literary pursuits. Baking pies was her province, not reading poetry. She shrugs at Hughes's stature. Worse, she takes his elusiveness as a sign that he has little respect for her husband's heroics. She regards the celebrity unforgivingly. Hughes is universally remembered as genial and fastidious, but Florence's hostility emerges in complaints that he is an awful houseguest who, undeservedly, expects her to serve him.

"Grandmother accused Langston of being lazy," Tony recalls. "She didn't like to take care of him. Clean your own dishes. Help out in the kitchen. He was above that kind of stuff."

To keep the peace, Battle arranges for Hughes to stay in Mrs. Taylor's guesthouse across the road from the cottage. He needs the time with Hughes because he has had infuriating difficulty focusing the writer to work on their project. An editor at Simon and Schuster has expressed "our keen—and unanimous—interest in such a book." Even more exciting, Battle has signed a deal with a screenwriter to develop a movie about his life. Still, he has gotten Hughes's attention only in fits and starts. What Battle does not know is that many others are similarly frustrated.

Four years earlier, in 1947, Hughes had scored success with *Street Scenes*, an opera about life in a Manhattan tenement produced in collaboration with Elmer Rice and Kurt Weill. *New York Times* critic Brooks Atkinson pronounced that Hughes's lyrics "communicate in simple and honest rhymes the homely familiarities of New York people and the warmth and beauty of humanity." Hughes's share of the proceeds, the largest sums he had ever earned, engendered hope that he had finally attained financial security.

Chasing ever harder after income, he collected in a book the most popular feature of a longtime column he had written for the Chicago *Defender*—imaginary conversations with a regular guy named Simple. He accepted a visiting creative writing professorship at Atlanta University and taught children from kindergarten through high school at the Laboratory School of the University of Chicago. With a one-thousand-dollar advance, he took on writing *Just Around the Corner*, a musical play about the Depression.

While the assignment should have been enough for any man, Hughes also agreed to collaborate with a young American musician on an opera commissioned by the American Opera Company of Philadelphia and the Pennsylvania Federation of Music Clubs, as well as to write two musical shows planned for Broadway. Despite everything, his income plummeted in the years following 1947, which is why he added Battle's life to a list of projects that was already too long and dispiriting. "I am a literary sharecropper," he complained to his good friend the novelist Arna Bontemps.[1]

Arnold Rampersad, author of the masterful *The Life of Langston Hughes*, explained, "Often subsisting in a dreary kind of neo-slavery, black sharecroppers toiled on land not their own. In the old days, Hughes had lived like a valiant runaway slave, owning nothing, wanting little besides freedom. Now, slavery apparently over, he had forty acres—but he was the mule."

Sorrowfully, Rampersad added, Hughes recognizes that "in many ways he was not working as a serious artist," a truth reinforced by publication of two landmarks of African American literature, Richard Wright's *Native Son* and Ralph Ellison's *Invisible Man*.[2] Instead of writing a similarly towering work, Hughes is consumed by the musicals, most of which come to naught, and by Battle's book, which he now finds a bore. Hounded by all of his collaborators and sponsors, Hughes works to pull together a manuscript, often monitored by Florence, whose disdain is surely as evident to Hughes as it is to Tony.

THE LESSON FOR Battle after the straw-hat eruption, as well as for Wesley Williams, was that the white man was never more prepared to open a door for a black man than if that particular black man had put his life on the line to save a white man. So be it. Battle studied at the Delehanty Institute with a new stature that extended high up the departmental ranks. At least one commander thought that this big, strong Negro could be of use.

Captain Cornelius Willemse, chief of the homicide squad, summoned Battle to headquarters. Willemse had joined the police force in 1899, learned the ropes in the San Juan Hill stationhouse, and participated in the antiblack police riot of 1900. "How those nightsticks worked—mine included!" Willemse recalled in a memoir.[3]

Now, he told Battle that he was looking for a man to go undercover as a prisoner in the municipal jail with the mission of wheedling a confession out of a black inmate accused of murder. Willemse promised Battle that the reward for putting his life on the line, locked in a cell with a hulking murderer, would be promotion to detective. Battle accepted the assignment. Leaving Florence with the four children, and having no idea when he might return, he marched into court in the guise of a criminal arrested for larceny. The magistrate ordered Battle held pending trial. Shackled, he trudged with accused killers, robbers, and rapists to an elevated passageway that connected the courthouse with the jail. It was known as the Bridge of Sighs.

As originally constructed in the first half of the nineteenth century, the jail was said to resemble the burial place of an Egyptian pharaoh and became known as the Tombs. The name stuck even as the structure was torn down and replaced. The incarnation in Battle's day had four tiers with stone floors. A long, rectangular area separated the cells from the outside wall. Light entered through high windows. Inmates doubled up in cages that were six feet wide and seven-and-a-half feet long.

Battle squeezed into an iron-bound space that was barely large enough for one person, let alone for the oversized Battle plus a violent man who was described by Willemse as a giant "far bigger and more powerful" than even Battle was. With a clang of the door, Battle began the work of gaining his cellmate's trust. The typical day moved from a cellblock breakfast of hominy, bread, and coffee, to a morning spent in the clamorous open area, to a cellblock lunch of lentil soup, mutton stew, and bread, to milling in the open area, to a dinner of corned beef hash and coleslaw before the cell door locked again for the night at five.[4]

This was to be Battle's life for the duration—although the duration proved not to last long. Willemse had recruited Battle because he needed a black police officer, but, with so few African Americans in the department, Battle was well known to blacks, both the law abiding and the law breakers. After a second day behind bars, someone recognized him. The accused murderer turned on Battle. Battle squared off, ready to fight. Up and down the tiers, inmates cried for combat. The warden called Willemse.

"Somebody's recognized Battle," he said. "The whole prison is howling and yelling. There's hell to pay here."

Racing to the scene, Willemse found Battle still in the cell. He was "unthinking of his danger but hopping mad that his trick had been discovered." Willemse wrote, adding, "He was so nervy that his enraged cell-mate hadn't attempted an attack."[5]

With yet another exploit to his credit, Battle could only wait for the department to award the detective's shield that Willemse had promised.

AS BATTLE HAD found a productive refuge in the stationhouse flag loft, Wesley took occupancy of the hose tower. The company was happy to see him climb alone to the rooftop. With Captain Brennan's encouragement, he equipped the space with barbells for working out and a chair and table for reading. His selections included

manuals filled with the information he would need to pass the fire
lieutenant's test as soon as he had racked up the required experience
on the job. He had a lot to learn. The exam topics covered the operation and maintenance of every variety of departmental truck and
equipment, along with proper procedures for fighting fires, ranging
from tenement blazes to conflagrations in varnish factories.[6] Company members scoffed at Wesley's ambition, with one saying that he
"would be an officer over white men when black crows turn white."
But Brennan encouraged Wesley to stick to his studies and to ignore
his tormentors.

Wesley swallowed the indignities until someone went one step
too far. Then he would challenge a white man's superiority by provoking the man into trying to settle the score physically. The company had rules of combat: two firefighters with a serious beef went to
the basement; the one who came up was deemed to have prevailed.
When men wanted to fight, Wesley accommodated them, each time
descending first and then climbing the stairs in triumph, leaving a
vanquished man to wash his bloodied face at a sink.

"I could not have stayed on the job if I lost," he would remember. "There was no Human Rights Commission, and you couldn't go
complaining to a civil rights group. They would have thought I was
a weakling and trampled me. In those days you stood up alone and
put knuckle to jaw."[7]

At the six-month mark, Wesley moved up from probationary firefighter to full-fledged member of the department. Around that time,
encountering a house fire while off duty in Williamsbridge, he led a
woman and six children to safety. The department withheld official
recognition. Then, Wesley happened by a fire while walking with a
white firefighter assigned to another company in the neighborhood
that today is trendy SoHo. Rushing in together, the two men guided
trapped people to safety. The department recognized the heroism of
Wesley's partner in the rescue, but Wesley's valor was chalked up to
routine action. It was the same when Wesley rescued a woman and
two children from a serious blaze while on duty.

Brennan, though, kept his commitment to fairness. After the company got a first gasoline-powered rig, he asked Wesley to adjust its

placement in the firehouse. Wesley drew on his experience driving a postal truck—experience unmatched by anyone in the company—to flawlessly execute a tight maneuver on a narrow, crowded street. Brennan ordered that from then on Wesley, instead of the company's senior man, would drive to fires. Someone took revenge by placing Wesley's helmet on the floor so that the truck crushed it.

The rig had no cab. The driver sat prominently in view on a high, exposed seat in front of a steam kettle that powered a water pump.[8] Wesley could not be missed as he raced to alarms. His visible place of honor infuriated many fellow officers. Once, a chief protested Wesley's arrival at a three-alarm fire by refusing to issue orders to the company, sidelining the men as others fought the blaze.

As Battle had predicted, Wesley had moved up on the merits. Many years later, when Wesley and Brennan were retired, Wesley would look back fondly on the decency shown by this one white man who "was the strongest influence in my rising to the rank of battalion chief" and who had "instructed and guided me as if I were his own son."

TWO HIGHER POWERS took command of Battle's future: the Democratic Party's corrupt Tammany Hall political machine and a ruthless police commissioner named Richard E. Enright.

Tammany Hall's roots trace to colonial America. After ratification of the US Constitution, New York upholsterer William Mooney organized a citizens' group around the theme of patriotic democracy. He called it the Society of St. Tammany, Tammany being the name of a mythical chief of the Lenni-Lenape Delaware Indian tribe. Tammany was celebrated for purportedly discovering corn, beans, and tobacco and for inventing the canoe.

A growing membership transformed Mooney's nonpartisan society into a political force. Espousing a philosophy that stood for the common man over the privileged, the organization eventually took control of the Democratic Party, along with governmental power and spoils. Tammany leaders awarded patronage jobs and moneymaking opportunities to members who contributed to the society's success.

They also engaged in excesses—a dip into the treasury here, a fraud on the taxpayers there—that pushed Tammany toward the infamous corruption of William Marcy "Boss" Tweed.

Tweed stole power by directing underlings to falsify vote counts when necessary, and he stole money through kickbacks on contracts: Vendors sold goods or services to the city government only if they inflated bills by as much as 65 percent and surrendered the over-payments to Tweed's ring. Estimates of the thefts ranged from $30 million to $75 million in the dollars of those days, with the cost of building a courthouse notoriously topping out at four times the price of the House of Parliament in London.

Eventually, the law caught up to Tweed. Once accustomed to sporting "a diamond like a planet in his shirt front," he died in the Ludlow Street Jail.[9] Tammany Hall wobbled for a few years after Tweed's downfall, but his successors soon restored its power, along with less blatantly rapacious plunder—at the center of which was the police department.

In 1870, Tweed had shrewdly engineered revisions to the city charter that placed the force under a four-member board of police commissioners. The panel was charged with setting policy and naming a superintendent, or police chief, to carry it out. On paper, the structure promised deliberative, independent policing. In fact, the arrangement empowered Tammany to approve or veto potential board members, dictate to superintendents, and introduce to stationhouses the favors and repayments, refusals, and retributions that were the currency of politics. The man who wanted a cop's steady pay, an easier assignment, or a promotion—or a break when he got into trouble—was well advised to be on excellent terms with his Tammany district leader.

The system produced William "Big Bill" Devery, who remains, more than a century later, the most flamboyant rogue in New York Police Department history.

A son of Irish immigrants, Devery was born in 1857 in a room over a saloon on the East Side, a grimy neighborhood seemingly populated in equal proportions by cripples and criminals. His uncle owned the saloon, as well as additional bars that catered to burglars, roughhousers, and thugs. Devery grew up running errands among the drinking spots, and then he followed a natural trajectory onto the force.[10] All around him, Irishmen and their boys found opportunity in policing, one bringing the next onboard until the group had hold of a good, secure workplace.

Just as important, Devery was raised in a household that swore allegiance to the Democratic machine. "I carried my father's dinner pail when he was laying the bricks of Tammany Hall," Devery would one day say, apparently remembering construction of the organization's headquarters.[11]

Fully at home, Devery won promotion to sergeant in 1884 and to captain in 1891. Quite likely, he paid his way up the ladder. In 1892, the *Mail and Express* reported that Tammany had set an informal rate schedule: $300 to join the force; $1,400 to rise to sergeant; and $14,000 to make captain, the last being a truly astonishing figure. Factoring in inflation, it is equivalent in twenty-first-century dollars to $350,000.

The sum is best seen as an investment that paid handsome returns. Graft was rampant. The higher a man rose in the ranks, the more money he could collect, and cash was plentiful because New York was bedeviled by commerce in sex, gambling, and alcohol.

To Devery, the vices were simply part of the human condition, none of the business of preachers and none of the business of police—except in taking a cut of the proceeds. This he accomplished with unprecedented efficiency after gaining the rank of captain at the youthful age of thirty-five.

The department posted Captain Devery at a stationhouse that served the Lower East Side, the world's most densely populated area, nine square blocks teeming with poverty-stricken Jewish immigrants, mostly from Russia and Poland. They crowded into squalid tenements, labored in garment sweatshops, kept faith in rudimentary synagogues, and patronized twenty-five brothels.

Devery's officers met a thick-necked bull of a man. He was five feet ten, had a fifty-inch waist, wore size seventeen shoes, and sported a moustache to do a walrus proud. As legendarily recounted, he laid down the law: "They tell me there's a lot of graftin' going on in this precinct. They tell me you fellows are the fiercest ever on graft. Now, that's goin' to stop. If there's any graftin' to be done, I'll do it."

The bill for a brothel was a $500 "new captain" initiation fee, plus $50 a month. The proprietors of gambling halls paid similar fees, some to offer wagering on horse racing, others to take bets on the numbers. Saloon owners made payments for the privilege of serving patrons at all hours, most importantly on Sunday, the lone day of rest for six-day-a-week workingmen.[12]

With money pouring in, Devery gave percentages to his police superiors and to Tammany Hall. The system of payments and protection applied in every precinct so that the vice laws became meaningless. Finally, the ruling-class Protestant elite recoiled. Asserting moral superiority, they held Catholic and Jewish immigrants responsible for debauching the city and set out to restore virtue, both for its own sake and as a means of regaining political prominence over the masses who powered the Democratic machine.

Devery bore the brunt of the reformers' assaults. Five years apart, two state legislative committees revealed him to be a lynchpin of organized graft. Two grand juries indicted him on criminal charges, once for neglect of duty, once for bribery. Through it all, Devery made a comic opera of attempts to bring him down. He laughed past legislative interrogations with the answer, "Touchin' on and appertainin' to that matter, I disremember." When juries acquitted him of criminal charges, he lighted enormous celebratory cigars.

By his brazenness, Devery personified the dark side in a fight for New York's soul. The struggle's opposing hero was brash young Teddy Roosevelt. After an accumulation of Tammany scandals, the voters installed a Republican mayor, who appointed Roosevelt in 1895 to the board of police commissioners. His colleagues then elected Roosevelt to serve as the board's president, and he set out not only to reform the force but also to conquer Tammany—and, still more, to improve the morals of New York at large.

The public cheered his swashbuckling—for a time. Huzzahs faded after Roosevelt relentlessly enforced the law that barred alcohol sales on Sundays, when the saloons were filled with good citizens enjoying what little time they had for leisure. Starting his second year in office, he marched to boos in the police department's annual parade, while Devery was a crowd favorite. Roosevelt grew more determined than ever to fire the Tammany grafter. All his efforts came to naught when

President William McKinley appointed Roosevelt assistant US secretary of war, ending his tumultuous twenty-three months as president of the board.

The next mayoral election restored the Democratic machine's grip on City Hall. Tammany boss Richard Croker took control of the board and engineered Devery's installation as chief of police, the department's highest-ranking uniformed position. "Too much praise cannot be given to the police department as presently administered by Chief Devery," Croker declared as Devery cast aside consistent enforcement of laws and regulations with a showman's flair.

Nightly, he ran the department from beside a fire hydrant, known as "The Pump" at the corner of Eighth Avenue and Twenty-Eighth Street in the Tenderloin. Often he displayed wads of cash. Captains, politicians, and gangsters came by to conduct business, of which there was plenty. As a noted writer for *Harper's Weekly* put it in 1898, "New York is wide open once more. Tammany Hall has at last secured its 'terrible revenge.'"[13]

The *New York Times* calculated that gambling interests alone were making protection payments totaling $3 million a year—an amount equal to more than $80 million today. Still more astounding, Devery went into the gaming trade directly by joining a syndicate with Frank Farrell, the city's preeminent professional bookmaker, and "Big Tim" Sullivan, a state senator and Tammany mainstay.

Often drunk, he brought hilarity to punishing cops found guilty of wrongdoing. He fined an officer who had recklessly fired a gun thirty days' pay for "not hittin' nothing," and he docked a second officer two days for kissing a girl in a hallway while on duty. "I would kiss a girl myself; there's lots of things I'd do and do do but I'll never get caught," Devery said. "And so I herewith fine you good and plenty for getting caught."

Most famously, he explained to a third officer the code he expected cops to uphold: "When you're caught with the goods on you and you can't get away with it, you want to stand up with nerve and take your medicine. You don't know nothin' then. No matter under what circumstances, a man doesn't want to know nothin' when he's caught with the goods on him."

Meanwhile, Roosevelt had left Washington to lead the Rough Riders at the Battle of San Juan Hill and had then been elected New York's governor. He took a final stab at cutting Tammany and Devery down to size by signing legislation that abolished the Board of Commissioners and gave the mayor power to appoint a single commissioner. To the relief of reformers, Mayor Robert Van Wyck, a Tammany man, named Civil War Medal of Honor winner Michael Murphy as commissioner, and then, to their horror, Murphy gave Devery full command as first deputy commissioner.

Devery's ride ended after Tammany lost the mayoralty in 1901. No longer a member of the department for the first time in almost a quarter-century, he took to civilian life with a hefty wallet. He bought an interest in a racetrack and joined with gambling syndicate partners Sullivan and Farrell in one of the most consequential New York investments ever made. Together, they purchased and brought to the city a Baltimore baseball team that would become the Yankees. Eventually, he would adopt the interlocking letters N and Y that remain the team's classic insignia.

LONG INDESTRUCTIBLE ATOP the department, Devery dominated the formative years on the police force of future commissioner Richard E. Enright. After Devery's ouster, Enright, then a young cop, saw the crowning and overthrow of a succession of commissioners who lacked either the savvy or the political muscle to bring the department to heel. He played a deft insider's game to win advancement. Promoted to sergeant, he organized a Sergeants Benevolent Association, part labor union, part lobbying firm, part society dedicated to aiding the widows and orphans of deceased members. Enright leveraged the functions to become the one man who spoke for the sergeants, and speak he did, portraying them in flowery orations as noble and graft-free protectors of the public. He furthered his influence by giving the commissioners who came and went a financial incentive to play ball, rewarding one who had promoted ninety-one men to sergeant with a silver loving cup and five hundred pieces of silver tableware.

As Battle weathered the silent treatment and exile to the station-house flag loft, Enright moved on to building a Lieutenants Benevolent Association into a still more potent force. His annual dinners in the Grand Ballroom of the Waldorf Astoria Hotel drew the rich and powerful, including President William Howard Taft. Among those who sent regrets were Devery, Andrew Carnegie, and Mark Twain.[14]

Enright became a casualty of war when voters threw the bums out. A reform mayor and police commissioner took office in 1914. Committed to tilting at the windmill of a corruption cleanup, the new commissioner established the department's first internal affairs unit. He called it the Confidential Squad and gave command to a warhorse of a captain known as "Honest Dan" Costigan.

With Sergeant Lewis Valentine at his side, Costigan identified commanders who were in Tammany Hall's pocket by raiding gambling houses in their precincts. He also seized the records of the Lieutenants Benevolent Association, infuriating Enright with an investigation that turned up no wrongdoing. The commissioner then denied Enright a promotion to captain, even though by exam score he was at the top of the list.

Enright would have his revenge. The machine prevailed anew on Election Day 1917, installing as mayor Mike "Red" Hylan, a hotheaded Brooklyn Democrat and former train motorman. Hylan stunned New York by appointing Enright commissioner, elevating him over 122 more-senior officers. With New York's governor studying whether to remove Enright from office out of that fear he would open the door to police corruption, Devery endorsed the appointment, saying, "It takes a former cop to make the department go. Enright is the boy to do it."

In short order, Enright disbanded the Confidential Squad, exiled Costigan and Valentine to grueling posts, and closed the department's honor roll to Valentine's partner Floyd Horton, who had been killed in the line of duty. When Devery died in 1918, Enright ordered flags lowered to half-staff, assigned the department's one-hundred-piece band to play on the day of the funeral, and made sure that a handpicked honor guard escorted his role model's casket from church to burial.[15]

Shrewdly, Enright established a closely held unit to handle sensitive investigations and to enforce the law—or not—as he saw fit. He called the squad the Special Service Division. High on its list of responsibilities were prostitution, gambling, and illegal alcohol sales, the vices where crime, money, and political power intersected. No police commissioner could ignore the statutes, but no police commissioner could enforce them with crusading zeal and expect to stay in office for long. Appointment to the unit was by Enright's invitation. He needed good cops and good superior officers who were more than that. He needed good cops and good superior officers whom he could trust.

And now Captain Cornelius Willemse put in a word for the big Negro, Sam Battle, who'd gone undercover to catch a murderer in the Tombs. Enright ordered Battle to report. No one in the department had ever opened a door for him without a fight, let alone a door to the commissioner's elite unit, but here Enright was saying that Battle had earned a coveted posting. He took the assignment as confirmation that a black man could endure to win his due. He was glad also to serve again as a beacon for others at a time when the post–World War I determination of the New Negro had produced a small surge in African American recruits.

Edward Jackson secured state legislation that enabled him to join the force after losing an eye on the battlefield. Wesley Redding, son of a high school teacher and a bank worker, emigrated from Atlanta to New York and worked as a Pennsylvania Station railroad cop before joining the department. Emmanuel Kline, son of a freed slave, arrived from South Carolina, studied English at Columbia University and French at the Berlitz School, and served overseas in the 376th Infantry Division. He came home to work as a redcap for Chief Williams at Grand Central and then followed Battle's path onto the force.

In 1918, the New York Police Department opened its ranks to a handful of women. They were issued badges but did not wear standard uniforms or perform standard patrol. A unit headed by the department's first female deputy commissioner focused on the "white slave traffic," abortions, fortune telling, "wayward girls," and "domestic relations cases." In 1919, Cora Parchmont, a graduate of the

University of Chicago and a former high school teacher, became the first black policewoman. "We will try to keep unfortunate ones from going to prison instead of aiming to imprison them," Parchmont told the Chicago *Defender*.

Unfailingly, Battle encouraged his fellow officers and Wesley to believe that they could secure fairer treatment. Now, the significance of Battle's membership in Enright's personal fief was profound. Headquarters duty was as distant from their posts as the peak of Everest is from a valley floor. More, they all knew that Battle was going to work for a hard man who played for advantage.

When Battle got the call in 1920, Tammany had shifted to less obvious, more lucrative corruption. Charles Francis Murphy, a former saloon owner, was now boss. He designated trusted deputy Tom Foley to be the machine's liaison to the underworld, and he relied on Arnold Rothstein, a genius of a gangster who participated in fixing the 1919 World Series, to serve as the primary contact between crime and politics.

Murphy conducted business with legitimate interests in "The Scarlet Room of Mystery," a private area of Delmonico's Restaurant, so named by the press due to the color of its plush upholstery. As recalled in M. R. Werner's history, *Tammany Hall*, it was "Murphy's great and lasting contribution to the philosophy of Tammany Hall that he taught the organization that more money can be made by a legal contract than by petty blackmail."

Enright was of like mind. He came by money with polish. A Wall Street broker bought five thousand shares of stock in a petroleum company with his own funds, sold the stock five days later, and, for reasons never credibly explained, cut a check to Enright for the resulting $12,000 profit. The broker also purchased a Stutz automobile for Enright's wife. Meanwhile, on an annual salary of $7,000, Enright found the resources to deposit $100,000 into bank accounts.[16]

Battle sized up what he was getting into without illusions. As excited as he was, the Special Service Division loomed as treacherous territory. He would roam the city in plainclothes, enforcing the law where he was told to or where he would have to divine the right side of an invisible line between an arrest that brought commendations and an arrest for which there would be hell to pay.

Battle's commanding officers gave him a desk and put him to work. At home, he told Florence, Wesley, and the Chief that Enright seemed a surprisingly fair-minded man, and he gained confidence that he would be measured by his performance. "I was assigned to cases without discrimination," he said years later.

Battle discovered great fun in being a cop who went about armed both with a gun and with political power—at times with orders from a mayor given to using the police to torment enemies. In one episode, Hylan mobilized the Special Service Division after learning that the Republican Club in his Brooklyn neighborhood was going to hold a stag party. "I was a Democrat, too, so I had no ardent objections to carrying out his orders," Battle told Hughes in recalling a raid that is quaint in its moralism, wild and wooly in the ease with which Battle fired his weapon, and wonderfully narrated by the poet:

> When I arrived at the Club, the midnight stag party was going full blast. Beer was flowing. Smoke was so thick you could cut it with a knife. The band was blaring. In the terminology of jazz, "the joint was jumping!"
>
> About five hundred men were feasting their eyes on three young ladies advertised as Little Egypt, Baby Doll and Fatima. These *artistes* were moving to the music with sufficient vigor to almost cause the walls to shake. As the music grew hotter, egged on by the men who threw dollar bills on the stage, the young ladies began to shed their garments, piece by piece.
>
> Each time a female garment fell, the men would cry approval, whistle, catcall and shout lewd remarks. As the music swelled in volume, one young woman threw her brassiere into the crowd and caused a stampede. Nobody got the brassiere. It was torn to ribbons in the melee. Excitement mounted as the same young lady stepped out of her step-ins.
>
> By now, the other dancers were vying with her in divesting them-selves of lingerie. Finally all three of the dancers were prancing around

the stage in nothing but silk stockings. At that point, I took a pistol from my holster and fired a couple of shots through the window—my signal to the detectives outside. The shots, the broken glass, the pistol flash, and the screams that went up caused pandemonium. But every exit was covered.

Those who jumped out of windows leaped directly into the arms of policemen. Those who ran—ran into a cordon of cops. Those who fainted were carried out headfirst. A few men did faint. The police department was not prepared for so large a catch. Since a single patrol wagon would not hold more than fifteen or twenty men, we had to telephone all the stations in Brooklyn for the loan of their wagons. On the way to the precincts, the Black Marias had to pass Mayor Hylan's home.

"Every time you go by the Mayor's house with a load, clang your gongs," I told the drivers of the patrol wagons. They did—all night long.

BATTLE'S HEADY DAYS of freewheeling police work slipped into eclipse when Florence noticed that three-year-old Teddy had a cough. Parents of today would hear little cause for worry in a three-year-old's rasping. Not so mothers and fathers in 1920. Teddy's jeopardy became clear when he gasped for air with a highly pitched sound, the signature of whooping cough.

The New York Health Department recorded 8,873 cases of whooping cough that year, while judging that large numbers escaped official count. The disease proved fatal for one of every fifteen afflicted children. A doctor took charge of Teddy on August 12, recommending the standard practices for helping a gasping child: mustard plasters on chest and back, forehead ice packs, and steam inhalations so primitive as to include traces of benzene or turpentine. After six days, Battle heard a child's last breath for a second time.[17] Gloom descended on the household. Florence was inconsolable. There was the room in which Teddy had died and there was the bed. Battle thought about taking her away, not for a vacation, but to live somewhere else.

* * *

HE HAD A place in mind: Harlem in its day of glorious promise.

Propelled by the Great Migration, New York's black population grew by two-thirds between 1910 and 1920, from 91,709 to 152,467 people, with more than half drawn to live in Harlem.[18] In front of Battle's eyes, critical mass produced a militantly proud, magnificently optimistic culture.

On Sundays, there was religion. People poured from their homes unified in expressing faith, some in storefronts with little more than a preacher, a Bible, and chairs, many in grand houses of worship that had been sold off by whites. Church-going could be an all-day affair. After the readings, preaching, and singing, the churches became social centers. Playing multiple roles, they were both "a stabilizing force" and "an arena for the exercise of one's capabilities and powers, a world in which one may achieve self-realization and preferment," wrote James Weldon Johnson.[19]

Sunday afternoons were taken up by The Stroll, and so, too, evenings when the weather was right. The place was Seventh Avenue, a boulevard of shops, restaurants, apartment buildings, and nightclubs. Up one sidewalk and then back down the other, people socialized with old friends and new acquaintances. Someone who knew someone always had word about something that had happened back home, and everyone on this "Great Black Way" shared Harlem's news and gossip.[20]

Some days the talk was of Paul Robeson. Still years from acclaim as an actor and singer, Robeson at the age of twenty-two was already a Renaissance man. He had attended Rutgers University as the school's third black student; had won fifteen varsity letters for football, basketball, baseball, and track; had twice been named a football All American; and had graduated as class valedictorian. He passed the time on Seventh Avenue while studying at Columbia University Law School and earning a living teaching Latin and playing professional football.[21]

Often the talk was of doers who were Battle's generational contemporaries.

Marcus Garvey, a Jamaican immigrant, age thirty-three, was building his ill-fated United Negro Improvement Association into the country's largest black nationalist movement with the message,

"We are striking homeward toward Africa to make her the big black Republic."

Fabulously wealthy A'Lelia Walker, age thirty-five, was running America's dominant business selling hair-care products to blacks. She had taken over the company on the death of its founder, her mother, Madame C. J. Walker, and she was soon to be renowned as a lavish hostess of the Harlem Renaissance.

Later to achieve a landmark in labor organizing with formation of the Brotherhood of Sleeping Car Porters, later to pressure President Harry Truman into integrating the US military, later to conceive of the 1963 March on Washington, A. Philip Randolph, age thirty-one, was urging radical socialism as the path to empowerment. He and a partner had founded the *Messenger*, "The Only Magazine Of Scientific Radicalism In The World Published by Negroes."

This being the takeoff of the Roaring Twenties, the neighborhood pulsed also with new cultural energy. Women cast off presumed propriety to wear their hair and their skirts shorter, so that, by one telling, a skirt sometimes "almost rivaled the bathing suit."[22] Saloons proliferated. Nightclub owners who had been tops in the Tenderloin found success in the Cotton Club, Small's Paradise, Baron Wilkins's Exclusive Club, and more. They provided drink and the best of song and dance at a time when a convergence of talent and creativity was remaking American popular music.

Jervis Anderson, author of *This Was Harlem*, encapsulated the leap forward: "Four musical styles appear to have met in Harlem by 1920 and to have influenced the emergence of jazz in the community: ragtime, stride piano, blues and some of the early Dixieland sounds of New Orleans. But until about 1922 the dominant forces in Harlem music were the blues singers and stride pianists."[23]

In the ferment, an upstart newspaper was giving the venerable *New York Age* a run for its readers. Where the *Age* was a sober broadsheet with a national vision, the *Amsterdam News* told the people of Harlem what the people of Harlem were doing in a tabloidlike voice. The paper bannered headlines like "Murdered Man a Bigamist" and chronicled ordinary events that had a touch of the extraordinary. Readers of a feature called "Items of Social Interest" learned, among endless other things, that Mrs. Harry Reeves, a member of the Citizen's Christmas Cheer Committee, was hosting a six-course dinner, that friends had thrown a surprise birthday party for Mrs. Laura E. Williams, and that twelve-year-old Clarence Propet had won a piano competition.[24]

Optimism trumped the social ills brought north by ill-educated Southerners, rent gouging by white landlords, and the low wages and closed doors that were the lot of most African Americans. Journalist George Schuyler recalled the era as a time "when everything was booming and joyful and gay."[25]

The buoyancy of 1920 made great things seem possible, and they certainly did seem so to James Weldon Johnson, who wrote in the *Age* that year: "Have you ever stopped to think what the future of Harlem will be? It will be a city within a city. It will be the greatest Negro city in the world within the greatest city in the world."[26]

And Battle, age thirty-seven, wanted to be there for it.

AROUND THE SAME TIME, nineteen-year-old Langston Hughes succumbed to Harlem's allure as he stood on the brink of adulthood after a lonely coming-of-age. Born in Joplin, Missouri, in 1902, he grew up in predominantly white areas of Lawrence, Kansas, and Cleveland, Ohio, knowing both antiblack bigotry and the friendship of whites. His parental bonds were, to put it mildly, frayed.

Early on, Hughes's father, James Hughes, abandoned his wife, his only child, and the America that denied him opportunity, and moved across the border to establish a successful life in Mexico. He was a man who scorned the poor, especially the black poor, seeming to view them as "lazy, undeserving cowards," in the judgment of Hughes's biographer Rampersad. Langston himself would write: "My father hated Negroes. I think he hated himself, too, for being a Negro. He disliked all of his family because they were Negroes."[27]

Hughes's mother, Carrie Langston, was a flighty woman who dreamed of a show business career and who often left her solitary son in the care of a loving neighborhood couple, or with his grandmother, a reserved woman who instilled in Hughes tales of ancestors challenging the white world's domination. She spoke most stirringly of her first husband, Lewis Sheridan Leary, who had ridden off from their home in Oberlin, Ohio, in 1859 to join white radical abolitionist John Brown's assault on the federal arsenal at Harpers Ferry, Virginia. For more than a half-century, Hughes's grandmother wore the bullet-shredded shawl that Lewis Leary had worn at his death, often using the cloth as a nighttime coverlet for her young grandson.[28]

Shortly after graduating from high school, Hughes read the stories of the French writer Guy de Maupassant and credited them with making him "really want to be a writer and write stories about Negroes, so true that people in far-away lands would read them—even after I was dead."[29]

In the summer of 1920, at the age of eighteen, he wrote his first poetic landmark, *The Negro Speaks of Rivers*, a work that captured the sweep of black history in thirteen lines. Audaciously adopting the personage of his race, he opened:

I've known rivers:
I've known rivers ancient as the world and older than the
flow of human blood in human veins.

Then he told of bathing in the Euphrates River, building a hut near the Congo, looking upon the Nile, and listening to the Mississippi when Abraham Lincoln traveled to New Orleans before concluding:

I've known rivers:
Ancient, dusky rivers. My soul has grown deep like the rivers.

Planning to study at Columbia University, Hughes arrived in New York City by ship from Mexico, where in 1921 he had left a father he admitted to hating.

"There is no thrill in all the world like entering, for the first time, New York harbor,—coming in from the flat monotony of the sea to this rise of dreams and beauty," he wrote four years later. "New York is truly the dream city,—city of the towers near God, city of hopes and visions, of spires seeking in the windy air loveliness and perfection."[30]

Hughes headed north to the subway stop at Lenox Avenue and 135th Street, the very stop where Battle had protected the white police officer from the angry mob. "I went up the stairs and out into the bright September sunlight. Harlem! I stood there, dropped my bags, took a deep breath and felt happy again," he would remember.[31]

In that moment, Hughes had unknowingly reached fertile ground for an unprecedented African American literary movement. Already, Jamaica-born Claude McKay had written poems of powerful emotion, none having more impact than his 1919 Red Summer sonnet, "If We Must Die." Already, Countee Cullen, an orphaned teenager who had been taken in by the Reverend Frederick Asbury Cullen, pastor of Salem Methodist Episcopal Church, was writing lyrical poems as editor of the student newspaper at DeWitt Clinton High School. His "I Have a Rendezvous With Life" had topped a national competition.

After completing two semesters at Columbia and resolving never to return, Hughes was repeatedly rebuffed in a job search because he was black. Over and over, he heard words to the effect, "But I didn't advertise for a colored boy." He wound up as a farm laborer on Staten Island, and then he landed, like Chief Williams and so many other young African Americans, at Charles Thorley's House of Flowers. There, he delivered orders costing more than a month's salary to the likes of the actress Marion Davies on her yacht and to the Roosevelts at Oyster Bay. He lasted a month before clashing with Thorley over showing up late one day.

Daring to believe that he could become America's first self-supporting black writer, Hughes signed on as a crewman on freighters that took him to Africa and Europe. The journeys opened his eyes to the continent of his ancestors and allowed him to vagabond through cities like Paris. On his travels, he wrote poetry that drew notice at home, while new voices of the black urban masses gathered in New York.

Destitute and hoping to work his way home from Genoa, he roamed the wharves at the age of twenty-two and wrote another of his masterpieces. The eighteen lines vibrantly opened with the poem's title, "I, too, sing America," and locked in his dream of being read even after death.

*   *   *

JUST THEN, AMERICA was embarked on the mad misadventure of Prohibition and the 1920s were starting to roar. On January 17, 1920,
when the Volstead Act took effect, the dry forces set out to prove
they could drain even drenched New York through criminal punish-
ments. New Yorkers were of a different mind. They drank as they
always drank, only in larger quantities and in clandestine bars that
came to be called speakeasies. "Be it known to the trusting and the
unsuspecting, New York City is almost wide open today," the *Times*
reported in a May 1920 story headlined "Making a Joke of Prohibition in New York City."[32]

Congress had expected that local police would help enforce
America's only attempt to use the Constitution to limit rather than
to protect personal freedom, but Congress could not require locals
like Enright to adopt federal law as a mandate of their own. Judging
him to be insufficiently enthusiastic, the "drys" persuaded the rural
politicians of New York's legislature to write a state prohibition statute onto the books.

Enright centralized enforcement in the Special Service Division.
Only the division chief would decide which speakeasies to target.
Enright promised two benefits: local cops would have fewer opportunities for graft, and the department's vice squad would apply special
expertise to clamping down. Concealed in the strategy was a third
goal: with the division firmly in hand, Enright could enforce Prohibition to the extent acceptable in a drinking city—and he could exempt
those parties who had the right connections.

Cynicism was well grounded. Aggressive or not, the mission of
stanching alcohol sales was doomed, its fate sealed all the tighter
as New Yorkers got into a partying mood. There was fun to be had
in the brighter time that followed the war, fun to be had as livelier
entertainment—these new movies, this new jazz, these new dances—
energized popular culture, fun to be had as young women broke the
shackles of sexual propriety, fun to be had in a round of cheer, or two
or four or six or more.

All you needed was a supply of alcohol and a serving place out
of the immediate reach of federal agents or cops. Ranging from the
seedy to the elegant, speakeasies grew so common that a *New York
Sun* columnist would eventually write that "the history of the United

States could be told in eleven words: Columbus, Washington, Lincoln, Volstead, two flights up and ask for Gus."[33]

Vast quantities of illicit liquor poured forth, none more plentiful than bootlegged goods financed by Arnold Rothstein. Described by his lawyer as "a man who dwells in doorways, a mouse standing in a doorway waiting for his cheese," Rothstein smelled plenty. He locked in contracts with distillers in Scotland, transferred the cargo to Irving "Waxey Gordon" Wexler, who controlled smuggling along the New York–New Jersey coast, and passed the alcohol to Lucky Luciano, who built a distribution network for clandestine drinking spots. Together, Rothstein and Luciano grew fabulously wealthy from a criminal enterprise that was unique for seeming a godsend to millions.

Each man's success was remarkable in its own right. Rothstein pulled his off despite being snared—and dodging jeopardy—in the gambling scheme that fixed the 1919 World Series. Luciano, meanwhile, organized a one-hundred-man army that would morph into a powerful Mafia crime family after Prohibition's repeal. With Rothstein selecting his wardrobe and instructing him in dinner table etiquette, Luciano enjoyed outlaw celebrity while purchasing ever more influence with ever more money—including cash delivered directly to police headquarters.

Reminiscing with Hughes, Battle cast alcohol enforcement as one more straightforward police duty. If he felt that the entire police department had been sent on a destructive fool's errand, he chose survival over principle amid the rising corruption. At home, he could talk to Florence, the Chief, and Wesley about cops who were selling protection to bootleggers, cops who were trafficking in seized contraband, cops who were letting cargoes drift ashore on the waterfront, but on the job Battle kept his mouth shut and followed orders. He took no action without express prior approval. Like every cop, he had seen how crossing someone big had very nearly destroyed a man who was as tightly wired at the top of the department as a man could be.

On January 19, 1919, Inspector Dominic Henry led a raid on a West Side apartment in which, he discovered, Rothstein was playing craps. As cops wielded a battering ram, someone inside opened fire

with a revolver. The shots wounded two detectives. Nothing came of
the bloodshed until newspapers questioned why the police and district attorney had failed to file charges. Finally, a grand jury indicted
Rothstein, only to have a judge dismiss the case amid reports that the
doorway mouse had bought his way out for $32,000. In the ensu-
ing furor, Henry was charged with perjury, convicted and sentenced
to two to five years in Sing Sing prison. He escaped that fate only
through the intercession of an appeals court, his near miss hammer-
ing home to cops the danger of barging through the wrong door.[34]

INSPECTOR SAMUEL G. BELTON commanded the Special Service Division. The son of Irish immigrants and a widower, Belton had joined
the force in 1891, the era of rampant vice and rampant graft; had
made good in the Tenderloin when Devery transacted business at
the street-corner Pump; and had bonded with Enright as a trustee of
the Lieutenants Benevolent Association. When a coveted lieutenancy
opened, Enright's influence gave Belton command of a fifty-officer
squad that enforced public health laws. When Belton was about to
be denied promotion to captain with the expiration of a civil service
list, Enright secured special authority to boost his friend's rank. And,
finally, Enright identified Belton as the cop he trusted to navigate the
shoals of politics and Prohibition.[35]

To the men of the division, Belton could be both a powerful patron and a protective shield. Wanting both, Battle could only strive
to meet his demands. Often, those entailed infiltrating a speakeasy,
gambling house, or brothel to observe criminal activity, an especially
tough challenge for Battle. Many a white-run joint wanted nothing
to do with a black man, and many a black operator knew who Battle was. He hit upon an audacious solution: Battle asked Belton for
permission to work with a raw black recruit who would be unknown
as a cop and who could be trained to go undercover where Battle
couldn't. The request went up the chain and came down with a pos-
itive response.

Battle found an excellent undercover man in twenty-one-year-old
Harry F. Agard. Although he was the son of African Americans, Agard
could be mistaken for Chinese because his skin tone was golden and

Samuel Battle speaks with famed poet Langston Hughes (left) for a never-published biography, as Hughes's secretary, Nate White, records the interview.

Renowned for feats of strength, Battle's protégé, Wesley Williams, fought his way up the ranks of the New York Fire Department with the help of his father, James "the Chief" Williams, head of the Grand Central Station Red Caps. Lieutenant Wesley Williams (left) in 1927.

Wesley Williams started as a pumper crewman in 1919.

Democratic Party boss Jimmy Hines exacted revenge after Battle raided a gambling den run by Harlem cabaret king Baron Wilkins in 1923.

Battle cracked the case when mobster Dutch Schultz (left) had Harlem gambling kingpin Casper Holstein kidnapped in 1928.

When rioting swept Harlem in 1935, sparked by false rumors that police had killed a black teenager, Battle and a detective posed with Lino Rivera to prove that the young man allegedly at the center of the violence was alive.

Daily News, L.P. (New York)

During Prohibition, Battle raided speakeasies while gangster Lucky Luciano lavishly paid New York Police Department brass for protection.

AP Images

Jesse Owens took up lodgings in Battle's townhouse after Owens stunned Adolf Hitler by winning four gold medals at the 1936 Berlin Olympics.

Bettmann/Corbis/AP Images

First Lady Eleanor Roosevelt impressed Battle indelibly at a public event in 1943, and she became an admiring friend.

Battle was in Joe Louis's corner the night the Brown Bomber defeated Billy Conn to keep the heavyweight crown in 1941.

Battle became the first African American member of the New York City Parole Commission in 1941. Family members attended his City Hall swearing-in: (left to right) son, Carroll; Carroll's wife, Edith; granddaughter, Yvonne, held by Battle; wife, Florence; and daughter, Charline Cherot, mother of Yvonne. Battle took the post previously held by Lou Gehrig.

Florence Carrington married Battle at age sixteen, in 1905. She anchored their family and supported her husband through all his many struggles. Here she is with Battle on the steps of their Strivers Row townhouse, around 1945.

Battle mentored young Sugar Ray Robinson and remained the champ's friend for life.

Daily News, L.P. (New York)

When his good friend the tap dancer Bill "Bojangles" Robinson died in 1949, Battle helped plan the dancer's funeral in Ed Sullivan's apartment. Robinson is seen here dancing for Chief James Williams (second from left), father of Wesley.

Rioting swept Harlem in 1943 after a police officer shot and wounded a black soldier, who was falsely reported killed. Mayor La Guardia summoned Battle to help restore peace.

Daily News, L.P. (New York)

Battle's grandson Tony Cherot (second left) with Councilwoman Inez Dickens (left) and New York Police Commissioner Ray Kelly (right) at a 2009 ceremony renaming the Harlem intersection where Battle saved a white officer's life in 1919.

his features had an Asian cast. Especially important: Agard had a memory that was almost photographic.

Under Battle's direction, they embarked on well-chosen investigations, Agard working his way inside a gambling operation or speakeasy and Battle staging a raid when signaled. Belton dispatched them on several occasions to bust fan-tan games in Chinatown, exploiting Agard's appearance and his initiative in learning rudimentary Chinese phrases. More often, Belton targeted drinking spots here, there, and everywhere in Manhattan.

On West Fifty-Third Street off Broadway, Battle remembered, "there was a certain loft where the best bonded liquors, choice wines and champagnes were sold illegally." Agard got in and emerged holding a bottle, the proprietor at his shoulder. Battle took the proprietor into custody and found "more than fifty-thousand dollars' worth of excellent stock."

"It took several patrol wagons to haul all this liquor to the stationhouse," he told Hughes, adding, seemingly with a chuckle, "Some of it never got there," as fellow officers made off with alcohol for their own enrichment. The courts disposed of the rest.

"No warrant, no evidence! Case dismissed," a magistrate declared over Battle's protest that he hadn't needed a warrant under the circumstances. "The place reopened that evening with a champagne party attended by large numbers of Broadway celebrities and politicians," Battle recalled.

As enforcement of an unpopular law undermined the criminal justice system, the vagaries became more pronounced. Battle won the conviction of Greenwich Village bootleggers after staging a raid that discovered barrels of whiskey and copper stills. But he was thrown out of court after busting a speakeasy on Third Avenue at 125th Street. He set before the judge a healthy sample of the liquor he had seized, along with three .45-caliber handguns. Again, he remembered, "The judge barked, 'Lack of evidence! Case dismissed.'"[1]

Then, a spectacular crime gave Battle the opportunity to prove his mettle as a detective. Shortly after ten-thirty on the night of December 18, 1921, three men bearing concealed guns walked through the majestic doors of the Capitol Theatre on Broadway. Built at a cost of more than $65 million (in twenty-first-century dollars) the Capitol had fifty-three hundred plush seats, a wide screen on which to display silent films, a broad stage for song and dance numbers, and a pit for a seventy-member orchestra. The imperious Major Bowes served as impresario. Later to gain fame by staging that era's *American Idol*, he drew throngs with movies featuring stars such as soon-to-be "King of Hollywood" Douglas Fairbanks.[36]

Man's Home, a drama about a businessman whose wife falls in with bad company, was playing as the gunmen donned masks and made their way to the theater's business office. "Stick your hands up and be quiet," the leader ordered as they burst in on three men and one woman.

The robbers bound the men with wire, left the woman untied, closed them in a closet, and escaped down a fire escape and into a cab with $10,000.[37] The newspapers played the story big. The detective squad of the West Forty-Seventh Street stationhouse got the case. They had little to go on. Then, through contacts among black New Yorkers, Battle met a source late at night in Central Park. The man named two of the bandits and said the Capitol's elevator operator, William Singleton, had laid out how they should pull the robbery.

Singleton was African American. Battle tracked him down, took his confession, and hauled him to the stationhouse. Brimming with excitement at having cracked the most publicized crime of the day, he delivered Singleton to the detectives, only to discover that the tough Irishmen had no intention of allowing an African American to outshine them. They spat that the case had been none of Battle's business and ordered him to get lost. Worse, the white detectives stole his accomplishment with lies. The newspapers reported that Daly, Cordine, Ferguson, Garrity, and Manning had identified Singleton and secured the confession.[38] Major Bowes showed his appreciation by giving Battle and Agard lifetime passes to the Capitol's shows. That was all the reward they got.

DESPITE THE DEPARTMENT'S overt racism, Battle continued to believe that Enright was a man of surprisingly liberal racial views. The commissioner had promoted former Pennsylvania Station railroad cop Wesley Redding to become the department's first full-fledged black detective. He had also given important recognition to African American officers in general. Then and today, cops formed associations based on ethnicity, religion, and other markers of group identity— Irish cops in one society, Italians in a second, Jews in a third, and so on. Battle's fellow officers broached forming an organization of their own. Initially, he resisted. The concept of blacks symbolically separating from whites seemed to run counter to his belief in integration. His colleagues told Battle they were seeking only an equal privilege that would allow for mutual assistance. Battle accepted their nomination as the man who would ask Enright for recognition.

Battle presented the petition. Enright said no. Blacks had numerous opportunities to join the many associations that were open to all cops, he said. Battle pressed his point, telling Enright that "like other groups we wanted our own distinctive organization." Enright reconsidered and gave departmental approval to the Guardians Society. Battle became the first president of an organization still in existence nine decades later, and he credited Enright for playing square.

ATOP ELEVEN STEPS, the front door opened into finer living space than Battle had ever imagined he could provide for Florence, Jesse, Charline, and Carroll. Parlors, studies, bedrooms, dining area, kitchen, baths, and two staircases filled four handsomely appointed stories. There was a full basement and a backyard with a garage that had been built for a carriage. On July 12, 1922, Battle placed the title to the townhouse in Florence's name, counting himself the beneficiary of the white man's race foolishness.

The family's new home was the work of a developer named David King, who had set out in 1890 to build an unparalleled neighborhood. With financing from the Equitable Life Assurance Society, he purchased a Harlem tract between Seventh and Eighth Avenues and commissioned three architects to design 146 row houses. King assigned the block front on the south side of West 138th Street to James Brown Lord, who had drawn notice for the Beaux Arts beauty of a now-landmarked Manhattan courthouse. Lord gave his residences a Georgian look and sheathed their exteriors with red brick and brownstone. The work of designing the north side of West 138th and the south side of West 139th went to Bruce Price, whose portfolio included a Yale University lecture hall. Price used yellow brick, white limestone, and terra-cotta to fashion houses in the Colonial Revival style. The renowned Stanford White, architect of the Washington Square Arch, drew from the Italian Renaissance for homes along the north side of West 139th. He covered them in rusticated sandstone and rose-colored bricks accented by pink mortar.

As beautiful as the row houses were, King found few takers amid a severe economic downturn. Equitable Life foreclosed, and the value of the company's investment fell further as developers flooded the area with new housing. This was the era when real estate mania swept Harlem in anticipation of subway construction. After the bubble burst, Equitable Life leased the properties to rent-paying businessmen and professionals. The company held to a whites-only policy for almost all of the next two decades. Finally, in 1919, relinquishing hope of a white resurgence, Equitable Life put the row houses up for sale to all comers. From September that year through 1920, blacks took ownership of fifty-four of the residences, with many more buyers soon to come, including Battle, who purchased 255 West 138th.

As Harlem was the place to live for African Americans, the row houses were the place to live in Harlem. Barbers, waiters, dressmakers, and domestics who aspired to upward mobility became neighbors to doctors and lawyers, as well as to a concentration of pathbreaking entertainers and racial "firsts." The homeowners were seen as strivers, and the blocks took on the name Strivers Row.

Harry and Ethylene Pace were among the first to welcome the Battle family. The Paces lived in an abutting townhouse. A year younger than Battle, Harry Pace was born in Georgia and studied at Atlanta University when Du Bois served there as a professor. He worked for a time as business manager of an ill-fated journal edited by Du Bois, then embarked on ventures in insurance and banking that took him to Memphis. There, Pace met W. C. Handy, the musician now known as "The Father of the Blues." Pace joined Handy in songwriting under the aegis of the Pace and Handy Music Company.

He saw their future in New York. The recording industry was coming to life in the city, but the phonograph companies were no more open to blacks than any other area of commerce. Handy would remember confronting "the beast of racial prejudice," while Pace recalled: "I ran up against a color line that was very severe." Undaunted, he founded a publishing and recording business for African American music. When the Strivers Row townhouses came on the market, Pace purchased 257 West 138th and Handy bought 232 West 139th. Pace set up shop in the basement and recruited twenty-three-year-old Fletcher Henderson to serve as music director of the Pace Phonograph Corporation's Black Swan record label. Henderson would soon purchase the row house two doors down from Handy's and go on to lead an orchestra that pioneered the smooth sound of swing. When Battle moved in, Pace had an eight-man orchestra and a sales network in major cities. He advertised with the slogan, "The only genuine colored record. Others are only passing for colored."[39]

Around the neighborhood, Battle shared the enthusiasm generated by Pace, Handy, and Henderson as they sold the talents of African Americans. Often, a fourth musical great would come across the street from 236 West 138th to revel in the burgeoning of blacks in entertainment. No one had enjoyed more success than Eubie Blake. The son of former slaves who took to the piano as a child, Blake had teamed up with Noble Sissle to write *Shuffle Along*, a musical comedy that took Broadway by storm in 1921 with tunes like "I'm Just Wild About Harry." As Battle moved onto Strivers Row, the show was within a few days of ending a 484-performance run. The chatter was about how Blake was taking *Shuffle Along* on the road for a tour that eventually extended for two years.

Across the rear drive, Battle met Vertner Tandy, New York's first licensed black architect and owner of 221 West 139th. Down the sidewalk, at 221 West 138th, he encountered Will Marion Cook, the preeminent black composer and conductor of an earlier generation. Harry Wills, the black heavyweight boxing champion, was around the block at 245 West 139th. Love of boxing drew Battle naturally to Wills. Known as "The Black Panther," Wills came up from New Orleans to become successor to Sam Langford, the black champion who had helped train Wesley for firehouse combat.

Now, as Battle joined him on Strivers Row, Wills was angling for a bout with reigning world champion Jack Dempsey. On the very day that Battle took the deed to his new home, the newspapers reported that Dempsey had signed a statement of intent that read: "The said Jack Dempsey agrees to box the said Harry Wills for the heavyweight championship of the world."[40]

Among all his neighbors, Battle had perhaps the most in common with Dr. Louis Tompkins Wright, who lived diagonally across the street at 218 West 138th. Eight years younger than Battle, Wright was born in Atlanta and raised as the stepson of a pioneering black doctor. He was fifteen when white-on-black violence swept the city. With gunfire crackling, his stepfather pressed a rifle into his hands with the order: "Son, you cover the front of the house. I'll cover the back. If anybody comes through the gate, let 'em have it."

Schooled at historically black Clark Atlanta University, he set his sights on studying medicine at Harvard. He submitted his academic transcript and letters of recommendation and arrived at the school for an interview, at which time the director of admissions discovered that he was black. Wright refused to leave without the interview he had come for. Finally, exasperated, the biochemist asked, "Mr. Wright, do you have any sporting blood in your veins? Will you agree, if I ask you a few questions here today that I will never be bothered with you again in life?"

Wright underwent a grilling about chemistry, won admission, and graduated fourth in the class of 1915. Setting out to specialize in surgery, he applied for positions at Massachusetts General Hospital, Boston City Hospital, and Boston's Peter Bent Brigham Hospital—and was offered only a laboratory job at Mass General, one that would deny him contact with patients. Regretfully, Wright put aside his principle that hospitals should be peopled by doctors and patients of all colors and took a position at historically black Freedmen's Hospital in Washington, DC. There, he proved wrong the widely held beliefs that African Americans were more susceptible than whites to diphtheria and that the recently discovered Schick test for immunity to the bacterial lung disease was useless on black skin. With the outbreak of World War I, Wright enlisted in the medical corps. His record included a study that taught how best to accomplish small pox immunizations.

Home from the war and married, Wright moved to Strivers Row and opened a practice on Seventh Avenue. His office was a short distance from Harlem Hospital, the community's sole health-care institution and part of the city's public hospital system. It may as well have been miles away. The staff was all white, while the patient census was increasingly black. Wright applied for a position. Under community pressure, hospital chief Dr. Cosmo O'Neill appointed Wright as Harlem Hospital's first black staff physician—but only as clinical assistant visiting surgeon, meaning that he could treat ambulatory patients for a few hours a week without pay or admitting privileges. O'Neill's attempt to blunt the impact of Wright's presence was to no avail. His superiors demoted O'Neill from hospital superintendent to monitoring ambulance traffic.

As happened when firefighters refused to work with Wesley, four staff physicians walked out. As happened to both Wesley and Battle, "When I first started no one would talk to me," Wright recalled years later. He not only held firm, he fought on. When Battle became his neighbor, Wright and the NAACP had organized an investigation that documented patient abuses at the hospital, along with tensions between white doctors and the seven black physicians who had followed Wright onto the staff. He wanted the ranks to grow, but, sharing Battle's dedication to racial equality, Wright rejected Mayor Hylan's plan to staff the hospital entirely with African Americans.[41]

Composer. Musician. Conductor. Entrepreneur. Architect. Boxer. Surgeon. Cop. An accomplished man among accomplished men, Battle could see futures of greater opportunity for Jesse, Charline, and Carroll. The children enrolled in public schools where stern women taught English, arithmetic, history, geography, science, and every other subject, including Latin. Many were the barriers still before the kids, but Battle could see the barriers breaking. And he could look past the swelling arrivals of poor uneducated Southerners to envision Harlem as the place where the barriers would first fall. He was glad to be raising the children here, to have placed them among tall-standing role models who were to be found nowhere else in such numbers.

*   *   *

A SUMMONS TO come home, to Anne, confirmed his thankfulness.

Gale-force winds buffeted New Bern. When a chimney flue caught fire, forty-five-mile-per-hour gusts whipped sparks into the air and down onto cedar shingle roofs in the preserve of New Bern's black citizens, including Anne, who still lived at 8 Primrose Street. A residence on this street caught flame and then a house on that one, and New Bern's Great Fire of 1922 was underway. Joe Gaskill McDaniel witnessed the inferno through the eyes of a twelve-year-old boy.

"Flaming shingles, careening on the breast of the gale, flew through the air for blocks and set widely scattered conflagrations," McDaniel remembered in 1992, adding, "Pitiful humans screamed everywhere, like trapped animals fleeing from a flaming forest." Anne joined the escaping throng.

The fire destroyed more than one thousand buildings. Thirty-two hundred people were homeless; nine out of ten were black. Battle's younger sister Mary Elizabeth, who was now principal of Beaufort, North Carolina's "Free School" for blacks, took Anne in. Mary Elizabeth was married to Curtis Oden, a shoe cobbler and Beaufort's first black undertaker.[42]

Traveling to New Bern, Battle found the family home to be a blackened pile in a blackened field. Only the chimneys remained standing. Those, Thomas had built to last, Battle well knew. All around, he told Hughes, "the pretty little cottages of my youth were no longer standing," and he added bitterly that "today where I was born there is a pickle factory" because the whites had broken a promise to create a park.

Battle invited Anne to live with him. Anne declined. She preferred the country to Harlem, the South that she knew to the North that she didn't. So, glad that Anne was in Mary Elizabeth's good hands, Battle returned alone to the distant universe where he worked as a Prohibition-era vice cop and where he lived side by side with trailblazers who were the pride of his race.

BATTLE RETURNED TO hard times as a New York cop. For months, black Harlem had been inflamed by the death in police custody of a nineteen-year-old transplant from Charleston, South Carolina. The passions that were to be unleashed by Herbert Dent's fatal encounter with blackjack-wielding detectives were more intense than any previously aimed at Battle and fellow members of the Guardians Society.

The pressures began building before midnight on December 19, 1921. The cops of Battle's former base, the West 135th Street stationhouse, were changing shifts. A few blocks away his friend Jasper Rhodes was leaving his beat for the night. He spotted two men in the shadows of a doorway.

"You two fellows come out here," Rhodes ordered. "I want to get a good look at you."[43]

One of the men drew a gun and opened fire. Bullets hit Rhodes in the stomach and shoulder. The pair fled. In Harlem Hospital, Rhodes told detectives that darkness had prevented a good look at either man, but he did know that his assailants were black. Rhodes was strong at the age of twenty-nine; doctors predicted a full recovery. Still, they all knew—Florence, Jesse, Charline, and Carroll knew, and Rhodes's wife, Isadora, knew—that two of New York's first three black officers now had been shot in the line of duty. Battle was the exception.

Crime was on the rise across New York and nowhere more so than in what the newspapers called the city's black belt. Over the next six months, young, male African Americans shot five more police officers, three fatally. Luther Boddy was the most notorious of the gunmen.

A swaggering twenty-two-year-old, Boddy had spent time in prison for burglary. Detective sergeants Francis J. M. Buckley and William Miller picked him up for questioning in connection with the Rhodes shooting. Boddy had hidden a gun in his coat sleeve, tied in such a way that the weapon would drop into his armpit if he raised his hands. Two hundred feet from the stationhouse, he fatally shot Buckley and Miller at point blank range.

All of twenty-five days passed between the murders and a jury's finding of guilt. Central to the trial was the question of why Boddy had shot the two white detectives. He testified that he saw the stationhouse as a torture chamber where, on previous occasions, police had beaten him with blackjacks and rubber hoses in hope of eliciting confessions or of coercing him into informing on others.

"They did not succeed in either," Boddy's lawyer told the jury, "but they did create in his mind a horror and fear of the police which meant physical agonies and torture of the human soul."[44]

Regardless, the jury convicted and the judge swiftly condemned Boddy to death. His fate had been doubly sealed when, in the middle of the trial, a mentally disturbed black man fatally shot a white cop through the head.

Police had arrested Frank Whaley for general disorderliness. They brought him to the stationhouse that covered southern Harlem. He appeared docile. Officer Otto Motz went about business seemingly without cause for wariness. Then, suddenly, Whaley snatched Motz's gun from his holster and fired.

The murder demanded explanation. A rationale quickly emerged. Calling Whaley a "crazed negro," the *Times* attributed his madness to racial rage. He was believed to have acted in "revenge for the arrest of Luther Boddy."[45]

Next, Officer Patrick McHugh was shot in the head while trying to arrest three armed robbers. Then, a janitor shot a lawyer in a fee dispute and wounded Officer Henry Pohndorf in a running gun battle.

Increasingly convinced that Harlem's criminal element had declared open season on cops, the men of the West 135th Street stationhouse patrolled on war footing. Detectives worked in three-member teams instead of pairs. Commanders beefed up night rounds under special supervision.[46] The full roster took up the mission of imposing justice on the perpetrator of the single unsolved shooting, that of Officer Patrick McHugh. Soon, detectives zeroed in on Herbert Dent, and a judge issued an arrest warrant.

Dent had but a few hours to live. The official account of his death appeared in the newspapers of June 28, 1922. Casting one of Battle's Guardians Society colleagues in a central role, the story was patently incredible: It is two-thirty in the morning. Wesley Redding, the city's first black detective, is alone in the stationhouse. An informant places Dent in a saloon five blocks away. Redding sets out to capture New York's most wanted man, an alleged member of Boddy's robbery gang, without back-up. Redding hauls Dent to the detectives' room. Still alone, Redding makes the same error that had proven fatal to Motz: He drops his guard, enabling Dent to grab his holstered gun. Fighting furiously, Redding yells for help. Detectives McGrath and Gorman rush into the room and subdue Dent with their blackjacks, saving Redding's life. A short time later Dent dies at Harlem Hospital. Chief Medical Examiner Dr. Charles Norris attributes the death to acute alcoholism. "If he had not been drinking the beating would not have caused his death," Norris says, and the district attorney closes the case as the unfortunate result of justified police action.[47]

One man would have none of it. *New York Age* editor Frederick Randolph Moore led the newspaper into challenging every aspect of the official account. Three days after Battle purchased his Strivers Row townhouse, he read that Dent had been an elevator boy and not a member of Boddy's robbery gang, that a white officer named Scott had actually arrested Dent, and that Dent had never snatched Redding's gun. Over the next months, Moore's revelations pointed increasingly toward homicide. People who lived near the stationhouse said they often heard screams as men and women were brutalized inside. A woman said that "moans and groans" and the "sounds of blows" had awakened her on the night Dent died.

Two doctors retained to review Dent's autopsy found a "cerebral depression," a break in "one of the principal veins leading to the brain," and no evidence of alcoholism. Then, a white US Secret Service agent who happened to have been in the stationhouse said that detectives McGrath and Flynn had struck Dent repeatedly with a blackjack and a nightstick to force him to confess. While Dent was prone, the agent said, McGrath broke the nightstick with a swing that hit both Dent and the floor. A black uniformed officer got a fresh baton.

"McGrath and Flynn continued beating this man with their blackjacks," the agent said. "Flynn broke his blackjack and then picked up the nightstick which the patrolman had brought back to the room, struck the man across the side of the head—and then everything was in silence for a moment."

Detective Gorman ran for some alcohol.

"Then they took the bottle and tried to force some whiskey down the colored man's throat by holding his jaws open," the agent recounted.

The *Age*'s revelations infuriated Battle's neighbors. Awaiting execution at Sing Sing, Boddy took on the quality of a folk hero who had answered the barbarism of white cops on behalf of all blacks. His corpse came home to Harlem in spectacle. Thirty thousand people filed by his casket, and thousands more lined Seventh Avenue to watch his hearse pass the corner where he had gunned down the two detectives.[48]

Battle suffered guilt by his association with the New York Police Department. Where fellow path breakers on Strivers Row basked in unequivocal admiration, he bore the stigma of membership in an institution seen as a muscular representation of white repression. Few were surprised when the district attorney ruled out proceeding against anyone involved in Dent's death.

BATTLE BID BON voyage to Sam Belton on August 25, 1923. The inspector sailed on the *Homeric* for a sixteen-week excursion to Paris, Rome, Venice, Vienna, Berlin, Copenhagen, Brussels, and London. Enright had announced that his Special Service Division chief would study "police conditions" on the continent in order to bring innovative crime-fighting strategies home to New York. The commissioner often took months-long cruises to the West Indies, Europe, or South America, sent off in staterooms overflowing with flowers, chocolates, fruits, and cigars. Now, he was similarly rewarding a trusted aide with the help of thievery more damning in its pettiness than the underworld cash flowing through police headquarters.

Enright had founded a charity whose stated purposes were to support the families of slain cops and to tide over officers who had run into financial difficulties. While the public had donated more than $95,000, Enright was on his way to providing all of $3,131 to widows and fatherless children. Instead, he was buying diamond-studded "honorary" deputy commissioner badges for influential New Yorkers. He also helped Belton tour Europe in style with $2,000 in spending money.[49]

Leading the high life, Enright and Chief Inspector William Lahey were among eighty-two thousand spectators who filled the Polo Grounds on September 14 to watch a heavyweight bout. Jack

Dempsey had held the color line against Harry Wills and instead was fighting Argentine Luis Firpo, the so-called Wild Bull of the Pampas. According to *The Last Testament of Lucky Luciano*, a posthumously published as-told-to autobiography some authors rely on and others trash as fiction, Luciano held court ringside at row A, seat 1. Having bargained his way out of an arrest for heroin possession, Luciano bought respectability again by distributing tickets to two hundred elite New Yorkers, including James Joseph "Jimmy" Hines, the broad-shouldered, ice-blue-eyed Tammany Hall chief from Manhattan's West Side. Stars of stage and screen came by to shake Luciano's hand. So did New York's top two police officials.

"It was a pretty big thing when Dick Enright, the police commissioner of the whole city, come over to see how I was feelin'," *The Last Testament* quotes Luciano as saying. "And right with him was Bill Lahey, his police chief. Why not, they were on our payroll."

In this telling, Luciano delivered $10,000 a week to headquarters in paper bags. While the figure is beyond confirmation, the coauthors of the well-researched book *NYPD: A City and Its Police* concluded that "few people have disputed [Luciano's] assertion that headquarters was for sale." More, the day before the fight, a court had subpoenaed Enright in a case in which two detectives were alleged to have demanded a $2,500 bribe to overlook a shipment of liquor and admitted they had released the bootlegged goods after being told that it was actually owned by three high police officials.[50]

AMID THESE ROILING TIDES, an inspector named Gaines took command of the Special Service Division in Belton's absence. He delivered an order directly to Battle. In Harlem, he said, wives had complained that husbands were playing craps in a gambling hall on West 144th Street. The women were black, the men were black, and Battle was the division's only black. Gaines told him to shut the place down.

This was no two-bit game. This operation was the property of Baron Deware Wilkins. More than a dozen years had passed since Battle had stood beside Wilkins, awaiting Jack Johnson's arrival at Grand Central after Johnson had defeated Great White Hope Jim Jeffries. Wilkins had been a big man then, and he was bigger now.

As his Little Savoy cabaret passed into history, Wilkins, his brother Leroy, and John W. Connor, who partnered with Wilkins in owning Negro League baseball teams, had opened clubs in Harlem. The musicians who were revolutionizing the American popular idiom followed to a nightspot at Seventh Avenue and 134th Street that would gain fame as Wilkins's Exclusive Club. There, dressed all in black at the keyboard of an upright, was Jelly Roll Morton, described by cultural writer Stanley Crouch as "the first theoretician of jazz and almost certainly its first great piano player." There, watching and listening in awe, was young James P. Johnson, soon to be known as a master of stride piano and composer of "Charleston," the anthem of the Roaring Twenties. And there, maybe, was a child prodigy by the name of George Gershwin. The future composer's first biographer, David Ewen, describes Gershwin as roller-skating past Wilkins's club as a boy about six years old. In this account, the strange new sound of jazz mesmerizes young George, whose itinerant family lived for a time in the white quarters of Harlem.[51]

As Wilkins knew, running a cabaret in New York City entailed buying the favor of the police and Tammany Hall. At first, the tab was fifty dollars a month, paid through Leroy, who was the front man for the Astoria Café near the corner of Fifth Avenue and 135th Street. Connor handed over seventy-five dollars a month as proprietor of the Royal Café, just down the block. In 1913, after the Manhattan district attorney indicted a Harlem police inspector, the prosecutor questioned Connor and Leroy Wilkins. Asked why he paid the bribes, Leroy "replied that he wanted to run an all-night saloon, and that even if he just wanted to run a straight, legal place the police, he was sure, could easily frame him up and put him out of business. To pay was the easiest way."[52]

Cultivating police and politicians was especially necessary for Wilkins because the good citizens of Harlem had mixed feelings about saloons. Straight-laced Frederick Randolph Moore, for one, was appalled by the rise in drinking. He railed in the *Age* in 1914 that Harlem was "infested" with more than eighty-five establishments that "thrive by selling whiskey principally to members of the race."

Headlined "Too Many Saloons in Harlem," Moore's editorial described the whiskey as "the kind that makes you fight your mother," complained that the businesses were dominated by white men who opened their "side door entrances" to black women, and reported that the "colored saloonkeeper seems to have a difficult time making a living at best."[53]

With rivals for the drinking dollar on every corner, Wilkins factored the purchase of police and politicians into the cost of doing business. The Exclusive Club stayed open to all hours, even as headquarters repeatedly hauled him into court. No matter the evidence, magistrates dismissed the charges or imposed nominal fines. Time and again, Battle and fellow cops watched Wilkins return unscathed to the scene of the party, seemingly untouchable.

Then one of Wilkins's friends brought two young men into the club. They drank liberally and went on their way. Over the coming weeks, they became familiar faces, stayed late, and took an interest in other pleasures available to the trusted. Finally, Wilkins opened that door. An associate brought the men to an apartment in the Tenderloin, where a madam welcomed them into the company of Linette, Rose, and Rosie. After the third such jaunt, the men came out from undercover as agents of the Manhattan district attorney.

For the only time in his life, Wilkins spent the night in jail. With characteristic panache, he complained only of personal betrayal, saying, "The man who turned me up was a man I would have trusted with $20,000. That is what hurts me." In fact, he had little to worry about. Time and again, anti-vice crusaders had targeted Wilkins, only to have Tammany magistrates dismiss charges for a supposed lack of evidence. This time, Wilkins dodged jeopardy with the announcement that he would run a simple bar, flamboyantly named the "Get What You Want."[54] But retirement was never the plan. The lesson learned was that a man could never have too much protection, so Wilkins began assiduously befriending politicians with well-aimed generosity. Most importantly, he bonded with Tammany Hall's Jimmy Hines.

BORN ON MANHATTAN'S East Side, Hines was the son of a police and fire department blacksmith. He captained a Tammany district that stretched along the Hudson into West Harlem. Refined manners put him in good stead with the business elite, while a gracious personality earned him the affection of the working class. He arranged for patronage jobs, fixed traffic tickets, made sure no one went hungry, and kicked off summers by hosting as many as twenty-five thousand people to hot dogs, soda, and ice cream in Central Park.

Hines was a rogue, too. He had mutually beneficial relationships with gangsters. They delivered money; he delivered services available only through the good offices of Tammany's most powerful chief. He had only to make a phone call to secure protection or inflict punishment. Both were crucial to Wilkins's cabaret ambitions, as well as to his determination never to take a fall again. When Prohibition dawned, they also helped propel his Exclusive Club to the top in the remaking of Harlem as New York's illicit fun zone.

Rebellion against temperance brought nightclubbing there to exuberant life. Hip and chic whites arrived late at night in limousines to let loose in a dark town pulsing with daring rhythms. Finely dressed and carrying fat wallets, they crowded into hot spots that catered to partiers from a hostile culture and that were off limits to regular folks. Few Harlem residents ever stepped through the doors of the Cotton Club, Connie's Inn, Small's Paradise, or Wilkins's Exclusive Club and into a universe where blacks entertained laughing, dancing, drinking revelers who had little interest in the afflictions of the lives around them.

To enhance the aura that his club was "exclusive," Wilkins limited admission to whites and light-skinned blacks, with the exception of darker-toned celebrities. A young woman whose name was Ada Beatrice Queen Victoria Louisa Virginia Smith was at the center of the action. Ada Smith had grown up in Chicago dreaming of show business, and she had made her way to New York in 1914 to see the legendary Baron Wilkins. She was not yet twenty-one and faked her way inside with two under-aged friends.

"Everything about his bar and back room was bigger and better than anything else in the neighborhood. He drew a crowd we called 'sporty,'" she remembered, adding, "Evidently I'd caught his eye. He was such a big, fat man that it wasn't easy for him to move around, but he managed to get over to our table. He said to Gertie and Anita, 'Whose's that cute kid?'"

They chatted and Wilkins pointed to Smith's red hair. "You know what," he said, "I think I'll call you Bricktop."[55]

For the rest of her long life in cabarets, Ada Smith would be known as Bricktop, most famously as barkeep and chanteuse to the Lost Generation writers who congregated in Paris of the 1920s. She was a favorite of Ernest Hemingway, F. Scott Fitzgerald, T. S. Eliot, Cole Porter, and, yes, Langston Hughes.

Before those expatriate years, Smith returned to the Exclusive Club in 1922. She found a place where liquor and music flowed freely in a land beyond the law. Much to Wilkins's anger, two headquarters detectives had staged a raid in March of that year. They arrested "ten white and two girls of color" plus "ten white and one man of color," accusing some of the women of "vulgar dancing." As ordained, a magistrate promptly dismissed the charges.[56] Still, Wilkins said, the police should have known better than to bust in. Next time, if there was a next time, the cops would learn the error of their ways.

The great man took Bricktop on as a singer. Patrons loved her and so did he. When Bricktop said that the club needed a better house band, Wilkins took her advice and imported a five-man combo from Washington, DC. They included a dashing and handsome young piano player; Edward Kennedy "Duke" Ellington stepped onto the launching pad for his career.

Al Jolson and John Barrymore were regulars, along with playwright Charles MacArthur, who wrote *The Front Page* with Ben Hecht, and Lucille LeSueur, a chorus girl soon to be known as Joan Crawford. And then there was the "nice quiet Irishman" who would say to Bricktop: "Bricky, come on let's you and me . . ."

"Oh, no that ain't the play," she would answer, knowing better than to get tangled up with Jack "Legs" Diamond, the killer who served as muscle for Arnold Rothstein.

"Sometimes the place would be full of gangsters," remembered Elmer Snowden, who led Ellington's combo. When the gangsters came in, he said, Wilkins "would close all the doors."

Everyone on both sides of the law spent wildly. Ellington recalled a scene that many recounted as a regular part of the fun: "People would come in who would ask for change for a C-note in half dollar pieces. At the end of a song, they would toss the two hundred four-bit pieces up in the air, so that they would fall on the dance floor and make a jingling fanfare for the prosperity of our tomorrow. The singers—four of them including Bricktop—would gather up the money and another hundred-dollar bill would be changed and this action would go jingling deep into the night."

Wilkins's world, one commentator wrote, was a place where "one easily forgets that all Harlem is not like it. Harlem, the Harlem of the poor, overcrowded, underfed, with children crippled with rickets and scurvy."[57]

ENRIGHT'S ORDER TO raid Wilkins's gambling joint set up a clash between two of Harlem's most prominent residents: Battle, who was both admired for breaking the police color line and tarred as an enforcer of the dominating structure; and Wilkins, who was both romanticized for outplaying the white powers on behalf of the race and as plugged into Harlem as one could be. He gave generously to charitable causes and to the needy, belonged to the same fraternal organizations as Battle, and was celebrated with Connor as owner of the Bacharach Giants, a popular Negro League baseball franchise. Even Frederick Randolph Moore, guardian of Harlem's rectitude, was a Wilkins fan. Selling alcohol to wealthy whites, promoting African American musical stars, and spreading the wealth close to home were no sins in the *Age*.

Battle looked for a way out of raiding Wilkins's joint. There was none. He could only hope that Enright would spurn demands for retaliation, but Battle had no basis for trust. In fact, he had fresh reason for wariness. The newspapers had just told the tale of Albert Pitt, a cop who had conducted a raid that had been fully approved by the commanding officer for Brooklyn and Queens, and still was made to pay. The department transferred Pitt from a post close to his home in the Queens oceanfront community of Rockaway Beach to the Harlem stationhouse, at least two hours away by elevated train and subway. Pitt wrote to Enright, hoping that the commissioner would correct the injustice, got no response, and resigned rather than suffer the misery of a long daily commute to and from work. For good measure, the department falsely accused Pitt of refusing to work in a black community because he was a member of the Ku Klux Klan.[58]

By then Battle knew that many of Enright's closest aides—his "understrappers"—had corrupt ties with powerful people.[59] Still, he sent an undercover investigator into Wilkins's game. The officer returned with more than enough evidence to persuade a judge to issue a search warrant. Armed with court authorization, swarming cops arrested Wilkins's lieutenants and more than fifty gamblers. One by one, a magistrate called the defendants before the bench and pronounced the charges baseless. They all walked free from a courtroom controlled by Jimmy Hines.

Long after his association with Hughes was over, Battle would ruefully tell an interviewer: "I didn't know what I was doing, I guess, because I thought it was honest and honorable to do your work correctly."[60]

Under more pointed questioning by Hughes, he explained: "The underworld whispered that both Wilkins and Connor were friends of Inspector Lahey. They predicted that in any case, since the game was protected by a 'Tammany fix' nothing would happen to it. They were right. The game continued to run."

And, then, on October, 14, 1923, the order came down: The department was booting Battle from the Special Service Division to a stationhouse in Canarsie, far out across Brooklyn, where the sewer pipes emptied into the bay. The building was known for that reason as "The Shithouse."

Battle took sick leave and requested an audience with Enright. When the commissioner refused a meeting, Battle turned to Charles Anderson, who had rallied behind Battle's fight to join the force and was still a Republican power broker. Anderson spoke with Enright and then reported back to Battle that "Enright advised me to go slow, lay low in Canarsie, and in due time I would be appointed sergeant and brought back to Manhattan."

His eyes on the prize of promotion, Battle swallowed the bitter medicine of exile to "the hind-end of New York" where "goats, chickens and turkeys ran unmolested down streets and lanes." He endured the hours-long ride to and from Harlem and the last stop on the subway line while waiting his turn on the promotion list. His new colleagues shared none of his hope about the future. They believed it was only a matter of time before he suffered a painful awakening.

A sergeant, "a very fine man, and officer," decided to burst the bubble, Battle remembered.

"He said to me, 'Battle, come here. What does it read over that station house?'

"I said, '80th Precinct stationhouse.'

"He said, 'No. Those words are not emblematic. What it should read is, "All Those Who Enter Here Leave Hope Behind," meaning that you're here for good.'"[61]

MANY SAID THAT Enright had played Battle for a fool. In Harlem and the Guardians Society, they said that Battle had been too willing to credit Enright with good faith. He had been a dupe, they said. Enright had given him a plum assignment and had let a handful of African Americans form their own organization, and from these small favors Battle had concluded that this commissioner would give black cops a fair shot.

Still more hurtful to Battle, neighbors and police colleagues drew a Shakespearean parallel to his relationship with Enright. They cast Battle as Othello and Enright as the deceitful villain who manipulated the tragically trusting, dark-skinned nobleman in order to achieve his own hidden ends. "Harlemites said that in sending me there Commissioner Enright had become my Iago," Battle recalled.

AS FALL MOVED toward winter in 1923, Battle looked toward the top of the slow-moving list for promotion to sergeant. He joined with Wesley, who was still studying for the fire lieutenant's exam, in believing that the civil service system offered the most certain route to advancement. Wesley was eager to match his brainpower against that of his fellows—plus he wanted to best them physically, black man against white men in the ring.

The fire department sponsored annual boxing championships. Hundreds of firefighters competed. The victors in each weight class went on to fight the men who had prevailed in police department championships. Both forces rooted for the combatants who bore the honors of the rival legions.

Wesley signed up in the heavyweight division. He had put to good use his private firehouse gym and was well coached. Battle's encouragement and Sam Langford's tutorials at the Colored Men's Branch of the YMCA sent Wesley to the bouts in top form. He disposed of opponents one after the other, until a single contender remained standing: Wesley.

This heavyweight crown, this thing that whites took so seriously as a badge of racial pride, now belonged to a black man. No one could deny Wesley the recognition in the way that his superiors had refused to acknowledge his life-saving valor on the job. More, by virtue of the victory, he would now represent the entire fire department in a duel with the police department's best.

On December 12, 1923, three thousand firefighters, cops, and dignitaries crowded into an arena to witness the spectacle. Battle was likely the only police officer pulling for Wesley as he climbed into the ring against the finest's legendary bruiser, Big Frank Adams. The bell rang. Wesley traded punches with Adams. Firefighters rose to their feet. Departmental pride trumping racial attitude, they urged on their man with roaring support. Here, he was their man because the blows he struck were their blows and the punishment he took was on their behalf. If Wesley won, they won. He stood proudly in until Adams was declared the victor. They cheered him then, too, for putting up a hell of a fight.[62]

On his next tour of duty, Wesley returned to a transformed firehouse. Men who had refused to speak with him outside the line of duty offered congratulations and included him in the give-and-take of comrades.

"Immediately everything changed," Wesley would remember, adding as only he and Battle might, "Why people seem to idolize brute force in preference to culture and intellect is beyond me."

EARLY IN THE evening on the 223rd day of Battle's banishment, May 24, 1924, Baron Wilkins passed the time outside the Exclusive Club with an associate nicknamed Yum Yum. Seventh Avenue was in full stroll. In the basement of a building down the block, five men played dice. One of them, William "Yellow Charleston" Miller, was a drug addict and thief. He went broke. The game's big winner spurned a loan request. Yellow Charleston drew a pistol, shot the man in the stomach, and fled.

What happened next was painted in bright and varying colors by the newspapers and in a retelling by the WPA Writers' Project. All agreed that Yellow Charleston ran toward Wilkins for help.

"Above all, he had been the best friend the little fellows in the underworld had ever known," the WPA author wrote. "He had helped them when they were in trouble, fed them, clothed them, had given them shelter, money to feed their families, and money even to beat the rap."

Wilkins saw no reason for fear as Yellow Charleston raced forward, gun in hand.

"Yellow's been hitting the dope again," Wilkins told Yum Yum.

Yellow Charleston stopped in front of Wilkins.

"Give me some money," he pleaded. "I've just killed a bird and I got to make a getaway."

"But I haven't any, son," Wilkins responded calmly.

Yellow Charleston clutched Wilkins by the lapels, crying in the dialect of the WPA account, "You got t' gie me some money. I jes' kilt a man. I got t' git away."

"Don't pull on my coat so hard," Wilkins answered. "I tell you I haven't any money. I simply don't have it now."

After one more refusal, Yellow Charleston pumped four shots into Wilkins and left him bleeding beside the Exclusive Club's doorway.[63]

The news spread rapidly. Battle's neighbors flooded into the streets. The stationhouse reserves cleared the way for an ambulance to bring Wilkins to Harlem Hospital, where he was pronounced dead. The next morning's newspapers reported that posses had fanned out to hunt for Yellow Charleston. Shortly, he surrendered and would go to his death in the electric chair.

Wilkins had not been a church-going man. Family members arranged for a funeral service in his home. Testimonials poured forth.

"Local charities in Harlem were benefactors of Wilkins' charity. Just recently he contributed 300 bathing suits to a local organization for the use of poor and needy children of Harlem," the *Age* reported, while the *Chicago Defender* wrote, "His money went to Race enterprises and helping his friends and the poor. . . . Baron Wilkins was a man who lived in the age fighting for the uplift of his Race."

In certainly his last good deed, Wilkins extended unsolicited help to Sam Langford. Nearly blind and approaching destitution, the boxer had arrived in New York to seek treatment by a prominent eye specialist. Just hours before Yellow Charleston opened fire, Wilkins had mailed Langford a twenty-five-dollar check to pay medical bills and had ordered his tailor to fit Langford for a suit. Two days after Wilkins's murder, Dr. James Smith began cataract treatments that would restore Langford's sight.[64]

An estimated seventy thousand people lined the sidewalks around the club on the morning Wilkins was to be buried. As happened in the outpouring for Luther Boddy, the crowd stood in admiration of a man who had violated Battle's unyielding sense of right and wrong. This time the affront was personal, and this time Harlem's most prominent men joined in paying testament to Wilkins.

Frederick Randolph Moore of the *Age*; Dr. Louis Tompkins Wright of Strivers Row and Harlem Hospital; Ferdinand Q. Morton, the first African American appointed to New York's Municipal Civil Service Commission; and Charles Anderson gathered around Wilkins's casket as honorary pallbearers. Members of Battle's Monarch Lodge performed a ritual Elks farewell. The noted Reverend Adam Clayton Powell, pastor of Abyssinian Baptist Church, led prayers. Then the honorary pallbearers walked solemnly behind casket of a man who had unabashedly supported Jack Johnson, championed black professional baseball, and promoted so many African American entertainers.

That Wilkins had also cast New York's first black police officer into the wilderness was of no moment to a group whose allegiance Battle deserved. They carried Wilkins's body one last time in front of the Exclusive Club. With understandable bitterness, Battle described the cabaret in a way that no one else did. He saw it in memory as having gone "downhill to become a sinister hang-out for gangsters and dope peddlers."

Under watch by the masses, the slow procession to a waiting hearse included a pallbearer whose bond with Wilkins grew not from the shared experience of America's racial crimes. He was a white man with ice-blue eyes, Wilkins's partner in political crime: Jimmy Hines.[65]

THAT FALL, IN September 1924, with the requisite five years on the job, Wesley sat for the two-day fire lieutenant's exam. Most of the 3,010 test takers were more experienced than he was and so would get an advantage in the scoring. He chanced it nonetheless, confident of his studies in the hose tower and eager to force salutes from white men who would refuse to acknowledge even a near-superhuman feat of heroism.

A month after the exam, Wesley and the Chief came upon a burning building in Harlem. Flames roared from the structure. The local fire company leaned a portable ladder against the facing and maneuvered their rig's hand-cranked aerial ladder toward nineteen-year-old William Thompson, who was silhouetted against flame and smoke at a window. Wesley sped to the top of the portable ladder but was still a considerable distance below Thompson.

As the crew brought the aerial ladder closer, Thompson jumped from the sill. His hands grasped the aerial ladder, only to be torn free by the momentum of his body. Instantly, Wesley leaped from the portable ladder, grabbed a rung of the aerial ladder with one hand, and caught the plunging Thompson with his other, holding fast to both with his muscular grip and rippled arms and shoulders. Then he carried Thompson to the street before climbing back up to help rescue five more people. A reporter witnessed the feat and chronicled what he had seen in a story headlined "NY's Only Colored Fireman Saves Six From Burning Building."[66]

Still, the department withheld a citation.

WITH PASSAGE OF the seasons, the police department's churn of retirements created openings for promotions, until finally Enright had

given sergeants' stripes to 342 officers—or found them not to his
liking. Battle was next for consideration at the 343rd spot on the list.

On June 5, 1925, a promotions order reached Canarsie. A sergeant, and only the sergeant, was to report to headquarters for elevation to lieutenant. The meaning was certain. Passed over again,
Battle would stay a cop for good.

Crushed and furious, he watched the lucky sergeant depart in
full-dress uniform. Adding to the insult, this sergeant drank heavily.
Battle would later hear that Enright recoiled on meeting the man.
The story went that he told a subordinate: "You take this badge and
put it on that bum. He's too drunk for me to do it."[67]

Battle would also discover that Enright had promoted three white
cops ranked lower on the list. Now the picture was clear to a man
who had been deceived by his own blindness as much as by his Iago:
never would Enright give a black man command of whites. Battle
would write with uncharacteristic vehemence: "Passed over by Enright, I cursed the day he was born, cursed all related to him, and
wished the wrath of God upon him."[68]

At home, Battle could only tell Jesse, Charline, and Carroll that
he would soldier on in the hard world they were coming to know.
Then the Municipal Civil Service Commission published the results
of the fire lieutenant's exam. Of the 3,010 men who had competed,
Wesley had ranked 189. The fire commissioner would get to his name
within eighteen months—and deny Wesley if he chose to. Wiser than
before, Battle urged Wesley to enlist allies immediately. Wesley wrote
to Frederick Randolph Moore, spelling out his rescues, boxing victories, and test score.

"Now will they promote me when my turn arrives?" he asked. "I
believe in preparedness, so I am notifying the Negro Press now as I
expect a fight about it later on."[69]

Quickly, the *Amsterdam News* ran a story headlined "Only Ne-
gro Fire-Fighter Passes Civil Service Exam for Lieutenant, Wesley
Williams Who Has Made Many Thrilling Rescues, Makes General
Average of 89.12—Over 1,200 Fail to Pass."[70]

Black New York's anger at the injustice done to Battle provoked
Enright to respond. A psychologist for the police department, E. E.
Hart, presented the commissioner's views in an article published by

the *Amsterdam News*. An extraordinary example of dishonest condescension, the piece hailed Enright as a dedicated benefactor of African Americans. Hart wrote that a black traffic cop stationed at the intersection of Lenox Avenue and 135th Street was a symbol "of the things that have enabled the Negroes of New York to so progress that word of their prosperity has spread to the dark-skinned peoples of the world around." Hart added that Enright deserved the applause of a grateful race for having allowed forty-five African Americans to join the force. "Thus he was the first city official to give them their place in the sun," Hart wrote.

As for Battle, Hart said that Enright had passed over several men, both black and white, "for good police reasons."[71] With these lies, Battle's hopes were dashed. But, suddenly, miraculously, Enright was gone two weeks later.

ON SEPTEMBER 24, 1925, after a then-record eight years as commissioner, Enright announced that he would head the newly formed International Police Association. Actually, he quit because the political wheel had turned. New York was about to install a new mayor for the Jazz Age: James "Jimmy" Walker.

Born into a Tammany Hall family, Walker grew into a handsome, stylish, witty, fun-loving man. Early on, he wrote songs, including "Will You Love Me in December (as You Do in May)?" In the state legislature, he presciently pronounced that Prohibition was a "measure born in hypocrisy and there it will die." He championed legalizing professional boxing and lifting a ban on Sunday baseball games. When the legislature took up a "Clean Books Bill," he declared, "I have never yet heard of a girl being ruined by a book."

After a hard-fought campaign, Walker deposed Red Hylan, who had fallen out of favor with the bosses. The *American Mercury* soon profiled him as a mayor who came not from the streets but "from the dance floors."

"His hair is black, thick and unruly," the magazine reported. "His eyes are dark and restless. He has the slim build of a cabaret dancer, of a gigolo of the Montmartre. He dresses in the ultra-advanced fashion redolent of the Tenderloin. He is a native New Yorker, smokes cigarettes continuously, has a vast contempt for the Volstead act, and reads nothing but the sporting pages. He looks, in brief, to be slightly wicked and is therefore charming."[72]

New Yorkers happily went along for the ride as the married Walker slept through mornings, stayed out late, and made the nightclub rounds with his showgirl mistress.

SPIRITS WERE HIGH in Harlem as well, at least among the elite.

Young black writers like Hughes and Zora Neale Hurston came into vogue. Publishers saw the promise of their work, as the American educated class hungered for all that was "new" in style and thought. No one fostered the phenomenon—this Harlem Renaissance—more than Charles Spurgeon Johnson. The son of a Baptist minister, Johnson secured a PhD in sociology from the University of Chicago and took over as research director of the National Urban League. In that position, he founded a journal called *Opportunity* and joined the *Crisis* in publishing the emerging writers.

In April 1924, Johnson organized a dinner at a downtown club to introduce the up-and-comers to white publishers, editors, and critics. The affair was a spectacular success. The editor of *Survey Graphic* magazine titled his March 1925 issue, *Harlem—the Mecca of the New Negro*. Guest-edited by Alain Locke, who had been the first African American Rhodes scholar, the magazine largely featured the writings of black authors, including Hughes. Brimming with optimism, Hughes's poem began: "We have tomorrow / Bright before us / Like a flame."[73]

Later that year, Spurgeon Johnson staged a literary competition "to encourage the reading of literature both by Negro authors and about Negro life, not merely because they are Negro authors but because what they write is literature and because the literature is interesting."[74] The competition offered monetary awards. A broad panel of judges included Fannie Hurst and Eugene O'Neill. More than three hundred people attended an elegant dinner at the Fifth Avenue Hotel. Hughes took first prize for "The Weary Blues," a masterpiece that captured the rhythms of a musical form infused with the American black experience. It opens and closes:

Droning a drowsy syncopated tune,
Rocking back and forth to a mellow croon,
I heard a Negro play . . .

And far into the night he crooned that tune.
The stars went out and so did the moon.
The singer stopped playing and went to bed
While the Weary Blues echoed through his head.
He slept like a rock or a man that's dead.

It was a heady time for the young writers. They were wanted at downtown A-list parties, and they were welcomed at fabulous soirées thrown by wealthy hair-care heiress A'Lelia Walker, later described by Hughes as "the joy-goddess of Harlem's 1920s." Amid the carousing and the high that came with being in fashionable demand, the writers took to calling themselves the "niggerati." Ever affable yet ever inscrutable because he was never known to have opened a deeply personal, let alone sexual, relationship with anyone, Hughes remained the movement's leading light. He spelled out its lofty ambitions in an essay in the *Nation* that declared: "We younger Negro artists who create now intend to express our individual dark-skinned selves without fear or shame. If white people are pleased we are glad. If they are not, it doesn't matter. We know we are beautiful. And ugly too. The tom-tom cries and the tom-tom laughs. If colored people are pleased we are glad. If they are not, their displeasure doesn't matter either. We build our temples for tomorrow, strong as we know how, and we stand on top of the mountain, free within ourselves."[75]

Soon, at the age of twenty-five, Hughes published a volume of poetry that biographer Rampersad described as "his most brilliant book of poems, and one of the more astonishing books of verse ever published in the United States—comparable in the black world to [Walt Whitman's] *Leaves of Grass* in the white."[76]

Evoking the lives and ways of poor African Americans, the book scandalized much of the black establishment with such starkly revealing poems as "Red Silk Stockings," which spoke of a black woman dressed to allure white men. Unfortunately titled "Fine Clothes to the Jew," a reference to poor people selling their clothing to pawnbrokers, most of whom happened to be Jewish, the collection was Hughes's declaration of freedom for his generation of African American artists. That it didn't sell well seemed of little consequence in a time when black expression was the essence of hip. A wealthy, elderly white woman, Charlotte Mason, known endearingly to Hughes as "Godmother," became his patron, funding him with $150 a month, asking only for an accounting and, far more important, a say over his writing projects.

Swept up as well, many in the black intelligentsia predicted that the cultural outpouring would lead whites, at long last, to see blacks for all their humanity. "I am coming to believe that nothing can go farther to destroy race prejudice than the recognition of the Negro as a creator and contributor to American civilization," wrote James Weldon Johnson.[77]

WALKER'S TAMMANY HALL background gave Battle little reason to hope for a reprieve, nor did Walker's unlikely appointment of George V. McLaughlin as commissioner. Then serving as New York State Superintendent of Banking, McLaughlin had no experience in policing and seemed ideally suited to act as Tammany's puppet. Regardless, the new commissioner summoned Battle.

"Officer, have a seat," McLaughlin said. "I want to ask you do you know why you were not promoted to sergeant when your turn came?"

"I do not," Battle answered.

"The only complaints I find against you in the files are anonymous letters. I have torn them up and thrown them into the wastebasket. Unsigned letters have no status with me. When I make my next appointments, Battle, I shall make you a sergeant. And when I appoint you, you will be a sergeant—not a Negro sergeant."

Battle's promotion came though on May 21, 1926. After almost fifteen distinguished years of service, including, by his count, two years, seven months, one week, and two hours in Canarsie, Battle was a sergeant, Shield No. 612, and for the first time the New York Police Department had authorized a black man to give orders to white men.

The Monarch Lodge of the Elks threw Battle a testimonial dinner. The Harold C. Clark Melody Orchestra played. The lodge's exalted ruler toasted Battle as "a symbol of benevolence, activity, truth, tenacity, love and elasticity." Dressed in a peach-and-orange crepe dress, Florence declined to speak, saying only that "one Battle a night was enough."[78]

Battle stood before his admirers as a forty-three-year-old man, almost twenty-one years a husband, the father of three children, one on the verge of manhood himself. He remembered that, in his days as a redcap, friends had warned him not to try for the police department, but he had tried, and today he had a higher rank than most of the white men on the force. He had been ostracized in the stationhouse and gawked at on the streets. They had not. He had been barred from a parade and threatened with death. They had not. He had been jailed with a murderer and saved a white officer's life. They had not. And he was a sergeant, and they were not.

In his pocket, Battle had a telegram, sent by Anne from Beaufort, where she was living happily with Mary Elizabeth. Anne reminded the son who had been born so large "that his good fortune was due to God and to prayer." And a quarter-century later, long after Enright had faded into obscurity, shortly before he would die at the age of eighty-two in a fall down a flight of stairs on Long Island, Battle would write of his tormentor, "I asked the Lord to forgive him."[79]

CHAPTER FOUR

COMMAND

TONY JUMPS INTO Battle's black, turtle-shaped Lincoln and across the front seat from his grandfather. Battle is taking the boy to see Sugar Ray Robinson, the world's greatest boxer, at his training camp in Greenwood Lake.

Battle first met the fighter when Robinson was a junior high school student. The Reverend Frederick Asbury Cullen of the Salem Methodist Episcopal Church had brought the two together. The neighborhood around Cullen's house of worship teemed with children who "were wild, bad, even vicious," Cullen would remember. The roughest had a headquarters "in a cellar deep underground" and called their club "The Crescent." Cullen persuaded the Crescent president, recalled only by the name Bunk, to take advantage of a gymnasium in the church basement. Thus was born the Salem Crescent Athletic Club.[1]

Then one day, Cullen found Robinson playing craps behind the church. The pastor took the boy to a cellar window through which he saw a boxing ring, punching bags, and a basketball court. Eventually, Robinson went in.

"About 20 guys were working out," he recalled. "Sparring in the old ring. Skipping ropes. Punching the bags. Doing calisthenics. And sweating, the perspiration dripping like leaky faucets off their bodies. Over the years, the sweat had permeated everything in the gym."

Robinson most remembered the smell. "The thick stale odor hung in the air and it hung in my nostrils," he told a biographer. "Later on, it would represent a strange perfume to me."[2]

Cullen recruited black police officers to keep the boys on the straight and narrow. Battle was at the top of the list. Boxer that he was, he got on famously with the fast-fisted boy and then the man.

"Robinson has been and still is a sort of protégé of mine," he told Hughes. "I have been close to him through the years as he rose to the championship, having been at one time champion of two classes at once."

TONY IS ACCUSTOMED to his grandfather's standing among prominent people. He meets Paul Robeson on a Sunday when he performs before the Mother AME Zion congregation for forty minutes. America's Communist blacklist has driven Robeson from the public sphere, but his brother, the Reverend Benjamin Robeson, is pastor, and nothing can stifle the tenor's powerful voice on this stage. On other Sundays, Battle takes Tony to the Polo Grounds. Grandfather and grandson sit in a box behind the dugout. There, Battle introduces Tony to Don Newcombe, the pitcher who followed Jackie Robinson onto the Dodgers and had won the 1949 National League Rookie of the Year Award.

But, clambering from the big Lincoln, Tony has never witnessed a welcome as extravagant as the one Sugar Ray Robinson extends to Battle.

"The entire program is choreographed to 'Sweet Georgia Brown,' with Sugar Ray dancing, skipping rope and sparring, all with the music going," Tony remembers.

Hughes, too, counts Sugar Ray as a friend. He's a regular at Sugar Ray's nightclub in Harlem. He makes his own trip to the boxer's camp in that summer of 1952, having returned to Greenwood Forest Farms for a few more weeks. Almost three years have passed since Battle began working with Hughes, and now finally, Hughes is showing Battle drafts of the manuscript in progress. Battle reads the stories that he has told to Hughes and that Hughes has put down on paper, and he goes over them with Hughes to get the stories right. Hughes promises that he has only one more chapter to write. Finally, Battle is happy.

OLIVE KEENE KNEW all about the sergeant who lived on Strivers Row, and she walked up the townhouse steps hoping to get help from the one cop who might provide it. Battle opened the door to find "an attractive brown skin woman" who had a story to tell about two powerful white men.

Joseph Roth and his son Herbert were pawnbrokers. They lent money at high interest rates to people pressed for cash. To guarantee repayment, they took property as security, "everything from pocket knives to diamonds." Although exploitive, the pawn business was legal. Another aspect of the Roths' trade was criminal. They worked as fences, buying stolen goods low at two shops, and reselling high elsewhere. Their version of the racket was particularly pernicious. They encouraged "domestic servants working in the homes of the rich to steal for them," and then blackmailed the servants into stealing more.

Olive Keene was one of the thieves. Now, though, standing on Battle's doorstep, she was furious that the Roths had paid her less for stolen goods than she had expected.

"Arrest me, Officer Battle," she said. "I want to give you a case against the Roths. First put me in jail—and protect me. I'm afraid."

Three months had passed since Battle's promotion. He was assigned to the detective squad in the familiar quarters of the Harlem stationhouse. His first homicide case had been an immersion in bloodshed: a locked apartment; a butcher knife, razor, and scissors; a man's dismembered body, head missing. The neighbors said they had heard the man arguing with his wife. Battle tracked her to Jersey City and made the arrest.

And, here, was Olive Keene, demanding to testify against two men who were connected to Tammany Hall. Harlem political leaders warned Battle to back off. He pressed on. Perhaps he felt safe because, to Tammany's horror, Commissioner McLaughlin was taking on the rackets without fear or favor. Or perhaps it was simply as Battle said: "I was a member of the Harlem community, not only as a policeman, but as a parent-citizen, and I felt it was my duty to help rid the community of the menace of men like the Roths."

Their vaults contained jewelry that wealthy New Yorkers had listed as missing, as well as firearms that had been reported stolen. Battle arrested father and son. When finally the trial was called, a judge dismissed the charges with the all-purpose case-fixing declaration: "lack of evidence." The pawnbrokers resumed business, and Battle set out to build a new case against criminals he saw as perpetrators of racial injustice.

THE HARLEM THAT he had pioneered and that had grown into the proud black metropolis was being transformed once more. For a time, spanning roughly the second half of the 1920s, social extremes abided side by side as if in competition, the hopeful culture of the middle and upper classes pitted against the arrival of poor and uneducated Southerners.

"It is a motley group which is now in the ascendancy in the city," Charles Spurgeon Johnson wrote in the March 1925 issue of the *Survey Graphic*. "The picturesqueness of the South, the memory of pain, the warped lives, the ghostly shadows of fear, crudeness, ignorance and unsophistication, are laid upon the surface of the city in a curious pattern."[3]

Less politely stated, many of the emigrants had neither the resources nor the backgrounds to meet expected standards of living.

"Whether it is apparent or not, the newcomers are forced to reorganize their lives—to enter a new status and adjust to it that eager restlessness which prompted them to leave home," Spurgeon Johnson continued. "It is not inconceivable that the conduct of these individuals which seems so strange and at times so primitive and reckless, is the result of just this disorientation."

From 1920 to 1930, New York's black population more than doubled to 327,706. The big city channeled the arrivals into narrow straits. Half of the working men held jobs as janitors, porters, messengers, waiters, drivers, and elevator operators. Six in ten of the employed women were laundresses or servants.

Meanwhile, housing demand soared as African Americans filled Harlem to its limits, and white resistance in abutting neighborhoods hemmed blacks into this limited territory. Built for large families, the neighborhood's spacious apartments were ill suited for an influx of young, single people. Tenants packed into shared rooms, driving the population density to a level 50 percent higher than in Manhattan at large. Rents doubled between 1919 and 1927.

All too predictably, disease and death followed. Harlem's mortality rate was 42 percent higher than the city's. Its infants died twice as frequently as babies elsewhere in New York. Tuberculosis, heart ailments, and pneumonia took lives with grim efficiency.

Meanwhile, across a class divide, some ten thousand people celebrated the dedication in 1925 of a newly constructed neo-Gothic church, still the landmark home today of Battle's beloved Mother AME Zion congregation.[4] Working and professional men swelled the membership of fraternal organizations like his Monarch Lodge. Wives appeared in the *Amsterdam News* gossip column for hosting bridge parties and participating in supper dances.

As the decade's halfway mark passed, James Weldon Johnson asked: "Will Harlem become merely a famous ghetto, or will it be a center of intellectual, cultural and economic forces exerting an influence throughout the world, especially upon Negro peoples?" He and so many others believed the latter, even as dreams were starting to die in the suffocating grip of race and economics.[5]

THIS TIME BATTLE INSISTED, and this time Anne came north to visit.[6] The townhouse was as fine a home as she had known in New Bern. Here, though, African Americans owned each and every house. Inside, Anne embraced three grandchildren whose progress in life reflected that they had been reared by two strong parents, unlike the many youngsters who were looked after by single mothers, often hanging about the streets "with keys tied around their necks on a ribbon."

Twenty-one-year-old Jesse was headed toward completing studies at Morgan State, the historically black university in Baltimore. Eleven-year-old Carroll was a junior high school athlete. Fourteen-year-old Charline was enrolled in a revolutionary institution dedicated to producing career "gentlewomen." Described by the *Times* as occupying "the finest high school building in the world," the Wadleigh High School for Girls had opened in 1902 to educate the offspring of Harlem's white upper crust. The student body remained largely white when Charline entered the five-story, elevator-equipped, French Renaissance–style edifice.[7]

Passing the spring through the fall of 1927 with Battle's family, Anne witnessed the start of an intensely eventful and newly happy phase of her son's career. He told astonishing tales about the Roths. After soliciting the support of wealthy whites whose stolen property had turned up in their vaults, Battle persuaded the district attorney to file a fresh indictment, and he stood ready for a new round of case fixing.

"A well-known Harlem go-between, who made his living arranging deals between gamblers, bootleggers, other law breakers and the politicians, came to me with the offer of a large cash settlement if I would back down on the Roths," Battle remembered.

He refused, and they persisted: "When it seemed clear that the Roths were going to trial, in spite of all, the word came down to me from higher sources that as much as a hundred thousand dollars would be available for division between the judge, the district attorneys, and myself—if the Roths were cleared."

Again Battle refused and, on May 31, 1927, the Roths faced judge and jury. After Olive Keene had exacted her revenge from the witness stand, Herbert Roth admitted guilt in a plea bargain, accepting a sentence of up to two years in prison. Joseph Roth was spared incarceration on the ground that he had a weak heart. Anne saw her son hailed in Harlem as a hero, with the *Amsterdam News* stating: "Credit for the arrest and conviction of Roth is due to the splendid work of Detective Sergeant Battle."

In July, there was more acclaim after Battle and fellow black detective William Boyden arrested career criminal Richard Daly on a robbery charge. "Hardly had Daly gotten in the doors of the stationhouse," Battle recalled, "when he said that he could 'put the finger' on the man who had murdered a grocery store clerk several months earlier."

Daly said that he knew the killer, a black man, only by the name "Blue." Battle, Boyden, and a white detective drove Daly up and down the streets until he pointed to twenty-five-year-old Leroy Leeks. Born in Richmond, Virginia, Leeks was literate enough to "read only a few words here and there." He lived in a tenement just south of Harlem, earned his keep in the building as a janitor and handyman, was active in the neighborhood Baptist church, and had no criminal record.

Battle rolled down the car window.

"Is your name Blue?" he demanded.

"No," Leeks responded.

"Yes it is. He done it," Daly said, adding that he knew Leeks as a fellow ex-convict. "He did two bits with me in Sing Sing."

With that Battle got out of the car, handcuffed Leeks, and searched his apartment with the other detectives. They found nothing. The next day Battle brought Leeks to the scene of the months-old homicide.

"You remember this place?" he asked.

"No, I have never been on West 140th Street before," Leeks answered.

Regardless, Battle hauled Leeks to court, telling him, as Leeks would swear, "I would never have arrested you if Daly did not say your name was Blue. You're not indicted by me, but by that boy, Daly."[8]

At that, Battle left Leeks to face a capital murder charge based solely on the uncorroborated word of an untrustworthy witness—and without investigating Leeks's protestations of innocence.

The newspapers bannered the arrest. Three months later, after Anne had returned to North Carolina, the headlines would be anything but complimentary. On the eve of Leeks's trial, Daly recanted, claiming that Battle and the other cops had bullied him into naming Leeks. Five witnesses, including Leeks's doctor, reported that Leeks had been sick at home at the time of the murder—none of which Battle had checked.

The *Times* blared:

Freed of Murder As Accuser Recants
Janitor, in Prison 3 Months, is Cleared when Negro Admits
    Identification was a Lie.
Police Beatings Charged
Prisoner Says He Pointed Out Innocent Man as Killer to Save
    Himself From Injuries.

The *Amsterdam News* reported: "A lie from the mouth of a known criminal without any supporting evidence nearly sent an innocent laboring man to the electric chair."[9]

Battle vigorously denied that he had laid a hand on Daly, told Hughes that the brutality allegations had harmed his reputation but never acknowledged in their joint storytelling that he had erred in solely relying on the career criminal's word.

WHILE THE LEEKS case was pending and Battle was still riding high, he had had the pleasure of introducing Anne to one of the most luminous of African American celebrities, legendary tap dancer Bill "Bojangles" Robinson. Battle and Robinson were just then starting a close friendship.

Born in Virginia in 1878, Robinson grew up shining shoes and dancing on street corners for pennies. He left home at fourteen to join a touring show that drew black audiences across the South. He arrived in New York around the turn of the century, danced at Tenderloin clubs, and followed the money into vaudeville. The traveling music and comedy shows enforced a "two-colored" standard that barred solo performances by blacks, so Robinson partnered with George W. Cooper. Rave reviews described them in terms like "real Ethiopians" and praised their "chuckling guffaws, pigeon wing steps and cachinnating songs." After a dozen years, Robinson broke the "two-colored" restriction, went solo, and began to dance more. He wore wooden-soled, slip-on clogs rather than laced oxfords with steel taps. His tapping began to draw audiences.

On the stage of New York's Palace Theatre, Robinson danced up and down a set of steps. The effect was stunning. Constance Valis Hill, author of *Tap Dancing America*, concluded that Robinson's "Stair Dance" was "the first tap masterwork of the twentieth century, one of the earliest tap choreographies to attune the listener to the precision, clarity, and rhythmic logic of a tap composition."[10]

Acclaimed as the "World's Greatest Dancer," Robinson was an incandescent figure in Harlem. He was noted for being able to run backward as swiftly as a fast man ran forward, and he was credited with coining the word "copacetic" to mean the "superlative of OK." Often called on to perform at public events, he happily obliged. That was how he and Battle began to forge their bond.

Sergeant's stripes on his sleeve, Battle had persuaded the Improved Benevolent and Protective Order of Elks to hold the group's 1927 national convention in New York. He organized the extravaganza during Anne's visit. Thanks to Battle, Harlem greeted the black Elks with "thousands of gaily colored electric lights stretched across the streets . . . and with flags, bunting and decorations in greater profusion than this section has ever seen before." Throngs watched the Elks parade up Seventh Avenue. Dressed "in a white flannel suit and stopping now and then to knit a dance step," Robinson led the way. Battle came next with New York's African American police officers in full-dress formation, giving Anne one memory above all to take home from her final trip to New York.[11]

THAT SUMMER, WESLEY'S name reached the top of the fire department promotion list. It would be only a short time before the commissioner elevated him to lieutenant or passed him over. His fears mounted when a deputy commissioner showed up at Grand Central to seek out white men who worked for Chief Williams as redcaps. How did this black boss treat his white underlings, the deputy commissioner asked, searching for like-father-like-son proof that placing African American Wesley in a superior role would bode ill for white firefighters. When finally the order came down, the news was good: Commissioner John Dorman awarded Wesley the rank of lieutenant.

He understood what he was up against immediately. "The Civil Service Commission cautioned me not to make a mistake or do anything wrong as it would throw a reflection on thirteen million colored people," he would recall years later. "I told them that that was not fair to the race or me. But I must admit that in this country that is the way it works, hard though it is."

Protests flooded into Dorman's office. Wesley got word that the commissioner planned to assign him to a water tower company, a post composed entirely of a single lieutenant and two firefighters. Further, Dorman would team Wesley with another lieutenant and a retired firefighter, thus denying Wesley command over any active member of the department. Wesley served notice that he would fight.

"I took orders from white officers," he told Battle. "White firemen will have to take orders from a colored officer."

Chief Williams contacted Patrick Cardinal Hayes, leader of the Roman Catholic Archdiocese of New York, and US senator Robert F. Wagner. Committing to speak with Mayor Walker, the senator told the Chief that Wesley should "continue on active service in a fire company as this was right and also necessary if a proper pattern was to be established."[12]

Hayes was even more specific about his wishes. "The cardinal, God bless him, told the mayor and fire commissioner that I was to stay in Engine Company 55, where I wanted to stay," Wesley recalled.

The commissioner gave Wesley command authority in the firehouse that had been his posting for eight years. He walked in as superior officer to men who had banished him to separate sleeping quarters, defecated in his boots, thrown away his eating utensils, abandoned him in a fire, and demanded transfers to escape working with a "nigger." There was a fresh revolt. A firefighter poured honey into a fire engine gas tank to prevent Wesley from responding to an alarm. Thirteen-year veteran John O'Toole walked out in disgust—and was rewarded with a transfer to working on a fireboat. Wesley's fellow lieutenants did worse than turn their backs. At the time, lieutenants belonged to an association that was akin to a union, but membership was by invitation. The association sent applications only to newly promoted lieutenants who were highly rated by friends or had political support. A man was guaranteed admission if an application came in the mail. If no application arrived, a man learned that he had been blacklisted. To Wesley's surprise, an application appeared in his box. He sent in the paperwork with an initiation fee. The association returned the money with an explanation: membership was limited to whites.

Celebrating Wesley's promotion, the *Amsterdam News* noted that he had recently finished reading *The Outline Of Science: A Plain Story Simply Told*, a best-selling work on the interplay of science and religion by Scottish naturalist Sir John Arthur Thomson.[13] His new duties placed him at the head of a company of men and kept him in harm's way. Early on in his command, an iron-columned structure went up in flames in today's SoHo. A superior officer ordered Wesley to lead his team inside. He pulled his men together. The chaos slowed them ever so slightly; then the building collapsed as they were about to enter.

"We would all have been lost as the entire nine stories fell," Wesley remembered of an escape so narrow that the Chief who had ordered the men in "came running up and said a prayer," because he had thought that the whole company, including Wesley, had been killed.

AT THE AGE of forty-five, in 1928, Battle plunged into two experiences that he vested with lifelong significance. The first was a pilgrimage.

In May, Battle joined the Reverend William Lloyd Imes, pastor of St. James Presbyterian Church, on a 290-mile drive into the Adirondack Mountains.[14] They stayed overnight in Saratoga before heading on with fifty travelers to North Elba, a tiny town near Lake Placid. Carrying a framed picture that depicted John Brown stopping to kiss a slave child as he was led to the gallows, they were headed to the radical abolitionist's gravesite on the 128th anniversary of his birth.

Brown had burned with hatred for bondage. His fervor brought him first to Springfield, Massachusetts, an antislavery bastion that he helped build into a major station on the Underground Railroad, and then to North Elba, where a wealthy abolitionist was giving land to poor blacks. Brown bought 244 acres with the goal of teaching the fledgling farmers to work the land. Seven years later in 1855, he went to war against proslavery militiamen in Kansas. The guerrilla conflict climaxed when he sanctioned the massacre of five prisoners. In 1859, Brown led twenty-one men on a raid of the Harpers Ferry federal arsenal with the vision that newly armed slaves would liberate the South. Marines commanded by Robert E. Lee squashed the insurrection, killing ten of Brown's men, including two of his sons, as well as Lewis Sheridan Leary, the first husband of Hughes's grandmother.

Six days after Brown was hanged for treason, his wife buried his body on the North Elba farm. Eventually, eleven of his raiders would also be interred there. New York State took over the property in 1895, but it was not until 1922, with the formation in Philadelphia of the John Brown Memorial Association, that the site got sustained attention. A small group began annual wreath-laying pilgrimages, and word spread to several cities, including New York, where a handful of African Americans joined the association. They named their chapter after Frederick Douglass, who had written of Brown: "His zeal in the cause of my race was far greater than mine—it was as the burning sun to my taper light—mine was bounded by time, his stretched away to the boundless shores of eternity. I could live for the slave, but he could die for him."

Battle joined an annual trek to Brown's farm as a member of the Douglass chapter. The pilgrims gathered first for lunch and an organ service at a restaurant. As a goodwill gesture, Battle presented the picture of Brown embracing the slave child to the Lake Placid Club, an organization of the area's leading citizens. Hosting the lunch, a local minister said with evident sincerity, "The black man who died in chains and the white man who died on the gallows both left the slave in bondage. Then beside these two marched a third martyr, and Abraham Lincoln died as the last shackle dropped from the last slave, and America was free." He left unspoken the fact that the Lake Placid Club barred admission to African Americans "except as servants."[15]

Later on the afternoon of May 9, 1928, standing before a roughly carved tombstone, Battle paid homage to a hero who was reviled by many as a murderous terrorist. He would tell Hughes of the events, and Hughes would barely reference them in a list of Battle's most cherished memories. Hughes's offhanded treatment of the episode was particularly startling because of his family's reverence for the raid at Harpers Ferry. Over and again, his grandmother had told the story of how Leary had ridden off from Oberlin, Ohio, to give his life fighting alongside Brown, instilling in Hughes the greatness of his lineage. Often, she had worn Leary's shawl, shown Hughes its bullet holes, used the cloth to protect him from the cold as he had slept. Then she had handed the shawl down to him and he had kept it in storage for decades until finally donating the cloth to the Ohio Historical Society.[16] Yet he limited the labor he exerted for Battle to mentioning the pilgrimage to Brown's grave to but two sentences.

FOUR MONTHS AFTER Battle returned from Lake Placid, he took on the most sensational case of his career, the kidnapping of Casper Holstein, one of the least remembered and most influential of the figures who guided Harlem's evolution in the 1920s. A native of St. Croix in the Virgin Islands, Holstein arrived in New York with his mother as an eighteen-year-old in 1894. He finished high school in Brooklyn and took a succession of jobs, including, by one account, reading to the blind matriarch of a well-to-do Brooklyn family. Working as a bellhop in a Manhattan hotel, he learned how to bet on horses from guests who owned thoroughbreds. Then he served in the US Navy, returned to bellhopping, and studied in Chicago to be an embalmer. By 1905, Holstein was in the gambling business. His name surfaced in a *Times* report about a black man who had reported a swindle in a joint called the Fair Play Club.

"Well, Sir, I jes' play a little monte and I had a roll ob $150 befo' me on de table when de lights went out," the story caricatured the man as saying. "Every nigger in de club then grabbed, and everybody got a piece of dat money."

The police charged Fair Play Club president Casper Holstein with running a gambling house. This was the first of the ten bookmaking arrests he would rack up by 1921. The busts came and went quietly. Holstein was a man of reserved demeanor. Showing none of the flamboyance typical of gamers, he maintained a low profile while building social and business ties both in Harlem, where he helped found the black Elk's Monarch Lodge, and in Chicago, where the men of the black gambling fraternity counted him among their kind.

They marked Holstein's visits with banquets. The *Chicago Defender* heralded him as a "well-known good fellow and club man of New York City."

Top among Holstein's Windy City comrades was yet another black man of outsized accomplishment. Oscar Stanton De Priest was an Alabama-born son of former slaves. He left home for Chicago at the age of seventeen, earned a living as a painter, and found his calling in the city's Republican machine, the equivalent of Tammany Hall. A talent for organizing gave De Priest command of votes in a growing African American population. He channeled his troops toward the party's candidates, all of whom where white until De Priest won election as a Chicago's first black alderman in 1914.

Known by then as the black district's "King Oscar," De Priest prospered through the collusion between politics and vice that dominated the era. In 1917, the state attorney charged him with masterminding a "conspiracy to allow gambling houses and houses of prostitution to operate and for bribery of police officers in connection with the protection of these houses." The renowned Clarence Darrow helped De Priest beat the rap at trial.

Whether visiting De Priest in Chicago, where he was hailed as a "well-known good fellow and club man," or working in New York, Holstein held a prominent place in the milieu of wagering. In the telling of a biographical sketch written for the WPA Writers Project, Holstein had substantial capital by the start of the 1920s and spent it charitably. Here, he comes to the rescue of the blind white woman to whom he had read as a young man in need of work. After the family goes broke in 1921, Holstein supports her and her loved ones in high style for a dozen years, and then he sits in the family's pew at her funeral.[17]

Even more colorfully, writing in the *North American Review*, black critic Saunders Redding depicted Holstein as working in 1924 as a building porter who "combined the prosaic traits of a financier with the dizzy imaginative flights of a fingerless Midas." Here, he sits "in his airless janitor's closet, surrounded by brooms and mops" as well as by stacks of old newspapers that published the daily tabulations of the New York Clearing House, an institution that transferred money among member banks.

"The thought that the figures differed each day played in his mind like a wasp in an empty room," Redding wrote of Holstein, until "he let out an uproarious laugh and in general acted like a drunken man."[18]

In that fabled instant, Holstein recognized that he could build numbers gambling around the Clearing House figures. The game was a precursor to today's quick-pick-style lotteries. Play was simple: A bettor would select a number from 000 to 999 and place a bet with a "banker." The banker would hold a drawing and pay anyone who had chosen the number that came up. Although the odds of winning were one thousand-to-one, the banker paid off at six hundred-to-one, all but guaranteeing a substantial profit.

For years, the game had had a relatively small following, in part because would-be players knew better than to trust that bankers would always conduct honest drawings. Holstein's flash of inspiration brought trust to the game, because no one could fake the Federal Reserve credit balance or the total amount of money the banks had cleared. Suddenly, with every banker and bettor tied to a single independent number—composed of the second and third digits of the clearance total and the third digit of the Federal Reserve balance—people of all walks of life began wagering vast quantities of pennies, nickels, dimes, and dollars.

"All Harlem is ablaze with 'the numbers.' People play it everywhere, in tenements, on street corners, in the backs of shops," wrote Winthrop D. Lane, author of "Ambushed in the City. The Grim Side of Harlem."[19]

Spent in volume, the coins and bills accumulated into riches for the bankers, with Holstein at the forefront. "In a year he owned three of the finest apartment buildings in Harlem, a fleet of expensive cars, a home on Long Island and several thousand acres of farmland in Virginia," Redding wrote.

Battle remembered Holstein as "a quietly well-groomed man of average size, light brown skin in complexion and amiable of manner, who neither drank nor smoked." Attended by housekeepers, he "entertained celebrities and national politicians and fraternal leaders" in a duplex apartment.[20] More tellingly, Battle recalled Holstein as "a kind of community Robin Hood, giving back a great deal of his

wealth to the neighborhood in benefactions of one sort or another—
such as building modern apartment houses at moderate rentals, spick
and span in their maintenance, with the brass always polished." Holstein was also revered for paying the college tuitions of deserving
young people. Battle knew so personally because, he wrote, "I had
sent many to him."[21]

Holstein was, in fact, a leading black philanthropist. He helped
build a home for orphaned children in Gary, Indiana; founded a dormitory for girls in a Baptist school in Liberia; and offered to finance a
sanitarium at which black doctors could practice in Harlem. He supported Marcus Garvey's back-to-Africa movement and distributed
as many as five hundred food baskets to Harlem's poor at Christ-
mastime. He paid for an annual boat ride for Harlem children and
donated money to historically black Fisk and Howard universities.
By donating the prize money for the *Opportunity* magazine annual
literary awards—won in 1925 by Hughes—the numbers king also
played patron to the Harlem Renaissance.[22]

HOLSTEIN SPENT THE evening of Thursday, September 20, 1928, at the
Turf Club, one of several Harlem cabarets he owned. Shortly before
midnight, a chauffeur drove him to an apartment building where he
planned to visit a woman. From that point, witnesses and newspaper accounts provide inconsistent details about everything from Holstein's abduction to his inexplicable release three days later. Battle's
account is the most authoritative: "As [Holstein's] car drove off, a
curtained black sedan pulled up to the curb. Four white men leaped
out, forced Holstein into the sedan and sped away."

A few hours later, on his day off, Battle rose at 4 a.m. to go ocean
fishing aboard a chartered boat off Long Island. He returned with "a
box full of iced porgy and weakfish" to find cops at the townhouse
with news of Holstein's kidnapping and orders to take command
of the investigation. Witnesses supplied only vague descriptions of
the curtained sedan. There was no ransom demand. Early Saturday
morning, more than thirty hours after the abduction, Battle theo-
rized that the kidnappers might force Holstein to make a bank with-
drawal. The manager of the Harlem branch of the Chelsea Exchange

notified banks across the city to alert Battle if anyone tried to cash a check signed by Holstein. Shortly, underworld beer runner Michael Bernstein presented a $3,200 draft at a bank in the Bronx.

Battle assigned two black detectives, Paul Moore and George Webber, to pose as members of Holstein's numbers crew. They visited Bernstein with a cover story about getting tipped that Bernstein was part of the kidnapping.

"Eventually Bernstein was convinced that my men were really racketeers like himself, that they were deeply concerned about the welfare of their backer, and would even be willing to payoff to have him released unharmed," Battle said.

After Bernstein set the price at $50,000, Battle took Bernstein into custody, "put the fear of God into" him, and arranged for Bernstein to be released on bond. Eight hours later, past one in the morning, after being held for three days, Holstein walked back into the Turf Club. Shortly, he stopped by the stationhouse to tell Battle a patently incredible story of being hit in the head, blindfolded, and then released by kidnappers who had returned his diamond ring, worth $2,000, and given him $3 for cab fare.

With good-humored obstructionism, Holstein said that he had paid no ransom and insisted that he could not identify any suspects, including Bernstein. When a reporter asked, "Mr. Holstein, didn't you recognize any of your captors?" the story related: "A smile overspread Holstein's face. 'Well, you know, how it is,' he said. 'I could'—a slow wink went with this—'but I can't.'"[23]

Regardless, Battle sent Bernstein to Sing Sing on the strength of the check he had attempted to cash. Relating the story to Hughes, he spared Holstein even a hint of criticism for refusing to cooperate with the investigation, and he placed the kidnapping into context as a turning point in Harlem history. There had been a hidden force behind the crime. Holstein's riches had gotten the attention of the brutal Arthur "Dutch Schultz" Flegenheimer. After using kidnapping, torture, and murder to seize control of bootlegging in the Bronx, Flegenheimer was moving in on Harlem's rackets at the vanguard of a white takeover. Holstein's comic postkidnap performance conveyed to an audience of one—Dutch Schultz—that he had no interest in a futile fight.

In the aftermath, despite his revulsion for the numbers game, Battle grew close to the very well-connected kingpin. Two months after the abduction, they had much to talk about when Holstein's friend, Oscar Stanton De Priest won election to the US Congress. No state, northern or southern, had sent an African American to Washington in the twentieth century. No northern state had done so in all of US history. Holstein told Battle about the tough man who had worked the levers of machine politics to make history. Battle shared with Holstein memories of the last African American who had served in Congress, George H. White, a lawyer who been principal of a school for blacks in New Bern during Battle's boyhood.

De Priest strode into the Capitol in 1929 and was immediately rebuffed. One after the other, House colleagues refused office space that adjoined the quarters provided to De Priest. Then a white man from New York, a colorful progressive from the Italian stronghold of East Harlem, spoke with moral clarity. Battle would long remember that Representative Fiorello H. La Guardia dispatched a telegram to the Speaker of the House, stating: "Have noticed in press agitation among some members against allotment office to our colleague, the gentleman from Illinois, Mr. De Priest. I will be glad to have him next to my office. It is manifestly unfair to embarrass a new member and I believe it is our duty to assist new members rather than humiliate them."[24]

Soon, supported by De Priest and "Bojangles" Robinson, Holstein recruited Battle into a drive to install Holstein as national Grand Exalted Ruler of the black Elks. With Holstein spending liberally, Battle jumped into electioneering at a convention in Atlantic City. Longtime incumbent J. Finley Wilson campaigned just as vigorously to hold his post. At an emotional high point, a Wilson bodyguard attempted to block Battle from mounting the convention platform, and Robinson backed up Battle by drawing a golden pistol that he was famed for carrying.

In the end, Holstein, Battle, Robinson, and De Priest went down to defeat. More important, Battle's association with these three leading figures at the time points to his arrival at a happy station in life. Back in New Bern, on the day of his last whipping for smacking a white who had called him "nigger," Thomas had worried that his bullyboy son would never learn to succeed among either his own race or the other. Now, no matter the *difficulties*, he was a New York Police Department detective sergeant, peer to Congressman De Priest, peer to gambler Holstein, peer to dancer Robinson, peer to all the Strivers—a Striver.

A GROUP OF detectives threw a party to celebrate Battle's forty-sixth birthday on January 16, 1929. The guest list mixed whites and blacks. The department now counted ninety African Americans in the ranks, mostly cops, five detectives, one sergeant, and one police surgeon, Dr. Louis T. Wright. Battle took pleasure in the dark-skinned faces who wished him well, and the moment was all the sweeter because an old friend, perhaps his closest white friend, had organized the event.

Way back at the beginning, Jimmy Garvey had defied the conspiracy of silence. After the department transferred Battle to Harlem, they had stayed close, Battle coming to Garvey's side when Garvey's daughter Helen, not yet two years old, contracted polio in the 1916 epidemic, Garvey offering moral support to Battle after Enright banished Battle to Canarsie.

Garvey was still an active cop. His wife would describe him as an officer who "never stopped looking for suspicious persons."[25] He had made detective in 1921 and had welcomed Sergeant Battle to the division five years later. He talked often about Helen, who wore a metal brace from left thigh to heel, and called home regularly to speak with her. She was a freshman in high school. Garvey wanted Helen to go college. Battle had the same hope for Charline, who was approaching graduation from Wadleigh High School.

True to form, Charline had ideas of her own. She talked about applying to schools in Boston. Battle and Florence balked at sending her so far away at the age of sixteen. Battle turned for advice to James Weldon Johnson. He counseled that Charline should consider New York City's Hunter College, a school that had been founded to offer free public higher education to women both black and white. Battle also introduced his daughter to a young woman who was as fine a role model for Charline as Battle could find. The granddaughter of a slave who had purchased freedom, Eunice Carter had earned both bachelor's and master's degrees from Smith College in Massachusetts, then and now an all-women's college, then and now among the most demanding of America's liberal arts schools. She was about to enter Fordham University Law School, perhaps kindling hope in Battle that his daughter might be the lawyer in the family. Carter would become Fordham Law's first black woman graduate, first black woman Manhattan district attorney, and the legal strategist behind racket buster Thomas Dewey's successful prosecution of Lucky Luciano in 1936. She certified Hunter as a fine choice, Charline won admission, and Battle savored sending the second of his children to college.[26]

THEN, THE TIDES of life turned. Mary Elizabeth telephoned with word that Anne had been stricken. Battle remembered, as only he could:

> In the summer of 1929 I was called to Beaufort to the home of my sister, Mary Elizabeth, where my mother had gone after the great fire. She had been overcome by a stroke. I found her helpless, unable to move, so I remained to lift and nurse and bathe her. Because of her modesty, even in her condition, she would attempt to push me away when she needed attention.
>
> The doctors had given her up. I knew that she resented a long and lingering illness. She never wished to feel that she was a burden upon anyone. I knelt beside her bed and prayed that for her sake this would not happen, that God in His mercy would not let her suffer indefinitely, and that I might remain with her until the end.
>
> On the eighth of August she died at the age of seventy-six—the best and loveliest mother in all the world to me. She lay in state at St. Peter's Church in New Bern, and was buried beside my father in the Cedar Grove Cemetery. Over the graves of our parents, we have built a monument of granite, but to their sons and daughters, grandchildren and great grandchildren, the example of their Christian lives will live longer and tower higher than any monument of stone we could give them.

Then the tides of history turned too.

On October 29, 1929, the Dow Jones Industrial Average plunged for a second day. Ten miles north and a world away, Harlem had scant reason to notice. Few of Battle's neighbors had ridden the stock market's tenfold rise during the 1920s, so sudden losses totaling $30 billion passed as the misfortune of people who lived in a distant world. There was, of course, more to it: Black Thursday marked the start of the Great Depression.

Shrinking businesses pushed 10 percent of the American workforce into unemployment during 1930. New York City was hit even harder, as one in every six workers lost jobs, and Harlem was pummeled harder still—the toll was one in four workers.[27]

"Men and women stand in line from 1:00 a.m. till 9:00 in near zero weather and fight their way past policemen in order to get a chance at $15.00 a week jobs," the New York Urban League reported, citing a pay scale that was less than half the amount deemed adequate for a Manhattan family of four.

Even so, the cumulative damage was slowly realized. For a time, the clubs poured illicit drinks and played swinging music, and church and The Stroll enlivened Sundays. Weldon Johnson, ever the optimist, wrote of Harlem in 1930 that "as a whole community it possesses a sense of humour and a love of gaiety." Confident that the writers, artists, and performers of the Renaissance were "helping to form American civilization," he predicted that "the Negro in New York ought to be able to work through discrimination and disadvantages."[28]

But hope was fleeting, and the party soon over. As if on cue, on August 17, 1931, a cerebral hemorrhage felled grand hostess A'Lelia Walker at the age of forty-six. More than eleven thousand people filed past the casket of the wealthy woman who had lived in high style and had invited Hughes into parties where, he would write in an autobiography, "Negro poets and Negro numbers bankers mingled with downtown poets and seat-on-the-stock-exchange racketeers."

Hughes took his place at the funeral, aware that he and black America had passed milestones. Having broken with his patroness, "Godmother" Charlotte Mason, in one of the most wrenching rifts of his life, he had seized full control over his destiny as a writer, one who would choose his own projects, one who would survive without patronage, one who longed for the approval of the African American masses yet who wrote verse that was challenging for anyone, one who saw the waning of white interest in things black.

A nightclub quartet called the Four Bon Bons sang Noel Coward's "I'll See You Again," and "they swung it slightly, as she might have liked it," Hughes remembered. A friend read a poem, "To A'Lelia," written by Hughes. And, seven years after its birth at the *Opportunity* magazine awards dinner, where Casper Holstein had endowed the literary prizes, the Renaissance came to a symbolic close.

Hughes would later write in his autobiography: "That was really the end of the gay times of the New Negro era in Harlem, the period that had begun to reach its end when the crash came in 1929 and the white people had much less money to spend on themselves, and practically none to spend on Negroes, for the depression brought everybody down a peg or two. And the Negroes had but few pegs to fall."[29]

THE SALARIES OF skilled workers fell by half. As a result, Harlem's median income in 1932 dropped 43 percent below its level three years earlier. For want of rent, landlords threw families into the street, touching off fights between police and newly energized activists, whose ranks included communists. "Police and riot squads come with bludgeons and tear-bombs, fights and imprisonments, and deaths," wrote Nancy Cunard, a British heiress who devoted her life to fighting racism and fascism.[30]

At the outset, government offered little help. Jimmy Walker, mayoral rascal of the good times, appointed a relief committee only after thirty-five thousand unemployed New Yorkers marched on city hall. Rather than tap public money, the panel solicited contributions from municipal workers in order to distribute food, clothing, and coal, and to stave off evictions. Harlem's churches and fraternal and social organizations provided similar assistance. Even white gangster Owney "The Killer" Madden, the power behind the legendary, whites-only Cotton Club, offered aid. He bought goodwill on Christmas Eve 1934 by having the nightspot hand out bags overstuffed with a four-and-a-half-pound chicken, five pounds of potatoes, five pounds of apples, and additional provisions.[31]

The demand for basic nutrition was overwhelming. President Franklin Roosevelt's New Deal programs were only then starting to take hold. Looking back, researchers for the Federal Writers Project drew a dire portrait: "When the Federal Emergency Relief Administration began operations, it found a majority of Harlem's population on the verge of starvation, as a result of the depression and of an intensified discrimination that made it all but impossible for Negroes to find employment."[32]

In 1935, New York City's jobless rate was 15 percent; Harlem's was 40 percent, an acidic level that combined with racism and governmental neglect to corrode the essentials. Public schools that had educated Jesse, Charline, and Carroll were now overcrowded firetraps. A visitor to one found an offensive odor, a dilapidated principal's office, and ten burned-out classrooms. Hungry children sat listlessly in classes or failed to show up at all. When police work took Battle inside Harlem Hospital, he entered an institution radically different from the one Dr. Louis T. Wright had integrated fifteen years earlier. Patients moved between floors in an elevator shared by garbage. The kitchen ventilation system was long broken. A doctor and nurse performed a bloody operation in a public area in front of twenty-five children. When Battle stepped out of the townhouse and walked east along Strivers Row to the corner of Seventh Avenue, he looked across the street at a block of apartment houses crammed with far too many people. On this block a few hundred yards from Battle's home, men, women, and children were massed at the city's highest human density, 620 souls per acre, all struggling for survival.[33]

BATTLE'S EIGHTEEN YEARS of indignities and successes had paid off in the job security guaranteed to senior members of the New York Police Department. After Jesse took a job with the US Post Office and moved out, never to become a lawyer, Battle took in two young redcaps as lodgers. Many in Harlem were renting space in their homes and apartments to stay afloat financially. Battle opened the townhouse to supplement a comfortable wage and to do a good turn, one old redcap to a new pair. His income placed Battle on an elevated social plane.

Three months after the crash, in celebration of Battle's forty-seventh birthday, Florence welcomed eighteen guests into the townhouse for a seven-course dinner followed by dancing. Less than a month later, Mrs. Maude H. Ferguson played hostess to the Las Estrellas Club in her family's home, located across the Strivers Row rear courtyard. As reported by the *Amsterdam News*, Florence was a "Mesdames" of this bridge-playing society. Just weeks later, Battle and Florence entertained sixty-five guests at a bridge party, dinner, and dancing in celebration of their twenty-fifth wedding anniversary. Charline served as tournament timekeeper.

A family friend doted on her. Henrietta Cachemaille was the wife of a Cuban émigré who made a living as a cigar maker. Charline knew the couple's son well. A rough contemporary in age, Enrique was a student at Lincoln University, the historically black school from which Langston Hughes had recently graduated. Henrietta, Etta to the Battles, shared their concern that Charline was struggling at Hunter. Charline had finished her first semester in January 1930, and was coming through her second term with disappointing grades: D in Composition, C in Greek and Roman Civilization, C in Elements of Economics. It was an unhappy time for Charline. In 1931, she withdrew from school for six months. Battle would write in longhand that she was "near breakdown" during her studies. To ease her burdens, Battle and Florence sent Charline on a grand cruise with Etta Cachemaille. On June 25, 1932, they boarded the SS *Pennsylvania* and set sail for Los Angeles via Havana and the Panama Canal. Etta had just lost Enrique to medical complications following a car accident and, grief-stricken, she was only too happy to have Charline's company.[34]

The steamer was equipped with the latest amenities, including en suite bathrooms in some first-class cabins and a swimming pool. Its course soon reached the heat of southern waters. Charline donned her bathing suit, only to be told poolside that the *Pennsylvania*'s five hundred passengers were welcome to swim as long as they were white. She dove in and "used the pool without question the rest of the trip." In Los Angeles, Charline and Etta attended the 1932 Summer Olympics before returning cross-country by train with stops to visit Yosemite National Park, the Grand Canyon, and Salt Lake City. There, they stayed in a hotel whose dining room was closed to blacks. Having no other choice, they ate in their room.

JIMMY WALKER AND his showgirl mistress Betty Compton were dining at a roadhouse popular with politicians, gangsters, and businessmen when someone fatally shot Arnold Rothstein in the Park Central Hotel. After midnight, Walker danced with Compton, who was in her stocking feet. A gangster whispered in the mayor's ear. Walker headed for the door. Holding Compton's fur, he told bandleader Vincent Lopez: "Rothstein has just been shot, Vince. And that means trouble from here on in."

Little did he know. Running for reelection in 1929, Walker faced the loud, pudgy Italian who had welcomed Oscar De Priest into Congress. Fiorello La Guardia ran as a Republican reformer. He relentlessly attacked Tammany Hall, charged that the police had shied from investigating Rothstein's murder for fear of finding ties to Tammany politicians, and proved that Rothstein had lent $10,000 to a Tammany magistrate. Few listened. A week after the stock market crash, Walker swamped La Guardia. Soon, though, hard-pressed New Yorkers fell out of love with their high-living mayor and Rothstein's ghost came back to haunt him.

The magistrate targeted by La Guardia proved to have deposited $165,000 into bank accounts on an annual salary of $12,000. Weeks later, Manhattan Supreme Court Justice Joseph Force Crater withdrew funds, got into a cab, and vanished forever. With the entire court system under suspicion, Governor Franklin Delano Roosevelt appointed a former judge renowned as a paragon of probity, Samuel Seabury, to investigate judicial corruption. Disclosures came quickly. A former waiter named Chile Acuna admitted that he had conspired with vice cops and magistrates to extort money from women by framing them on prostitution charges. The commission discovered that numerous judges had impossibly large bank balances. With evidence of widespread payoffs, Roosevelt expanded the commission's authority to cover all municipal affairs. Now, New York learned that zoning variances were for sale and that many office holders had swollen accounts. In October 1931, the commission questioned $12,000-a-year Sheriff Thomas Farley about deposits totaling $396,000. The money came from a tin box in his house, he explained, famously adding, "It was a wonderful box."

ANARCHY REIGNED ON the streets as the corruption came to the fore. In May 1931, a cop killer named Francis "Two-Gun" Crowley had a two-hour gun battle with police from inside a West Side apartment. Warring between Dutch Schultz and Vincent "Mad Dog" Coll killed a five-year-old boy and wounded four children in a shootout. In August 1931, payroll bandits fatally shot a police officer, then led cops on a twelve-mile chase, killing a second cop and a four-year-old girl and wounding twelve people. All told in 1931 and 1932, gunmen killed sixteen police officers and wounded sixty-one. They also hit forty-three bystanders, killing four, in the nineteen months leading up to July 1931.[35]

Walker's police commissioner—Edward Mulrooney now had the job—responded by introducing a momentous technological advance to the New York Police Department. Mulrooney equipped two hundred fifty police cars, harbor launches, two airplanes, and the departmental blimp, *Resolute*, with two-way radios. The vehicles hit the streets on February 23, 1932, the first dispatch stating: "Motor patrol 500 respond at once to Room 1, ninth floor at 20 Exchange Place. Two men attempting to pass a forged check."[36]

As chief of detectives, Mulrooney had been Battle's superior officer. Now, he elevated Battle from detective sergeant to acting lieutenant with command of a twelve-man crew known as a Radio Gun Squad. The assignment moved Battle from solving crimes after the fact to heading a forerunner of today's SWAT teams, on the front lines, where gunmen were killing or wounding cops at a rate faster than one every two weeks.

Standard radio patrols called for pairs of officers to drive fifteen- to fifty-square-block zones.[37] The Radio Gun Squads had larger territories and served as backup on the most serious calls. Typically, four plainclothes detectives and a chauffeur manned a "high pow-ered automobile, with radio, tear gas bombs, sawed-off shotguns, gas masks, night batons and revolvers," as Battle described the ve-hicle. Siren blaring, Battle rode with his men where and when he chose. They made "excellent arrests, also assisted many policemen in trouble," and once took a man into custody after a 2 a.m. gun battle by gangsters associated with Dutch Schultz. The man turned out to be a cop who was working for Schultz. "Much pressure was brought to bear on me that morning to have this policeman released," Battle remembered. He stood his ground, won the cop's conviction—plus a five-hundred-dollar raise.

NEW YORKERS WERE so fed up with crime and corruption that Walker canceled the police department's annual parade. The springtime march of thousands, from which Battle had been barred, would never be revived. Two weeks later, on May 25, 1932, the corruption com-mission called Walker to the stand. "There are three things a man must do alone," he smiled. "Be born, die and testify."

There was a brokerage account to be explained. A company with a city contract had set up the fund and had generated $26,500 in profits for Walker without a penny's investment. The mayor had no credible explanation. There was a second brokerage account to be explained, this one opened by a businessman seeking a subway system contract and producing $247,000 for Walker, again with-out a penny's investment. The mayor had no credible explanation. Nor could Walker charmingly chat his way past a Paris vacation financed by a man to whom he had granted a bus franchise, or the $451,000 his brother had amassed on a $6,500 salary. Walker faced removal from office by Roosevelt in the thick of his first win-ning presidential campaign.

"Jim, you're through," former governor and White House con-tender Al Smith told him.

On September 1, 1932, Walker resigned and sailed with Compton for an extended European stay. Two placeholders then occupied the mayor's office. Who would be police commissioner, the second was asked. "I don't know. They haven't told me yet," he answered.

The power vacuum extended until November 7, 1933, when Fiorello La Guardia, "the Little Flower," as his first name translated from Italian, won election and filled the void to bursting.

THERE WAS NO telling what Battle would meet on leaving for duty. The anxieties of a street cop's wife heightened for Florence as the roll of the murdered grew. Gunfights with holdup men killed Officer Peter De Carlo in Brooklyn, Officer George Gerhard on Manhattan's Upper West Side, and Officer Joseph Burke in Harlem, on Seventh Avenue, two blocks south of Strivers Row. Although the shootings abated in 1933, they extended a long shadow over life.

Danger was equally real for Wesley. Increasingly, misfits filled his company. The department transferred in men who "had bad records or were always in trouble, or men who had no friends political or otherwise," he remembered. None too happy, Wesley's conscripts faced among the city's most challenging firefighting duties. Flammable materials filled the loft buildings that surrounded the station, creating traps prone to smoky blazes and collapse.

Wesley and his men had stood their ground in the cellar of a five-story SoHo loft where fire had broken out between the floor of a restaurant and the basement ceiling. They retreated from the flames when ordered by a chief, regained their breath, and plunged back into the inferno.

Twice, Wesley reached the brink of death. At one fire, he led Company 55 in rescuing four families from a burning tenement. Smoke inhalation killed one of his men and knocked Wesley unconscious. The crew placed an oxygen mask over his face as he lay supine on the sidewalk. Two hours elapsed before he revived. In 1933, the company answered an alarm in a loft building occupied by firms that worked with fabrics. Wesley led seven men to the fourth floor, only to have the blaze come up behind them. Blinded by smoke and choking on the fumes of burning cotton waste, the eight raced to the roof. Several were incapacitated. The sole hope was rescue from below. Wielding hoses and carrying inhalators, squads ascended fire escapes. They administered oxygen before Wesley and his men scaled to safety behind streams of water.[38]

By then, the word was out that Wesley had aced the captain's exam and was sure to get called for promotion, assuming that the fire commissioner was of a mind to grant blessings. Battle heard the news while vacationing over Labor Day. He wrote to his former protégé on September 6, 1933: "It is my earnest desire that you will receive your promotion in the near future. Don't rest on your oars, continue until you have attained the very highest rank as I know that you deserve same. . . . With kindest regards to your dear family and also your good father."[39]

Off duty, Battle maintained the social life of a Harlem burgher. He introduced Etta Cachemaille and Fannie Robinson, Bill's wife, to the police commissioner when they needed a permit for a fund-raising dance. He and Florence hosted several hundred guests for dinner and dancing at a club in celebration of their twenty-eighth wedding anniversary, and they donated a silver cup, the "Battle Trophy," to be awarded to the winners of a bridge tournament.

At home, Carroll had worked his way through high school. He was a popular teenager and had inherited Battle's athleticism. Battle insisted that Carroll would follow Jesse and Charline in earning a college degree, because that was what Sam Battle's children did. Carroll enrolled in New York University, where he played basketball and joined the Rameses Club, a social organization that had hosted a dance for five hundred in Harlem, entertained by Nappy and his Orchestra. Meanwhile, on better psychological footing, Charline was finishing a bachelor's degree in political science. All was in order, and then a young man came calling.[40]

Thornton Cherot was graceful and charming. He moved through a color-ruled world with a light skin tone and European features. On surface inspection, Jim Crow would easily have overlooked the African American lineage handed down to the son of Baldomero Cherot and the former Fanny DuPont.

Baldomero could be traced to Ecuador; he was of Quechua Indian and French extraction. Fanny was likely the descendant of a white grandfather and black grandmother. She appears to be white in a photograph taken later in life. Thornton Cherot was the fourth of Baldomero and Fanny's children. The contributions to Thornton's DNA explain his appearance, while his social place derives from racial strictures. The state of Virginia delineated those, first setting a standard that a person was white unless more than one-quarter black, then lowering the mark to one-sixteenth, and then, in 1924, decreeing that "the term 'white person' shall apply only to the person who has no trace whatsoever of any blood other than Caucasian."[41]

In this era of the "one-drop rule," the four children of Baldomero and Fanny Cherot joined the Great Migration north. By 1930, twenty-two-year-old Thornton had rented a room, or perhaps just a bed, among twenty-one lodgers who shared a townhouse down the block from Battle's.[42] Preferring to be called Eddy rather than Thornton, he found work tap dancing at the Cotton Club and playing semiprofessional baseball.

By family lore, Eddy took an interest in Charline after admiring her legs when he saw her dance. Charline began a relationship with a young man who had a playboy reputation and was estranged from a first wife. Eddy set out to get schooled in chemistry at New York University in hope of embarking on a well-paying career and, perhaps harder, earning his potential father-in-law's respect.

BATTLE'S RANK OF acting lieutenant was a milestone—it made him the first African American to climb that high in the department—but only full lieutenant would suffice. More well-read than ever, richly experienced in policing and welcomed to study at Delehanty's Institute, he was confident that he would ace the lieutenant's exam, and the captain's exam after that, but hard experience had taught him not to go it alone. Aware that the higher he tried to climb, the steeper the climb would be, Battle sought the help of the most-connected friend he knew: Casper Holstein, the numbers baron.

Gambling in Harlem had changed radically in the five years after Holstein's kidnapping. At first, the kings and queens of the industry did business under the threat of Dutch Schultz's ambitions. Then, in 1931, Schultz found the opportunity for a takeover. A common superstition linked the numbers five, two, and seven with Thanksgiving. When five-two-seven came up on the Wednesday before the holiday, the numbers bankers owed more than they could pay. Schultz made an offer they couldn't refuse: he would cover their debts and, in return, take part ownership of their operations. Many agreed, and soon they were no longer his partners. Schultz reduced them to salaried employees.

"So Harlem's numbers business goes back into the hands of a white king after the valiant effort of the Negro bankers to keep the money in Harlem," the *Age* reported in August 1932.

To solidify his hold, Schultz summoned Tammany's Jimmy Hines to his Upper East Side apartment. "I can arm these different bankers in but I can't protect them in the courts, or protect them from the police making raids," Schultz told Hines, using the word "arm" to mean that he could use violence to force the bankers to work for his organization.[43]

Schultz's lieutenant, George Weinberg, told Hines that the gang wanted "to show the people in Harlem that are working for us that we had the right kind of protection up there." He wanted the cops to lay off and the magistrates to dismiss big gambling arrests. Hines's price would be a thousand dollars a week. Schultz paid the first installment and put out word that his operation was untouchable.

African American numbers bosses fought back, none more vigorously than Harlem's fearless policy queen Stephanie St. Clair. Vowing to drive out the white gangsters, St. Clair hired muscle, waged a public relations campaign against the interlopers, and hid from would-be assassins. In February 1933, Schultz called his resistant black operatives to a meeting overseen by machine-gun- and shotgun-bearing gangsters. He announced that he was restructuring the business. No longer would runners move about Harlem taking bets; the players would instead place wagers in central locations like candy stores. Schultz saw profit-boosting efficiencies. His listeners heard a ruthless white man say he was throwing hundreds of African Americans out of work in the teeth of the Depression. Worse, he was tossing them out of Harlem's sole homegrown industry. Twenty independent bankers met to plan resistance.

"Harlem will be the scene of a long drawn out gang war waged on the one side by white racketeers who are determined to continue their domination of the rich takings of the game and on the other side by the Negro bankers who are working hard to exist and to win back for themselves the game which they once controlled," the *Age* predicted.[44]

Sporadic violence broke out. Both sides appealed for support, St. Clair urging the public to spurn Schultz's operation for the sake of black Harlem, and Schultz's forces purporting to offer better-funded, better-protected gambling. St. Clair won the day. Public sentiment turned against Schultz at a time that was, for him, disastrous. Special Prosecutor Thomas Dewey was in relentless pursuit, and, with Prohibition ending at the close of 1933, illicit alcohol revenue was drying up. Schultz had staked his future on the numbers, only to see his take drop as black bettors wagered with black bankers. Starved for cash, he told the so-called controllers who collected bets that he was cutting their percentage of the wagering from 10 percent to 5 percent. In January 1935, the controllers went on strike.

"They were the only people I ever knew who had the nerve to stand up and fight the Dutchman," Schultz's lawyer Richard "Dixie" Davis later said.[45] Within a week, Schultz backed down, hastening a decline that would lead to his gangland execution.

Far more profound, the numbers rebellion represented Harlem's first mass action in pursuit of a tangible goal. Harlem had declared that Harlem's money and Harlem's self-determination were to stay in Harlem. This was a fight of pride and of the pocketbook—and a harbinger of struggles to come.

NO FOOL, HOLSTEIN had receded from prominence in the numbers game by the time he and Battle put their minds to ensuring Battle's promotion. Holstein recruited his old friend Oscar De Priest, now in his fifth year as the first African American elected to Congress in the twentieth century.

De Priest saw La Guardia's mayoral election as a significant opportunity for New York's African Americans. In February, about six weeks after the inauguration, he visited New York to urge Harlem leaders to form a committee that would present the community's needs to the new mayor. When De Priest returned a month later, Holstein welcomed the celebrity congressman into his duplex apartment for an overnight stay. Battle joined the host and his guest, and then, on Saturday, March 17, 1934, the police sergeant and the politician traveled downtown to city hall.

Battle walked up the building's broad steps and through tall doors. Inside, the rotunda where Abraham Lincoln and Ulysses S. Grant had lain in state was quiet. On weekends, the building emptied of politicians, except for a mayor who was storming to the end of his first one hundred days in office.

A police officer escorted Battle and De Priest toward the high-windowed room designated for the city's chief executive. La Guardia sprang from behind a desk piled with reports, correspondence, a pipe ashtray, and a magnifying glass. Battle looked down at a round, rumpled man with jet-black hair. La Guardia was five feet two yet moved with more confident authority than many larger men.

"Oscar," the mayor said, gripping De Priest's hand.

"Fiorello," De Priest responded, his voice warm with affection for the former colleague who had welcomed a black representative to Congress.

Even now, the House enforced segregation. Recently, the Capitol dining room had barred entry to one of De Priest's top aides, and the restaurant had ejected "an educated, refined colored woman who sat down to eat with white friends," the Age reported.[46]

De Priest gestured toward Battle, saying by way of introduction: "Here's a young Negro sergeant on the current list for promotion to lieutenant. I want you to make him a lieutenant, the first among Negroes. You'll be making history for New York and for the country."

A breed apart from all of his predecessors, La Guardia struck Battle as, quite possibly, the mayor to guarantee his promotion.

BORN IN GREENWICH VILLAGE in 1882, La Guardia was the son of immigrants. His father was Achille La Guardia, an Italian of lapsed faith and prodigious musical talent. His mother was Irene Luzzatto-Coen, a woman of Austrian descent who was raised in the Italian culture of Trieste. She was Jewish. Achille La Guardia escaped the teeming lot of New York's ethnic poor by enlisting in the US Army to serve as the chief musician of a regiment stationed in South Dakota. The family followed him there and then to a base near Prescott, Arizona, where Fiorello spent his boyhood in the waning days of the Wild West.

At the outbreak of the Spanish-American War in 1898, Achille prepared to ship out for Cuba to entertain the troops. Sixteen-year-old Fiorello insisted on accompanying his father into the war zone, but tainted beef severely sickened Achille before they could sail. The illness forced Achille's discharge into a civilian life of limited prospect. He returned with his family to Trieste and made a living as a hotel proprietor. Approaching the age of twenty-four, Fiorello sailed back to the United States, attended New York University Law School, and worked as an interpreter of Croatian, Italian, and German on Ellis Island. He also knew Yiddish.

After graduating from law school, La Guardia stood up for tenants against landlords, immigrants threatened with deportation, and workers who had been mistreated by bosses. He picketed on behalf of strikers and joined a political club—a Republican club because he loathed Tammany Hall's corrupt bossism. Soon, social justice activism led to politics, and bare-knuckled politics led in 1916 to winning a seat in the House of Representatives. La Guardia was now New York's unorthodox gentleman from East Harlem.

Wedged between the East River and a rim of Harlem, East Harlem was like its larger neighbor in name alone. An invisible dividing line separated dark skins from lighter ones and Southern-inflected speech from the rhythms of mixed European ancestries. Foreigners and the children of foreigners from two dozen backgrounds, Italians first, Jews second, packed into tenements that were less fit for habitation than Harlem's once-upscale housing stock.

La Guardia carried the straits of his constituents to Washington. He dreamed of milk stations for children, public housing for families, and parks and playgrounds for all, none of which was on the agenda of a government that expected self-sufficiency of the poor. Regardless, he combined a flair for skewering comment and a capacity to outwork virtually anyone to stand in favor of benefits for the downtrodden and against succor for the powerful.

After President Wilson asked Congress for authorization to lead America into World War I, La Guardia enlisted as a lieutenant in the army's nascent aviation unit to fly combat missions over Europe. He returned with the rank of major. Homecoming consigned La Guardia to life in a lonely minority in Congress. When the presidency of New York's Board of Aldermen came open, he escaped an outsider's frustrations in Washington with a campaign heavy on ethnic appeal and bruising statements. "I can outdemagogue the best of demagogues," he told an aide.[47]

Typically, La Guardia made more of the post than anyone had before. As Thomas Kessner chronicled in his authoritative *Fiorello H. La Guardia and the Making of Modern New York*: "La Guardia refused to allow a small office to make an unimportant politician of him." But calling for public housing, supporting labor unions, backing women's rights, and urging progressive taxation was not to the liking of the Republican establishment. The party dumped the renegade at the next turn of the election cycle. Overcoming the additional and devastating blows of the deaths of his wife and infant daughter from tubercular infections, La Guardia engineered a return to Congress. There, he ridiculed Prohibition as unenforceable, railed against Washington's refusal to adopt then-radical policies like unemployment insurance and relief for the poor, and unstintingly attacked Tammany Hall's corruption.

Then came the Depression, and a change in attitudes about government's obligations to citizens in need. Suddenly, the public showed a new willingness to consider for mayor a man who had right to crow, "I told you so." On November 7, 1933, La Guardia secured 42 percent of the vote in a three-way contest, enough to be crowned winner.

New Yorkers soon discovered that everything about their ninety-ninth mayor was full-bodied and frenetic. His words, energy, humor, and temper were outsized. So, too, his optimistic, can-do spirit. Quickly, his whirlwind touched down in Washington and returned from Franklin Roosevelt's newly opened spending bank with enough money to put two hundred thousand New Yorkers to work on public projects.

The Little Flower, yes, a shrinking violet, no—La Guardia capped Inauguration Day, January 1, 1934, by unceremoniously announcing to the Tammany-controlled Board of Aldermen, "In this administration, I'm the majority." Immediately, he embarked on a fight to secure from the boss-dominated state legislature unprecedented powers to reorganize the government and cut costs. He dispatched hard-charging Robert Moses to speedily repair parks, playgrounds, and recreation areas with FDR's funding. And, sporting a black sombrero that harkened to his formative years in Arizona, he dashed about New York inspecting city services. Woe be it to anyone whose work was found wanting.

Of paramount importance to Battle in the opening days of La Guardia's administration was the question of what the volcanic new mayor intended for the police department. On Inauguration Day, La Guardia swore in as commissioner General John O'Ryan, a spit-and-polish World War I commander. Referring to a boundary that supposedly fenced off Lower Manhattan's commercial district from criminals, he also gave marching orders to police commanders: "I have been told that Fulton Street is considered the deadline for crooks. That deadline is now removed. It is replaced by the Hudson River on the west, the Atlantic Ocean on the south, the Westchester County line on the north and the Nassau County line on the east." Referring to organized crime's political connections, La Guardia added: "We are removing that protection. Now see that that kind of crime is ably handled. If not—get out."[48]

O'Ryan's first directives included an edict that, come summer, police officers would continue to patrol in full-dress woolen jackets. "Every member of the department will have to stand up like he-men and take it, and like it," O'Ryan declared. La Guardia soon countermanded the order and began to work his will on the force through Lewis Valentine, the scourge of Tammany Hall whose fortunes had risen and fallen even more violently than Battle's had. Come August, La Guardia would dump O'Ryan to name Valentine commissioner.

Well before that, Battle watched La Guardia stamp the police department with his preferences. The organized crime syndicate had installed some twenty-five thousand slot machines in storefronts across the city, reaping an estimated $37 million in annual revenue. La Guardia hated the one-armed bandits for bilking people who could least afford to lose money. He ordered Valentine to be rid of the devices, led sensational raids, and personally took a sledgehammer to seized machines.

Battle admired the formidable little mayor's grit, and La Guardia was broadly gracious, if noncommittal, at their meeting. Although he generally made sport of spurning special pleaders, La Guardia wished Battle well and encouraged De Priest's plan for a Harlem citizens committee. Then, as quickly as it began, the session was over. La Guardia was not one for small talk and he had no time to spare.

The next night De Priest and La Guardia appeared at a dinner marking the twenty-fifth anniversary of the NAACP's founding. Addressing the celebrants, De Priest called La Guardia "the greatest asset to the NAACP that we have ever had in this city." La Guardia told the gathering that his former House colleagues had an "obsession" with race that bordered on insanity.

Joking that "57 varieties of Negro leaders" had besieged him, La Guardia endorsed forming a committee to serve as his point of contact. Two weeks later, the Harlem Civic Union elected a mayor's panel. The twelve members included A. Phillip Randolph, chief of the Brotherhood of Sleeping Car Porters; Frederick Randolph Moore of the *Age*; Reverend William Lloyd Imes, the minister who had joined Battle's John Brown pilgrimage; and Dr. E. P. Roberts, the physician who had delivered Jesse and Florence D'Angeles and who had signed Florence D'Angeles's death certificate.[49] What more could Battle need? He had the support of America's leading black politician, who was a personal friend of the mayor, as well as the allegiance of the Harlem leaders who were promised the mayor's ear. Likely unique again in the New York Police Department, Battle would have a place on Fiorello La Guardia's agenda. He was sure of it.

THERE WAS A wedding to plan, a church service, and a grand celebration befitting the marriage of Samuel Battle's daughter. The date was set for Charline and Thornton Cherot to exchange vows. Florence took charge of deciding the niceties with Charline—her dress, the reception hall, the favors, the menu, the music. Battle would give Charline away in style.

But first there was a funeral to attend. Shortly before 6 p.m. on April 21, 1934, Battle's dear friend Detective Jimmy Garvey called home to speak with his daughter Helen. For eighteen years he had borne the guilt of believing that he had afflicted her with polio during the 1916 epidemic. That evening Helen wasn't feeling well. Garvey touched base to cheer her up, and they spoke for a good, long time.

"See you later," Helen said before hanging up.

Garvey and his partner, Detective Francis Gleeson, left the stationhouse to patrol Broadway in plainclothes. Around 11 p.m., near the corner of West Seventy-First Street, they spotted two men who seemed excessively watchful.

"We decided to question them," Gleeson would tell investigators. "We thought we could do a better job if we followed the men down a side street rather than stop and question them on Broadway, where a crowd might collect."

Garvey and Gleeson had no way of knowing that they were tailing two hit men who had been brought in from Detroit by Louis "Lepke" Buchalter and Jacob "Gurrah" Shapiro, the top men of the infamous Murder Incorporated killers-for-hire. The target was a double-crossing mobster.

"When the two turned east on 75th Street we decided to close in on them," Gleeson recounted. "Garvey advanced a step or two. He tapped one of the men on the shoulder. He said, 'Hey,' but before he could add anything else the two drew revolvers from under their coats and fired."

Six years later, one of the shooters would say on his deathbed, "We didn't intend to kill cops. We thought they were friends of [the mobster's], so we let them have it."

Shot through the heart, Garvey fell dead on the curb. Gleeson survived chest and head wounds. The next day, Garvey's widow, Pauline, spoke to a newspaper reporter in the family's apartment. Helen, a New York University freshman, was with her.

"Killed on duty." Pauline pondered the phrase. "He was always on duty." Then she said of her husband, "He was always saying that if he had to go before retirement, and that would have been in four more years, he wanted to die in the line of duty—in harness. I don't mean he didn't want to live. I mean, if he had to get it, he wanted it to be that way."[50]

Amid skirling bagpipes, Battle passed down the ranks and into Garvey's parish church for a solemn requiem Mass. Officers in full-dress blues filled the pews. All were agreed: Jimmy Garvey had been a cop's cop and a brave man. For Battle, there was more: Jimmy Garvey had been a brother.

TURNED OUT IN a black tuxedo, white waist jacket, white tie, white gloves, and white carnation, Battle extended an arm to Charline. She took hold at his elbow. The organist played the opening notes of the "Wedding March" from Wagner's *Lohengrin*. All heads turned toward the rear of Mother AME Zion Church. Battle and Charline stepped forward in slow cadence, her matron of honor spreading the long train of Charline's ivory satin gown. Four bridesmaids in powder-blue gowns and picture-book hats followed under a canopy of pink June roses and white peonies.[51]

Thornton Cherot waited at the altar. He too wore a black tuxedo, white waist jacket, tie, gloves, and carnation. A top hat waited nearby to perch at jaunty angle on his head. He had won over Florence completely, and Battle had warmed to a young man who had left behind the early swing of a carefree male. Cherot had secured a divorce from the woman he had married too young in life, and he had completed studies in chemistry at New York University. The NYU credential had enabled Cherot to win a well-paying position as a foreman for a fabric-dying company—the NYU credential plus his light skin. The firm was whites-only. Cherot had felt no obligation to explain the calculus of his bloodlines to its managers. Let them jump to their own conclusion. In the parlance of the day, he was "passing."

No one knows how many people met the mathematical definition of black yet moved through society as white. Walter White, longtime secretary of the NAACP, would estimate that "approximately twelve thousand white-skinned Negroes disappear" from the black census annually. He wrote that virtually every discernibly black American "knows at least one member of the race who is 'passing'—the magic word which means that some Negroes can get by as whites, men and women who have decided that they will be happier and more successful if they flee from the proscription and humiliation which the American color line imposes on them."

Born with light skin, blue eyes, and blond hair, White committed to a black identity as a young teenager while imperiled by white-on-black rioting that swept Atlanta in 1906. "In that instant there opened up within me a great awareness; I knew then who I was," he wrote. "I was a Negro, a human being with an invisible pigmentation which marked me as a person to be hunted, hanged, abused, discriminated against, kept in poverty and ignorance, in order that those whose skin was white would have readily at hand a proof of their superiority, a proof patent and inclusive, accessible to the moron and the idiot as well as to the wise man and the genius."[52]

There were degrees of passing. Some would deny blackness entirely; some would work in the white world and otherwise live in the black. Cherot had chosen the latter course in order to overcome the Depression's narrowed opportunities. Having suffered the trauma of working in hostile company, Battle had to admire the fortitude displayed by his soon-to-be son-in-law in sublimating identity, forced to silently accept an antiblack culture, in order to support family. It was inconceivable that an employer would have given Cherot authority to supervise whites had his racial makeup been known. That, too, Battle understood.

On Mother AME Zion's altar, the Reverend James W. Brown watched the wedding party's approach beside Battle's brother, the Reverend William Battle, pastor of the Columbus AME Zion Church of Boston. This was William D., who had shared Battle's dormitory cot way back when Battle was a redcap and William D. was a Pullman porter. At the appointed spot, Charline handed a bouquet of hanging gardenias and lilies of the valley to her matron of honor. Battle kissed her and then gave the hand of the "pretty born" baby he had wheeled so proudly in her baby carriage to the man who would be her husband. Then Battle slipped into a pew next to Florence. Twenty-nine years earlier, at sixteen years of age, she had kept him waiting for two hours while she shopped for clothing. Then he had married her in the home of the Reverend George Sims. And here she was, in a flowered chiffon gown, in a church filled to overflowing, her two sons in white-tie formal attire; her daughter, a college graduate who was looking forward to a master's degree. They smiled to reminisce, and when the vows were exchanged, the pronouncement was made, and the organist had keyed the recessional with Mendelssohn's "Wedding March," Battle and Florence welcomed five hundred guests to a supper reception at a banquet hall. It was the place to be on this night in Harlem because this was the wedding of Samuel Battle's daughter.

THE LADIES OF Harlem stood up first. The black community had expanded across 125th Street, the prime commercial boulevard. Although departed whites returned to buy clothing and household necessities, the customer base had shifted toward African Americans. Employment had not followed suit. The color line remained drawn at the sales counter.

Women shoppers took note and gave rise to a "Don't Buy Where You Can't Work" campaign. The numbers operators had faced down Dutch Schultz; now, led by the indomitable Effa Manley, the women mapped a drive to boycott stores that limited blacks to menial positions, if that.[53]

Manley was the wife of a numbers runner. A light-skinned woman, she was believed at the time to be the daughter of a black father and white mother. Today, it is generally believed that Manley was the progeny of an extramarital affair between her white mother and a white paramour. Raised among mixed raced siblings who were counted as African American, she maintained an enduring racial allegiance by passing for black. She and her husband would become co-owners of the Newark Eagles of the Negro Baseball League. After her husband's death, she would manage the team and, eventually, would sell the contract of star player Monte Irvin to the New York Giants. In 2006, long after her death, Manley would become the first woman inducted into Major League Baseball's Hall of Fame.

While still in her thirties, she brought the grievances of Harlem's women shoppers to the Reverend John H. Johnson, vicar of St. Martin's Protestant Episcopal Church. She was looking for action. Today, the tactic of applying united public pressure would be taken for granted; in the spring of 1934, it was revolutionary. Society took for granted that employers were free to hire based on race or ethnicity. In Harlem, there was debate about the wisdom of the women's strategy. Some predicted that white-run companies would retaliate by hiring fewer blacks. African American merchants complained they would lose a competitive advantage if white-owned stores put blacks on the payroll.

Enlisting eighteen churches, forty-four fraternal and social organizations, and Frederick Randolph Moore of the *Age*, Johnson convened a mass meeting, out of which emerged the Harlem Citizens League for Fair Play. Participants included Battle's friends the Reverend William Lloyd Imes and Etta Cachemaille, as well as his long-ago whist instructor Arthur Schomburg, who announced: "In years to come, our children will look into our records to see if we have done our part. Do not let them find us lacking."[54]

The Citizens League targeted Blumstein's Department Store, the largest, oldest, and most influential business in the neighborhood. After collecting receipts to document how much the store relied on black shoppers, Johnson led a delegation to meet with proprietor William Blumstein. He stressed that the group wanted Blumstein to hire qualified African American salesclerks of his own choosing without displacing whites presently on the staff.

"Indignantly, Mr. Blumstein stated that he had been in business for many years, knew how to run his business, and would not be dictated to by anyone," Battle recalled.

Backed by the *Age*, the Citizens League set up picket lines. A month of falling sales brought Blumstein's around. The store agreed to hire fifteen African American salespersons immediately and twenty more in several months. Battle and the Citizens League celebrated the victory. To Reverend Johnson's dismay, others then took up a rowdier fight all along 125th Street. The Reverend Adam Clayton Powell Jr., whose father was pastor of Abyssinian Baptist Church, became a force. So too did communist activists, who tapped into Depression-fueled anger. So, too a turbaned figure who went by the street-theater name of Abdul Hamid Sufi and claimed to be Egyptian. Sufi—real name Eugene Brown—demanded jobs for his followers and would come to be called the "Hitler of Harlem" because of the anti-Semitic cast of his rhetoric.

Scuffling broke out between shoppers and picketers. The police department assigned Battle to keep the peace, once again placing him across a divide from fellow Harlem leaders. Although Battle was as deeply committed to the cause as they were, duty required him to enforce disturbance-of-the-peace laws that favored the merchants. The Reverend Powell's wife, Isabelle, challenged him from the picket line:

"Lieutenant Battle, are you going to arrest me for carrying this sign?"

"Not as long as you picket legally. I am here to protect both the pickets and the picketed," he responded.

Battle was less even-handed when answering complaints from the other side.

"Storekeepers would rush from their shops crying, 'Officer, can't you stop this picketing?'" Battle remembered. "More than once I replied, '*You* can stop them by hiring some of them. Your business lives on community money. Haven't these people a right to live, too? I am here to *regulate* the pickets, not stop them.'"

Finally, in a ruling that highlights how limited mass activism was then, a court barred further picketing on the ground that the law permitted only labor unions to picket. Historic in their own right, the demonstrations stopped. Blumstein's failed to live up to its commitments, the color line stayed largely intact—and a fuse was lit.

CHAPTER FIVE

RESPECT

WHILE WAITING FOR Hughes to finish the manuscript's last promised chapter, Battle announces that he's going to take Tony on a drive to the South. Tony hears that he is going and that is all there is to say. When the morning of departure arrives, he climbs into Battle's black Lincoln and heads into a grandfather's past and a grandson's future.

Map points and the names attached to strangers who are somehow attached to him have faded from Tony's memory. Recollections lead to country roads. The big car draws stares as they pass hand-built houses and vegetable patches. Homes overflow with people. Wherever they stop, someone moves out so that Battle and Tony can share a bed. Food is prepared in large, fried portions. Between meals, the little store down the road sells Nehi sodas. In a few weeks, a skinny boy becomes a pudgy one.

On Sundays, there's long, hot church on hard benches. The men dress in jackets and ties; the women wear white dresses and hats and wave paper fans. There is singing and the preacher goes on and on in spiraling repetitions. In private, Battle talks to Tony about the drawling rhythms of his relatives' speech. He orders the boy never to speak with the Southern inflections that confirmed backwardness to white people.

One bit of bustle is New Bern. Battle's hometown now boasts that Caleb Bradham's drugstore was the birthplace of Pepsi-Cola, and it shows off the residences of a society from which African Americans are still largely excluded. The old "Black Second," the congressional

district that sent African Americans to Washington in Battle's boyhood has never done so again.

He moves in a swirl of the childhood memories that Hughes has
rendered on paper. His mind's eye sees an older half-brother, Tom,
who was "wild like myself and *loved* to fight" and who "loved
women and they loved him." He conjures his father whipping him
and his brother John Edward for fist-fighting so much they became
known as "The Battling Battles." He recalls breaking the Sabbath by
"swimming with the melons in the river until they got cold" and then
sitting "on a shady bank to eat their sweet, juicy hearts." He remembers his first sexual experience, at the age of fourteen, with a girl who
worked in the fields picking peas and beans. He looks back on a boy
with a penchant for thievery who learned a life's lesson in a favorite
vignette that Hughes has written into the manuscript in Battle's voice:

One autumn I got a job with a Negro businessman, John Dixon, who
cured and tanned hides. Since I was a grammar school pupil with
more education than his other employees, I was soon entrusted with
paying off his help, counting out the money and recording the sums
paid out in a ledger.

When my father learned I was good at figures, he also trusted
me with keeping his accounts. My father was the treasurer of the
Masonic Lodge in which he held thirty-two degrees. I kept the books
for him.

I also kept small sums of lodge money for myself. Sometimes,
when I could get away with it, I pocketed bits of extra change be-
longing to Mr. Dixon, too. Hating to see money lying idle and not
being spent, also desiring to treat the girls, I pried open my father's
trunk and helped myself to a considerable portion of the lodge
funds. This was soon discovered of course, and I was punished severely—but not cured.

What broke me of my thieving were not the whippings that my
father gave me. For, increasingly severe as they were, they rolled off
my shoulders like water. The cure came from a few bitter words from
an employer that suddenly struck me harder than a switch.

My father's friend, Isaac H. Smith, had given me my first really
responsible job. Mr. Smith had been in the House of Representatives

at Raleigh, being the last Negro Representative in the state before the Red Shirt era came that drove colored men out of politics. Mr. Smith was a real estate man who owned a large building in the heart of New Bern's main business section, Middle Street, directly across from the white Episcopal Church.

One day he drove up in a big open barouche, and he had a white footman, a white coachman—I'd never seen anything like that in the South. He was a big, stout black man, very wealthy, highly intelligent, well liked by everybody.

The front of his building was leased to a white dry goods store, another portion to a Negro shoemaker, John Havens. Mr. Smith's offices were in the rear of the building where he carried on a brisk business, buying and selling houses and lending money to whites as well as Negroes. I became a kind of protégé of his, working in his office at a salary of five dollars a month. Meanwhile, my father aided Mr. Smith in the building of a suburban residential section called Smithtown.

Mr. Smith took a great interest in me because my father was much older than he and had given him excellent advice. The result was, the first month's salary, $5 a month—he made me put this $5 in the bank. He said, "I'm going to start you on a bank account and make you save money every month, and someday I'll have you lending money and buying houses and renting them in your own name, if you stay with me."

Well, I thought this was a good opportunity. But I got real smart—as I thought. I used to open up the offices, and I used to watch Mr. Smith—he had a big, high, yellow safe, about four and a half feet high—and he kept all of his records there, important records. He also kept his hand cash. I used to sit on this high stool adjacent to the safe, and I watched him using the tumblers, and I remembered in my mind the way he turned the tumblers.

When I'd open up the office in the morning, I got so that I could open this safe myself, and I began to pilfer from the safe from time to time—nothing that he would ever miss or anything like that. I thought he had no idea that I would have sense enough to even try to remember or to get into his safe. As a matter of fact, he had a lot of confidence in me.

Later on, however, he began to miss his money. He was smarter than I. He was shrewd, very shrewd. So he made a plant for me. He placed a certain amount of money in this safe where I would naturally find it, and he knew the exact amount that was there. And when he came, he opened this safe and he found that, sure enough, somebody had been there. It couldn't be anyone excepting me.

He accused me of it. I wasn't smart enough to tell a lie about it, and I admitted it was true. He said to me, "If you weren't Tom Battle's son—the son of my good friend—I would put you in jail. But you're young, your life is in front of you, your father is my good friend, and I'm not going to do that."

But he said, "I'm going to discharge you, and I never want you to work for me again." He said, "Young man, before another year rolls over your head you'll be in state prison."

He said that to me. That was the turning point of my life.

My father came—my father prayed and almost cried, because this was his good friend and I'd stolen from his good friend, and his good friend wouldn't have me arrested. The result was that I said to myself:

"From this day on, I shall always be honest and honorable, and I'm going to make Mr. Smith out a liar."

With these and many more memories, Battle drives with Tony to Beaufort, North Carolina. There, they stay with Battle's younger sister Mary Elizabeth. Long ago, after their father's death, Battle had sent money home for the two years of college that enabled Mary Elizabeth to make her mark as a school principal. Mary Elizabeth had taken in Anne after the great fire, and Anne had died there with Battle at her side. They reminisce about Battle's life and talk about the biography that the great Langston Hughes is about to finish; Mary Elizabeth will be part of the story. So will Thomas, and so will Anne. Then they imagine making Battle's life story into a movie. Can you believe it, a movie? Yes, Battle could.

Six decades on, Tony remembers the long car trip with his grandfather as one of the formative experiences of his own life. He sees a boy who had yet to reach the moment when a young African American awakens to racism. W. E. B. Du Bois reached the milestone at ten. A white girl spurned him as classmates exchanged greeting cards and he realized that he was "shut out from their world by a vast veil." Hughes was six when a teacher stopped a white boy from eating licorice sticks, saying, "You don't want to eat these, they'll make you black like Langston. You don't want to be black, do you?"[1] Battle introduced Tony to Jim Crow on the drive, and Tony believes that his grandfather may have taken him to the South for just that purpose.

He remembers a roadside restaurant in Maryland or Virginia. Tony runs inside while Battle parks the Lincoln. There is a sign on the wall. Tony does not understand what it says. He takes a place at the counter. No one notices because he has light skin. The server, a boy, places a glass of water and silverware in front of Tony. Then Battle sits down. The manager, the boy's mother, refuses Battle service.

On discovering that Tony is Battle's grandson, she scolds the boy: "You know better than to serve him." Then Tony hears Battle talk about the United States of America and tell the woman: "I could buy your whole store."

Farther south, Tony recalls an Atlantic Ocean beach. Battle is on his way to visit someone. He gives Tony permission to swim until Battle returns. Tony skips up a ramp, crosses a boardwalk, and skips down a second ramp to the sand. He rides the waves. Then there's a commotion on the boardwalk.

A man in a sheriff's uniform has blocked Battle from going down the ramp. It's a whites-only beach, the uniformed man says. Speaking in a strong, sure voice, Battle explains that he is a retired police officer. The uniformed man refuses to relent.

Finally, Tony sees Duke University in Durham, North Carolina. The campus is quiet for the summer. Battle stops the Lincoln in front of an administration building. He goes inside and returns accompanied by a man who, Tony believes, is the university president. He introduces Tony to the man and introduces the man to Tony. He tells Tony that, one day, he should attend a school like Duke, and then he tells the man, cordially but forcefully, that all-white Duke should admit blacks students like Tony.

*   *   *

ON JANUARY 7, 1935, the last day of his eligibility, ten months after Battle met the mayor, Valentine handed him the blue badge and single gold bar of a New York police lieutenant. The next morning he was "greeted with slaps on the back and warm handclasps" at the Harlem stationhouse, where many of the department's 125 black officers now worked. The *Times* reported that he planned to study for the captain's exam, undeterred by "the prospect of having to meet college men as competitors."[2]

Wesley, too, had moved up. He had made captain in the fire department. There, the roster included only six African Americans. The commissioner assigned three to a firehouse on the Lower East Side. Its captain barred them from a communal table.[3] Battle and Wesley agreed there was a fight to be had—but only after more blacks joined the fire force.

For now, Battle concentrated on his own accomplishment. An article in the *Nation* magazine pleased him most. The author was Oswald Garrison Villard, one of the white activists who had founded the NAACP. Because of the police department's social significance in enforcing the laws, Villard stamped Battle's breakthrough as a milestone in civil rights and said of Wesley, "He, too, was told that he could not last."[4]

Battle took command of the stationhouse at night, mounting the desk as figurehead of the New York Police Department, whose work, La Guardia declared, was not for the faint-hearted.

This mayor was comfortable with nightstick justice. In the month after he met with Battle and De Priest, La Guardia had spoken about Jimmy Garvey's murder to an organization of Catholic cops: "I want you to put so much fear into the heart of every crook in New York that every time he sees a cop he'll tip his hat," the mayor said, adding, "Out where I was raised, we didn't have much of a police department. . . . Our sheriff was quick on the trigger, if you know what I mean."

Valentine had gone further. After observing a well-dressed, finely groomed suspected cop killer in a lineup, the commissioner told his troops: "When you meet such men, draw quickly and shoot accurately. . . . When you meet men like this, don't be afraid to muss 'em up. . . . Blood should be smeared all over that velvet collar. Instead, he looks as though he just came out of a barbershop."

La Guardia was fully in tune after police carted a half-dozen suspected jewel thieves with pummeled faces to headquarters. "When six gangsters meet six policemen and the gangsters are mussed up it's just too bad for them," the mayor said. "We have no room in the police department for sissies."[5]

Battle was still partial to brawling when necessary. He felt the need after a saloon opened in a Strivers Row townhouse, complete with a transvestite review. No fan of the Jitter Bug Club's "parade of she-men and a chap who could do tricky things with an alleged piano," Battle strode into the joint at four in the morning and "turned the place inside out."

"It was a one-man raid, but it was handled as effectively as if it had been done by a squad from headquarters," the *Amsterdam News* reported.[6]

Battle's officers were sporadically brutal and got away with it.

Thomas Aikens had waited on a bread line for three hours before a group of men shoved him aside. Cops ordered Aikens to the back, behind several hundred people. He protested. An officer called Aikens a "smart nigger," and the squad pummeled him unconscious, destroying his left eye. Valentine backed the cops, who were white.

After drinking heavily, Edward Laurie threatened the manager of a Lenox Avenue restaurant. Officer Abraham Zabutinski arrived. Laurie, who was black, took a drunken swing at Zabutinski, who was white. The cop clubbed Laurie, killing him. Valentine ruled that Zabutinski had applied justified force.

When the mother of a Scottsboro Boy came to Harlem, five thousand people showed support for the nine young men wrongfully imprisoned in Alabama for raping two white women. A white police officer provoked an hour-long melee by throwing a tear-gas canister into the crowd. Valentine concluded that the officer had used unjustified force, yet he took no disciplinary action.

Still more grinding on the people of Harlem, the police had little use for civil liberties. A black man in the company of a white woman, or a black woman in the company of a white man, well knew to expect a challenge from a cop. More broadly, police barged without warrants into homes and stopped people on the street to search for gambling slips.[7]

Finally, on March 19, 1935, Harlem had had enough.

That afternoon, Battle rode the subway to Delehanty's to prepare for the captains' exam. While Battle was in class, a brown-skinned, sixteen-year-old Puerto Rican boy named Lino Rivera walked into the S. H. Kress five-and-ten-cent store on 125th Street. A pocket-knife on a counter drew Rivera's fancy. He slipped the trinket into his jacket and headed for the door. From a balcony above the shopping floor, the store manager saw the theft. An assistant blocked Rivera's exit and took the knife.

The two white men struggled with Rivera in front of black customers. Clinging to a pillar, Rivera bit his captors. When they had subdued him, store personnel summoned a cop and called for an ambulance to treat the bite wounds. The cop and the manager brought Rivera to a back room. The manager wanted Rivera released after taking his name and address. The officer agreed. Avoiding a crowd that had gathered out front, the cop escorted Rivera downstairs to leave by a rear basement door.

Then, in the first of three tragic misinterpretations, a woman cried out that the officer had taken "the boy to the basement to beat him up." The rumor quickly spread to the people in the street. An ambulance arrived to care for the men Rivera had bitten, seeming to confirm that Rivera had been brutalized. Then, someone noticed a hearse parked behind the store. When its driver entered Kress's to visit his brother, who worked in the shop, the conclusion seemed obvious: the cop had murdered Rivera. It was "just like down South where they lynch us," a woman said.[8]

A group of men started a public meeting on the corner. Police dispersed them. They assembled again in front of the store. Atop a lamppost, white City College student Harry Gordon fired up the crowd with stories of brutality and victimization. A bottle flew through the air. Kress's plate-glass window shattered. Looters rushed in and, as Battle told Hughes, "the Harlem riot was on."

Inflamed by the belief that police had murdered a black teenager, people massed on 125th Street. Looters smashed storefront windows and made off with what they seized. The police department ordered more than five hundred uniformed cops, two hundred detectives, and fifty radio cars into Harlem. Downtown, Battle left Delehanty's assuming that he was headed for a routine night. He emerged from the subway to find chaos. Inspector John De Martino had command in the stationhouse. Battle had answered to De Martino while leading the division's Radio Gun Squad, and the two men had come to respect each other. Now, Battle assumed the pivotal spot on De Martino's stationhouse desk, relaying reports from the field, booking prisoners, and dispatching reserves as they reported for duty. Suddenly, La Guardia and Valentine burst in.

"What are you doing here on desk duty on a night like this, Lieutenant?" the commissioner asked Battle.

"This is my assignment, Commissioner, according to the chart," Battle answered.

Valentine saw a mission that only Battle could carry out. He wanted his black police lieutenant on the street, where everyone could see him and where, he hoped, Battle could be a calming presence.

"I don't need to tell you what to do," Valentine said. "You know."

Mobs roamed the neighborhood. Bricks, bottles, and flowerpots rained from widows and rooftops. There was sporadic gunfire. Marauders set buildings ablaze. Black merchants posted "Run by COLORED people" signs; white retailers tried to escape damage with signs reading, "This store employs Negro workers."

Battle persuaded saloons and pool halls to close and exhorted cops to distinguish between African Americans who engaged in lawlessness and the much larger number who were bystanders. He ordered "that there be no wholesale clubbing of Negroes."

Battle's pleas had little effect, and sixteen-year-old Lloyd Hobbs paid with his life. Lloyd and his brother Russell had found refuge from the rioting in a movie theater. When the show let out, they approached a crowd in front of an auto parts store. Looters were passing merchandise through a broken window. A police car pulled up. Officer John McInerny jumped out, revolver in hand. The crowd ran. McInerny opened fire. A bullet passed fatally through Lloyd's body.

Police brass set out to locate Lino Rivera in order to prove that the teenager was alive and well. Cops found him at home at two in the morning. Battle paraded Rivera around the streets and posed with him for newspaper photographers. Even then, many refused to believe. They insisted that the police had murdered another teenager—that the cops had forced Rivera to claim falsely that he had been the boy in the store.

Mayhem subsided as dawn approached. By afternoon, Harlem was quiet. After almost twenty-four hours on duty, Battle reported to a stationhouse where La Guardia and Valentine had set up base. Valentine ordered Battle "to remain on outside duty the remainder of the week," by which the commissioner meant that he wanted his lone African American lieutenant to serve as the reviled department's goodwill ambassador to Harlem.

LA GUARDIA APPOINTED a commission to investigate why Harlem had exploded. The panel included Dr. Charles H. Roberts, a black dentist who had run for Congress; Oswald Garrison Villard, the white former newspaper publisher who had celebrated Battle's promotion to lieutenant; A. Philip Randolph, president of the Brotherhood of Sleeping Car Porters, who was approaching victory in his quarter-century fight to win a contract with the Pullman Company; Eunice Carter, the former Fordham Law student who had counseled Charline to study at Hunter College and was now engineering Lucky Luciano's prosecution; and Harlem Renaissance poet Countee Cullen.

This Mayor's Commission on Conditions in Harlem probed employment, housing, health, schools, relief for the poor, and the police department. Civil rights lawyer Arthur Garfield Hays chaired the police inquiry. He summoned Valentine to testify. Valentine refused. Instead, the commissioner ordered surrogates into the lion's den: Battle and De Martino.

Hays held public hearings in a Harlem courtroom and announced that audience members could interrogate police witnesses. "Those colored people had a chance to speak up and to grill the authorities who for years had dealt with them with little sympathy and often with brutality," he recalled in a memoir. "Sometimes the intensity and excitement were reminiscent of a revivalist meeting and the statements of witnesses were greeted with loud 'Amens!' and 'Glory be to the Lord!'"[9]

The chamber was filled to bursting when Battle and De Martino took their places. Battle bore the brunt of the fury. When he spoke of Lino Rivera at the first session, an outcry made clear that many of the four hundred spectators believed Battle was covering up the true murder. City College student Harry Gordon testified that he had been clubbed by a police officer outside the department store and beaten by cops in the stationhouse. As Gordon described their alleged blows, the audience shouted angrily at Battle.[10]

By the commission's final hearing, he was the police department's convenient shield and the crowd's handy sellout. Hays came armed with a letter sent to La Guardia by a Harlem man. He reported that three plainclothes officers had entered his home without a warrant, searched his dresser drawers, bed, suitcases, and china closet and left without a word. A representative of the Citizens League for Fair Play told Hays that cops would simply "pull citizens into hallways and search them for policy numbers."

"That's true!" spectators yelled.

Hays asked anyone who had been searched that way to stand up. Twenty-five people got to their feet. Turning to Battle, Hays asked whether he permitted his men to make such searches.

"No," Battle answered, touching off boos and catcalls.

At that, Hays challenged Battle and De Martino to explain the circumstances under which the law authorized police to enter a home without a warrant. They responded that officers could force entry if they had a reasonable ground to suspect a felony had been committed. Hays read aloud the Penal Code. It clearly limited cops to entering a home without a warrant only if they knew—not just suspected—a felony had taken place.

"You know very well that you would not do it if the person lived on Park Avenue or was someone who was well-known," Hays said.

Then he lectured Battle: "I think that you, as a colored officer in the police department, should charge yourself to see that these things don't happen, especially to your people."

The spectators cheered Hays and jeered Battle.[11]

Hays further pressed Battle on the case of a man who had been jailed for two days based solely on an anonymous—and false—telephone tip that he was wanted for murder. Battle and De Martino

defended the arrest, provoking a new uproar. The commission concluded in its final report that "their interpretation of the law . . . was
not in accord with the statute" and that the "large audience was
justified in shouting that the law was not being applied in connection
with the arrests of Negroes."

Ultimately, the commission reported: "The cases which have been
cited here indicate to what extent the police of Harlem invade the
rights of Negro citizens. This invasion of the rights of Negro citizens involves interference in the association of whites and Negroes,
searching of home without a warrant, and the detention of innocent
men in jail, and even the mutilation and killing of persons upon slight
provocation."[12]

La Guardia withheld the document. Instead, he recruited Harlem
Renaissance scholar Alain Locke to write an appraisal of the findings. Ruefully, Locke recalled the time when "Harlem was full of the
thrill and ferment of sudden progress and prosperity." He found "it
hard to believe that the rosy enthusiasms and hopes of 1925 were
more than bright illusions or a cruelly deceptive mirage." Charitably
accepting La Guardia's expressions of good intent—plus preliminary
steps toward upgrading Harlem Hospital, opening new schools, and
building public housing—Locke endorsed the commission's cata-
logue of discrimination in education, housing, relief, health care, and
employment. He focused on Battle in discussing the police.

After citing the death of Lloyd Hobbs, Locke wrote that "a series
of police shootings in Harlem, continuing down to two quite recent killings of children in the police pursuit of suspected criminals,
has brought the community to the point of dangerous resentment
toward the police." The hostility ran so deep, Locke wrote, that
"many in the Harlem community feel as much resentment toward
Negro police as toward white police, and even toward the Negro
police lieutenant, who sometime back was a popular hero and a
proud community symbol."[13]

THE STING OF Locke's conclusion must have been profound. Fifteen
years later, Battle would tell Hughes about the riot of 1935, while
making scant mention of the hearings. No doubt Battle recognized

Valentine's cynicism in making him the brown-skinned face of the police department after he had served for only eighty-two days as a lieutenant. Certainly, Battle also felt the injustice perpetrated by Hays in placing the burden for correcting police abuses on his shoulders rather than on those of the no-show Valentine and of every member of the white power structure who had allowed Harlem to fester. And, quite surely, with emotions running justifiably high among African Americans, Battle never felt so hurtfully the antiblack guilt by association that came with wearing a police uniform.

ONCE AGAIN, he could only make the most of the black man's straits, and in this circumstance he took advantage of the value that the mayor and police commissioner suddenly found in having a ranking African American cop at their service. After the riot, Battle never returned to a standard assignment. He took on the functions of visible presence and wise leader as the dour 1930s headed blindly toward the genocides and wars of the 1940s.

The department turned naturally to Battle when the Reverend Major J. Divine—the wildly flamboyant Father Divine—asked the police commissioner to assign fifty officers on horseback to escort his annual Easter parade in 1935. Father Divine preached that he was "the written word" who had come "to comfort you, bless you, give you homes for your bodies, rest for your souls, relief from all sorrow." He ran grocery stores, barbershops, and newsstands. Many of his adherents lived in "heavens," where he served lavish meals. He was wildly popular.

Tactfully, Battle informed Father Divine that the department would not call out the cavalry on his behalf. Instead, he marched beside Father Divine's $25,000 Rolls Royce, "while on one running board a beautiful white female angel waved, and on the opposite running board a beautiful brown female angel smiled."

Similarly, City Hall called on Battle when racial tensions split the Democratic Party. Tammany Hall had never nominated an African American to serve as a district leader, partly because of prejudice, partly because black enrollment had never reached a critical mass in any district. But, with Harlem's growth in a district that also included white communities, blacks had gained a shot at a place in the party hierarchy. African American restaurant owner Herbert Bruce stepped forward to challenge a longtime incumbent. Orders came down: Battle was to be on hand when party members convened to elect their leaders.

"The white folks saw that Bruce was about to win and they wanted to walk out and close the meeting," he remembered. "I said to the captain of the precinct, 'Captain, I'm only a lieutenant but I'm sent up here to help you. I want to avoid interracial disturbances, so if I was you, tell them they can't close this meeting."[14]

The captain did as Battle recommended and Bruce broke Tammany Hall's district leader color line.

Shrewder than he once had been and more comfortable in the gray areas, Battle bid farewell when Casper Holstein went to prison on a gambling conviction in 1936 and found useful common ground with Tammany's Jimmy Hines, who would soon be on his way to prison as well.[15]

"Many times when poor people were being dispossessed for lack of rent, many times when poor people didn't have coal or fuel, I went to Jimmy Hines, and Jimmy Hines would call the city marshal and say: 'Come and see me, don't dispossess those people.'" Battle recalled. "He did so many things from the humanitarian standpoint for those people. All those things are overlooked. Of course, we know he had to get the money from somewhere, and where he got it from—well, he suffered for that afterwards."[16]

Battle also forged a deep bond with Inspector John De Martino. When the moment was right, Battle told De Martino a story from his rookie days on the force. He recalled that half a dozen men had pulled up at his post in a car with a police insignia. One of the men had said he was a commissioner, had asked Battle whether he would like to join the detective division, and had ordered him to appear at headquarters. Battle told De Martino that he had done as instructed, only to be turned away, humiliated.

Then he asked a question about which he had long wondered: Had De Martino been one of his tormentors?

De Martino laughed, "You know who it was?"

"I think it was you." Battle smiled. "You were one of them."[17]

De Martino would say no more, and Battle let the matter rest—
no hard feelings toward a man who had become a friend.

AT THE MIDPOINT of the decade, Battle stood proudly with Florence at Carroll's wedding to a fellow New York University student. Edith, whose maiden name was not to be found in either the
census or news accounts, had finished four years of classes and
had graduated. To Battle's displeasure, Carroll had left school after
three years and was setting out to build a future in Washington,
DC. Trying to dissuade him was futile. So, resigned to the ways of
young people who were sure they knew best, the Battles wished the
best for their youngest son and his wife.[18] Battle and Florence were
rapidly approaching the twenty-fifth anniversary of his joining the
force and their thirty-first year of marriage. An *Amsterdam News*
reporter interviewed Florence "among her plants in the yard behind
her home" on Strivers Row. "She is a modest, charming woman—
the sort of woman who strides side by side with her mate over roads
that are built for those unafraid of life," the journalist reported.
"And, you know, he is still studying," Florence said of her husband.
"He hopes to be a captain. Perhaps after he achieves that, we can
have a home in the country where I can have an honest-to-goodness
garden."[19]

Mother AME Zion Church was packed on the afternoon of the anniversary, June 28, 1936. More than eight hundred people rose to their
feet when Battle came forward to speak. "Too often we Negroes have
allowed ourselves to look upon ourselves as an inferior race," Battle
pronounced, adding: "I've lived with you, prayed with you, socialized
and fraternized with you. I've done everything with you, including
arrest you. Make your own opportunities. When you see them, take
hold of them and never give up."

When an interviewer asked about racial prejudice, Battle responded optimistically, "I couldn't conceive of it being wholly
eliminated. But it is gradually decreasing as Negroes are improving
themselves educationally and financially. But we do not seek social
equality. What we want is an equal opportunity to enjoy life and to
make our own way."[20]

*   *   *

GIVEN HIS PROMINENCE in Harlem and his love of sports, boxing most of all, it was all but inevitable that Battle would cross paths with two of the greatest black athletes of the era: Joe Louis and Jesse Owens.

At twenty-one, they called Louis "The Brown Bomber." In the spring of 1935, he donated the proceeds of sparring matches to enable Sam Langford to undergo surgery for a detached retina after a reporter had found the retired champ sitting in a food distribution center, "a fat old fellow in a tattered overcoat and decadent shoes, with a black cap pulled down over his curly gray wool."[21] Louis staged the exhibitions at Harlem's Pioneer Sporting Club. They were great fun to watch for Battle, who was a charter member, as well as for Eddy Cherot, who had played his semipro baseball for Pioneer teams.

On June 25 that year, Louis fought former world champion Primo Carnera at Yankee Stadium. As with any heavyweight bout featuring a black contender, the public transformed man-to-man combat into a racial and political drama. Carnera was Italian and, taken as the personification of dictator Benito Mussolini, was particularly noxious to many African Americans because fascist Italy had invaded Ethiopia. Louis knocked out Carnera in the sixth round. In September, again at Yankee Stadium, Louis dispatched a second former champ, this time sending Max Baer to the canvas in four rounds. Ernest Hemingway described the fight as "the most disgusting public spectacle outside of a public hanging" he had ever seen.[22]

Nine months later, Louis climbed into the ring against Max Schmeling, a German and symbol of Adolf Hitler's doctrines of Aryan superiority. In the second of his autobiographies, *I Wonder as I Wander*, Hughes described how towering a hero Louis was to African Americans, writing that "thousands of colored Americans on relief or W.P.A., and poor, would throng out into the streets all across the land to march and cheer and yell and cry because of Joe's one-man triumphs."[23]

It was taken for granted that, after defeating Schmeling, Louis would next fight for the world championship, because Louis was the better fighter. Unfortunately, Schmeling was the better prepared.

He knocked out Louis in the twelfth, throwing black America into mourning, including Hughes who had watched the fight at the stadium. Afterward, he remembered in his autobiography, "I walked down Seventh Avenue and saw grown men weeping like children, and women sitting on the curbs with their heads in their hands. All across the country that night when the news came that Joe was knocked out, people cried."

Joy soon returned. In August, in Hitler's Germany, Jesse Owens took the 1936 Summer Olympics by storm. Born in Alabama, raised in Cleveland and not yet twenty-three, Owens was the star of a US track-and-field delegation that included outstanding black athletes. He led his fellows onto a pressure-packed world stage. These Games were more than games. The stadium in Berlin was seen as a proving ground for Hitler's master race theories. It wasn't to be. Over a span of seven days, with the future fuehrer looking on, Owens took gold in the one-hundred-meter dash, the two-hundred-meter sprint, the four-by-one hundred-meter relay, and the long jump.

His accomplishments brought the back of white America's hand. The Amateur Athletic Union stripped his amateur status, along with his ability to compete, after Owens declined to participate in fund-raising exhibitions in European cities. Instead, he sailed home on the *Queen Mary*. His father, Henry; his mother, Emma; and his wife, Ruth, traveled from Cleveland to meet the ship in New York. There, four hotels denied them rooms.

The press turned out in force at the *Queen Mary*'s berth. Reporters wanted to find out: Had Hitler snubbed Owens? Owens would say no, but later in life he would say yes. They also wanted to discover whether Owens would cash in on his celebrity. In fact, he had been swamped with money offers—$40,000 to appear in song-and-dance man Eddie Cantor's act, $25,000 to play joke-telling warm-up for a California orchestra. As the *Queen Mary* approached the harbor, Bill Robinson had cabled Owens: "Don't do anything until you see me!"[24]

About to set foot in an overwhelming city, Owens placed his trust in the New York icon. Robinson arranged for police to escort Owens to Robinson's apartment in Harlem, where police stood guard. All day, notables paid their respects, no doubt including Battle, who might well have commanded the security detail. That evening, Owens headed home to Cleveland for a parade. Columbus staged one as well. Then he set up base in Harlem to pursue commercial opportunities. For a time, Carroll Battle remembered, his father welcomed Owens to stay on the top floor of the great old townhouse.

The minister of Owens's church urged President Roosevelt to invite the American victor to visit the White House. FDR demurred. Running for reelection while seeking good relations with the South, the president offered not a word of public recognition. La Guardia stepped into the breach. On September 3, 1936, New York threw a ticker-tape parade for the entire US Olympic team.

Owens and his wife Ruth took pride of place in an open car at the head of the motorcade. The route stretched from the Battery at the foot of Manhattan up Broadway to Harlem and then across the Triborough Bridge to an athletics stadium on Randall's Island. Almost four weeks had passed since Owens had won his fourth medal. By this time, the reception was more curious than passionate—except in Harlem, and there it was mixed. Many a spectator was offended that parade organizers had placed Jack Dempsey in the lead car with Owens. Worse, the organizers had seated the other black Olympians in cars toward the rear of the procession.

"Jesse Owens, Jim Crowed. Jesse Owens, Jim Crowed," some in the crowd chanted.[25]

On Randall's Island, the audience cheered Owens warmly.

"Jesse, on behalf of New York City, I hail you as an American boy," La Guardia said.

Deeply moved, Owens gave the friendliest face in a hostile world—that of Bill Robinson—the first of the gold medals he had won.[26]

Now, Owens needed to earn a living. One by one, the money offers extended to the black phenom evaporated. He accepted a healthy sum to stump for Alf Landon, FDR's doomed Republican challenger. Over the next months, Owens moved in and out of Harlem, accepting fees at promotional events and crossing paths with Battle.

He threw out the first ball in the second game of a Negro National League doubleheader at the Polo Grounds, a portion of whose proceeds benefited Sam Langford. The Pittsburgh Crawfords and the New York Black Yankees took the field, the Crawfords getting the win behind the pitching of the legendary Satchel Paige. "Samuel Battle was on hand in all his regalia directing the police activity," the *Amsterdam News* reported.[27]

Weeks later, Owens served as a starter and Battle as chief marshal at a five-mile footrace that rounded through Harlem, and he addressed the congregation of Battle's Mother AME Zion Church, telling his listeners about thrills they could only imagine, as well as about trials they knew only too well.

ON JULY 16, 1937, Charline gave birth to a girl as "pretty born" as she had been. Charline and Eddy named their daughter Yvonne and brought the baby home to the great old townhouse. Passing for white, Eddy still worked as a textile factory foreman, while Charline had enrolled in Columbia University's Graduate School of Arts and Sciences in pursuit of a master's degree in psychology. She left her studies to tend to Yvonne, along with Florence.

Charline and Eddy invited Bill Robinson and his wife, Fannie, to serve as Yvonne's godparents. The Robinsons accepted and opened a bank account for the infant.[28] Robinson was then at the peak of his popularity. He had played roles in five movies, most notably with child star Shirley Temple in hit films like *Rebecca of Sunnybrook Farm*. Later that year, Battle and Florence drove to Los Angeles to visit Bill and Fannie at their new $65,000 home.

FIRST LADY ELEANOR ROOSEVELT was coming to Harlem. The date was November 7, 1937. The place was the Young Women's Christian Association. Battle was to make sure that all went smoothly. He arrived early at the YWCA. Financed partly by John D. Rockefeller, the building featured a gymnasium, pool, residence for 260 women, and a packed auditorium. The Y had opened the room for a meeting of the National Council of Negro Women.

A stout, ebony-toned woman who carried a cane as an affectation greeted Battle. He saw in Mary McLeod Bethune a most formidable woman. The fifteenth of seventeen children of former slaves, she grew up picking cotton in South Carolina. When her elders recognized her intellectual gifts, they enrolled Bethune in Presbyterian-based education. She excelled, moved on to schools that trained missionaries, and, in 1904, opened a school in Daytona Beach, Florida, "with $1.50, faith in God and five little girls for students."[29]

Stressing "Self-control, Self-respect, Self-reliance and Race Pride," the Daytona Educational and Industrial Training School for Negro Girls grew to offer college and teacher preparation on a twenty-acre campus. Eventually, Bethune merged Daytona Educational with the Cookman Institute to lead a school that developed into today's Bethune-Cookman University.

In 1934, Mrs. Roosevelt invited Bethune to join the staff of the National Youth Administration. She accepted and would eventually become its director of Negro affairs. The post and a growing bond with Mrs. Roosevelt installed Bethune in FDR's so-called Black Cabinet. She spoke frankly to both Roosevelts and, from her first visit to the White House, became known for a singular sense of rightful place. As she walked up the lawn, the sight of a black woman headed toward the main entrance disturbed a gardener.

"Hey there, Auntie, where y'all think you're going?" he called.

Bethune walked up to the man, studied his face, and asked: "I don't recognize you. Which one of my sister's children are you?"[30]

In 1935, Bethune united twenty-nine organizations with eight hundred thousand members under the umbrella of the National Council of Negro Women. She invited Mrs. Roosevelt to address the group's New York chapter. That evening, the First Lady ran late. Dorothy Height was assigned to greet Mrs. Roosevelt at the front door. Newly hired as the Y's assistant executive director, she instructed the receptionists to notify her as soon as Mrs. Roosevelt's car pulled up.

Born in Richmond, Virginia, Height came of age in a working-class, integrated, steel-mill town near Pittsburgh. At the age of eight, she learned that she was a "nigger" in the eyes of her best friend, the blond girl next door. At twelve, the Pittsburgh YWCA barred her from its pool. At fifteen, a Harrisburg hotel denied her a room when she visited the state capital to compete in—and win—the Pennsylvania high school speaking competition. At seventeen, she won a national speech contest, came away with a four-year college scholarship, secured admission to prestigious Barnard College, and was turned away because Barnard had filled its quota of two black students. Instead, Height earned bachelor's and master's degrees at New York University.

Now, she was anxious to flawlessly escort the First Lady from the front door. Mrs. Roosevelt upset those plans. She drove to Harlem in her own car and entered the Y through a service door. Alerted by a janitor, Height intercepted the First Lady and showed her into the auditorium. There, Battle saw how deeply the women adored Mrs. Roosevelt.

The First Lady was a vocal civil rights advocate. In 1934, she hosted an unprecedented White House meeting at which America's black leaders discussed issues of pressing importance, including high unemployment and the low amounts of money provided to schools attended by African American children. She had tea with the Hampton Institute choir and lunch on the patio with the NAACP's Walter White. And nothing resonated more with black America than Mrs. Roosevelt's activism against lynching.

The 1930s brought a resurgence in white-on-black mob killings. Congress took up legislation that would have empowered federal authorities to prosecute local officials who let a lynching pass without prosecution. Mrs. Roosevelt supported the bill; her husband declined to get behind it for fear of alienating powerful Southern members of the House and Senate. Two years later, the First Lady again pressed FDR after particularly savage lynchings gave the legislation new urgency. Again FDR refused to act. The antilynching bill died an ignominious death. Hitler scoffed that Jews were better off in his pre-Holocaust Germany than blacks were in the United States.

Palpable anger swept black America—exempting Mrs. Roosevelt. Fighting the good fight generated the genuine affection for the First Lady that Battle witnessed at the YWCA. When the evening was finished, the audience sang "Let Me Call You Sweetheart" to her.

As Mrs. Roosevelt prepared to leave, Bethune turned to Height. "We need you at the National Council of Negro Women," she said, making a fist to indicate that women should bond against injustice. "The freedom gates are half ajar. We must pry them full open."

Battle spoke quietly to the First Lady. "Mrs. Roosevelt, where are you going from here, and what can I do?" he asked. "I want to know your itinerary."

"Lieutenant, I'm going to Hyde Park," she answered, referring to the family home north of New York City.

"This is night, and you're going to Hyde Park alone?"

"Yes."

"I will get you an escort to Hyde Park, to drive behind you while you drive," Battle said.

"If you'll let your escort just go as far as the parkway with me and get me on the parkway, I'll be all right from there," Mrs. Roosevelt directed.[31]

Battle humored the First Lady. He ordered a contingent of officers to stay with her not just to the parkway but all the way to the city line, and there he arranged for Westchester police to follow her home unseen.

For Height, the evening's event marked the start of a life of civil rights activism. Drawn into Bethune's "dazzling orbit of people in power and people in poverty," she would serve as president of the National Council of Negro Women from 1957 to 1997, would be the only woman on the dais when the Reverend Martin Luther King Jr. delivered the "I Have a Dream" speech to the 1963 March on Washington, would be honored with both the Presidential Medal of Freedom and the Congressional Gold Medal, would be on the dais at President Barack Obama's first inauguration, and would be lionized by Obama as "the godmother of the civil rights movement" on her death at the age of ninety-eight in 2010.[32]

For Battle, the night's consequences were less sweeping and more personal. He had started a relationship with Eleanor Roosevelt that he would come to treasure.

WITH RANK AND recognition came the opportunity to keep making a difference for the race.

In 1938, Battle joined a fight to integrate the Baltimore Police Department. For almost a decade, the local black-oriented newspaper, the *Afro-American*, had railed that governors, mayors, and police commissioners had maintained an all-white force.

Finally, Republican governor Harry Nice promised to integrate the department. When action was slow in coming, black Republican power broker Marse Calloway helped organize training that would prepare African Americans to take the civil service hiring test. Numerous blacks enrolled. As they were completing the course, Governor Nice wrote to La Guardia, asking that Battle be sent to address the class.

La Guardia granted permission for Battle to make the trip, advising Valentine, "He is going into unfriendly territory and I repeat must make a good showing, guarding against being a 'Show-Off.' We will help him with it."[33]

Black leaders scheduled a rally at Baltimore's Bethel AME Church. On the stage, Battle rose to offer his seat to Governor Nice, but "Marse Callaway said, 'Don't move, Lieutenant Battle. You are the guest speaker here. The governor is only incidental. Let him sit on your left.' So that is where he sat."

Battle recounted his history and described the service of fellow black officers. Local leaders spoke and the audience signed petitions to the governor, mayor of Baltimore, and police commissioner.

"The very next day, for the first time, several Negroes took the examinations for the police force. And it was not too long before two plainclothes men and a Negro policewoman were appointed," Battle recalled.

His satisfaction at helping to push Baltimore toward equal opportunity gave way that summer to the thrill of Wesley's elevation from captain of a single firehouse to battalion chief overseeing half a dozen companies, each led by a captain and lieutenants and staffed by a total of almost two hundred men. The milestone produced a delicious moral victory. As battalion chief, Wesley had charge of a fire company that was led by a captain named O'Toole. Way back at the start, this same O'Toole had tried to humiliate Wesley by asking why his commanding officer would have anything to do with "that nigger" and urging that Wesley be driven from the force.

When Wesley won promotion to lieutenant, O'Toole's brother John had walked out, pulling strings to get a new assignment. Now, after serving under Wesley at a single fire, Captain O'Toole retired in order to escape taking further orders from a black man.

THE FIRE DEPARTMENT was changing. In 1936, the New York State legislature had reduced the standard workweek from eighty-four hours to forty-eight and had given the department three years to hire large numbers of firefighters. Propelled by the Depression, African Americans had stepped forward to brave the hostility that ruled firehouses. The number of blacks on the force rose from four to twenty at the end of 1937 and to more than fifty in 1940. Some fire companies required African American members to sleep in Jim Crow beds. Silence prevailed except in the line of duty. Lieutenants assigned blacks to porterlike duties, such as cleaning toilets and tending firehouse furnaces.

Wesley visited captains of the offending firehouses to urge fair treatment. When the captains ignored him, Battle and the Reverend John H. Johnson, who had helped orchestrate the "Don't Buy Where You Can't Work" campaign and who had been sworn in by La Guardia as a police chaplain, agreed that Wesley should organize New York's fifty-plus black firefighters into an advocacy group similar to the police department's Guardians Society.

The effort proved difficult. Some firefighters objected that joining a blacks-only organization would amount to self-segregation. Some worried about career-ending retaliation. Some were assigned to companies where they were fairly treated and saw no need to organize. Wesley told the reluctant warriors: "There will be a Negro fireman organization even if it ends up that I am the only member in it."

Soon, he knit the men into a unit. In 1940, he founded the Vulcans, naming the organization after the Roman god of fire. When, finally, the commissioner recognized the society, Wesley presented a benign and unthreatening list of objectives. They included reducing fire deaths, developing good fellowship among members, promoting athletics, studying fire department regulations, and providing a death benefit to members' families. There was not a word about demanding equal rights, but that would come.[34]

* * *

MOST POLICE OFFICERS looked forward to retirement and a pension as they approached thirty years on the job. Not Battle. He was no ordinary lieutenant. His duties as La Guardia's troubleshooter were unique.

In February 1940, tension mounted in Harlem after two white cops shot to death a black fellow officer. They were responding to a burglary in the building where John Holt lived with his wife and three young sons. A neighbor summoned Holt to capture the thief. Holt left his apartment in civilian clothes. Jumping to the conclusion that he was the burglar, the responding officers opened fire. The authorities deemed Holt's death accidental. It fell to Battle to explain the circumstances in the hope of defusing beliefs that the white officers had executed Holt. Battle led the funeral procession. La Guardia joined the march, as did Wesley, who was active with the fire department's basketball team and had known Holt as a competitor on the police squad.[35]

Four months later, in June 1940, the NAACP invited La Guardia to speak at its annual convention. The mayor flew with Battle to Philadelphia, happy to have a well-known symbol of fairer treatment as his side. The six-day conference called for integrating the US military, passage of federal antilynching legislation, and abolition of the color line in federal employment.[36]

Overseas, Hitler had conquered Denmark, Norway, Holland, Belgium, and France, just as he had earlier taken Austria, Czechoslovakia, and Poland, and just as Mussolini had invaded Ethiopia. The NAACP voted a resolution in support of people "who have been enslaved in the labor armies of Germany and Italy whose governments are functioning on the basis of a master race." The delegates also awarded the NAACP's highest honor, the Spingarn Medal, to Battle's Strivers Row neighbor Dr. Louis T. Wright. Much lauded at the convention, Battle returned to New York proud of both his performance on a national stage and his stature with La Guardia.

* * *

IN JUNE 1941, he was ringside when Joe Louis, who had come back in 1938 to knock out Max Schmeling in one round, faced a title challenge from light heavyweight Billy Conn. Louis and Conn met at the Polo Grounds. Battle escorted Louis from his dressing room to the ring and stayed at the champ's corner to watch the fight.

Conn had the better of Louis for twelve rounds. The smaller man seemed likely to win, but in the thirteenth, trying too hard for a knockout, he gave Louis the opening he needed to send Conn to the canvas.

"I lost my head and a million bucks," he told reporters after the fight.

Speaking with Hughes, Battle filled in what had happened at ringside, suggesting that he had played a decisive role in Louis's victory:

> During the fight and between rounds, I rested on the knees of Harry Ballou, the announcer. One of the fans nearby yelled to Conn: "Kill the Nigger." I was near the fan and in full uniform. I called to him: "You are a fine sport." Others nearby voiced the same sentiment.
>
> Conn was like a will-o-the-wisp and Joe was not able to catch up with him. He was ahead on points. The crowd yelled to Conn: "Stay away from him." Realizing that Conn had out-pointed Joe up to that time, I whispered to Jack Blackburn, his trainer, and also to John Roxborough, one of his managers, that I thought Joe was losing the fight. Blackburn whispered something into Joe's ear. When Joe entered the thirteenth round he acted groggy and weak. Conn rushed him. Joe delivered a left uppercut and right cross and down Conn went for the count.

THAT NOVEMBER AN all-black football team sponsored by Battle and fellow Harlem sports enthusiasts took the field in the Polo Grounds to compete against an all-white squad. The white players earned wages as members of a professional team that was called the New York Yankees, although it was unrelated to the baseball organization. For this game, they played under the banner of the Yankee All Stars. The black team consisted largely of young men who had been college football standouts and was dubbed the Colored All Stars.

The game drew 22,800 spectators who had never seen interracial competition on this scale. Walking amid the African American squad, which narrowly lost 24 to 20, Battle encountered Kenny Washington, who had shined for four years as a running back for the Bruins of the University of California at Los Angeles.[37] Nearby he saw Woody Strode, a tall decathlete who was renowned for his physique and who had been a great wide receiver on the same Bruins team.

Washington and Strode would break the National Football League's color line five years hence by signing with the Los Angeles Rams. Washington would then go on to work as a police officer and Strode to an acting career, costarring with John Wayne in *The Man Who Shot Liberty Valence*, with Burt Lancaster in *The Professionals*, and with Kirk Douglas in *Spartacus*.

Washington and Strode had been celebrated as members of the 1939 Bruins' "Gold Dust Trio." Their third comrade had been by far UCLA's best running back—perhaps the best running back in all of college football. He was a quiet man, slightly distant. He extended a hand to Battle. His name was Jackie Robinson.

FIVE YEARS OF selling shoes was all that Carroll could stomach. He had taken up the work after moving to Washington with his wife, Edith, who had found employment as a waitress, and he had continued in the trade after returning to New York for an apartment in Brooklyn's new black community, Bedford-Stuyvesant. It was a living—but the pay was poor, chances for advancement were slim, and measuring feet wore on the spirit of an outgoing twenty-five-year-old athlete. Carroll wanted more.

Having witnessed the trials that Battle had overcome through the eyes of a young son, he now appreciated his father's courage from the perspective of a man who was roughly the age Battle had been when breaking the police department's color line. Carroll also admired Wesley for embarking on his own brave struggle at an even younger age. The exploits of both men had opened doors that were there for him to walk through. He spoke with his father. Battle responded that he would be happy were Carroll to join either the police or fire department—for the salary, for the respect, for the betterment of the race. Battle envisioned passing the torch so that the men of a new black generation would carry on the fight. Carroll chose the fire department. Wesley was delighted. He had known Carroll ever since Carroll had taken his first breaths with a touch of old Mrs. Wagner's gin on his lips. He was sure that Carroll had the physical, mental, and emotional qualities to win appointment and to succeed in the roughest of environments. So, coached by Wesley, Carroll scored well on the fire department exam and was called for appointment. In 1941, three decades after his father had weathered exile in the flag loft, Carroll took hold of Battle's torch on a force that still insisted on "black beds."

THAT YEAR, 1941, Battle crossed paths again with Mrs. Roosevelt. The First Lady was on hand for the dedication of a new branch library. Battle made sure to be there. She remembered him. They chatted. She stood at his side to have their picture taken.

EVER MORE DEVOTED to Florence, Battle threw a surprise birthday party for her at a Seventh Avenue club. Attire was formal. The menu for the one hundred guests included filet mignon and ice cream molded in flower designs. An eight-piece Cotton Club orchestra entertained with swing music, supplemented by a quartet that played sentimental tunes. Battle had the cake topped with sixteen candles in remembrance of Florence's age on the day they had married.[38]

Charline and Eddy broke the news that Charline was pregnant again. Florence had eased Charline's return to master's degree studies at Columbia by helping to care for Yvonne. Now, Florence tended to the new needs of her daughter and three-year-old granddaughter. On January 8, 1941, Charline gave birth to the boy for whom Battle would be a lifetime influence. They named the baby Thornton Cherot, after his father. They called him Tony.

A REVERED MAN died on the night of June 2, 1941. Pride of the Yankees during the team's most fabled era, Lou Gehrig had meant the world to New York. They called him the Iron Horse for playing in 2,130 straight games. He put muscle into the "Murderers Row" of the legendary 1927 Yanks, chasing Babe Ruth's sixty home runs with forty-seven of his own. He racked up a lifetime batting average of .340, knocked in an average of 147 runs a season in his thirteen full seasons, and set the record for career grand slams. Moving from a partnership with Ruth to one with Joe DiMaggio, Gehrig was a constant as the Yankees built a spirit-lifting World Series–winning dynasty and the United States emerged from the Depression.

Then, in 1939, he stayed on the bench at his own insistence. After months of subtle deterioration, his athletic body was weaker and less responsive than the body of a major league player had to be. He was suffering from amyotrophic lateral sclerosis, the fatal neurodegenerative condition that came to be called Lou Gehrig's disease.

The Yankees announced his retirement on June 21, 1939, and declared that July 4 would be Lou Gehrig Day at the stadium. There, after numerous tributes, he delivered an address for the ages, beginning with the famous words: "Fans, for the past two weeks you have been reading about the bad break I got. Yet today I consider myself the luckiest man on the face of the earth."

Soon after, La Guardia appointed the dying Gehrig to an honored position. He had been born in East Harlem. He had completed a year at Columbia University in an entering class whose members had included Hughes. He was an idol to the young. The Yankee great was ideally suited to serve on New York City's Parole Commission, whose mission included steering youthful prisoners in the municipal jail into productive freedom. Gehrig fulfilled the role superbly until the disease forced a leave of absence. He never returned to work. On June 3, 1941, New Yorkers awoke to the news of Gehrig's death. La Guardia mourned with the city and turned to the task of naming someone to assume Gehrig's duties.

He chose Battle.

While he was "loath to leave" the police department, Battle could hardly decline an opportunity to achieve another first for the race. La Guardia said that he had selected Battle because he was the best man for the job, not because he was black. Battle credited the sentiment, even as the mayor added of Battle: "He knows all the children of

Harlem from the time of their birth and has been very active in social work in addition to his police duties."[39]

Battle saw different racial implications. "I shall try to conduct myself so that this job may be perpetuated for a colored man, and that greater rewards will not be denied us because of anything that I may do during my term," he promised.

Speaking on the *Wings Over Jordan*, a groundbreaking nationally syndicated radio show that featured gospel choir music and interviews with notable African Americans, Battle told listeners: "The Negro must be better qualified and do a better job than the white man, to compete. Then, if you render service, it means more service and better service in order to always keep advancing. The reward for service is more service. That is reward beyond glory and power."

Battle inherited Gehrig's secretary, "an estimable white woman" who reported "that she had been asked if she wished to continue as secretary to a Negro as commissioner." He became good friends with Margaret Kelly.

"My office was a corner one with large windows through which I could hear the cooing of pigeons and the sounds of traffic below," he remembered, adding, "In the pulsing heart of the greatest city in the world, I sat at my desk and studied many of the problems of its less fortunate ones."

DECEMBER 7, 1941. Pearl Harbor. The Day of Infamy. World War II came to the United States, came to Harlem, and came to the great old townhouse.

A quarter-century had passed since Battle had helped found the regiment that became the Harlem Hellfighters and had marched with Needham Roberts in a spectacular parade, the two walking beside the car carrying Henry Johnson, who wore the *Croix de Guerre avec Palme*. Then, so many believed that the unit had earned America's respect for the race and that everything would be different for New Negroes.

Hopes had, of course, been dashed.

Harlem was more crowded than ever. From 1930 to 1940, the city's black population climbed by 131,000, pushing the total complement toward a half-million. Fully 40 percent were on relief or making due with temporary jobs.[40] Most of the city's workplaces remained closed. Worse, industries supplying the British in hope of repelling Hitler's air assault had hired whites while shutting out blacks. "We have not had a Negro working in 25 years and do not plan to start now," North American Aviation informed the Urban League.[41]

The color line was as rigidly enforced in the military. Secretary of War Henry Stimson wrote in 1940 that segregation "has been proven satisfactory over a long period of years and to make changes would produce situations destructive to morale and detrimental to the preparations for national defense." Separately, he elaborated that "colored troops do very well under white officers but every time we try to lift them a little beyond where they can go, disaster and confusion follows."[42]

Hearing echoes of the Third Reich's doctrine of Aryan superiority, black leaders grew more militant. The NAACP's Walter White and A. Philip Randolph, president of the Brotherhood of Sleeping Car Porters, planned an unprecedented mass action: a march on Washington. Eleanor Roosevelt and La Guardia attempted to dissuade them at a meeting in New York's city hall. But after White described the abuses suffered by blacks, the First Lady promised: "I will get in touch with my husband immediately because I think you are right."

In June 1941, White and Randolph went to the White House. Face-to-face with Roosevelt, they said the march was set. White remembered:

> The President turned to me and asked, "Walter, how many people will *really* march?"
>
> I told him no less than one hundred thousand. The President looked me full in the eye for a long time in an obvious effort to find out if I were bluffing or exaggerating. Eventually he appeared to believe that I meant what I said.
>
> "What do you want me to do?" he asked.[43]

One week later, Roosevelt issued an executive order barring defense contractors from discrimination in hiring and training, but he left military segregation intact. Some two hundred thirty thousand strong, the peacetime armed forces included fewer than five thousand blacks, and a lone African American general. The navy limited blacks to serving as messmen. The Marines were all white. Even blood donations were segregated. The military reserved plasma refined from African American blood donors for black recipients, never for whites. It made no difference that an African American doctor, Charles Drew, had recently perfected the science necessary to create blood banks.

Still, after the United States went to war against Japan and Germany, African Americans joined the rush to serve. Many were inspired by the first American hero of World War II, Dorie Miller, who was black. The twenty-two-year-old son of a Texas sharecropper, Miller labored as a messman on the USS *West Virginia* at Pearl Harbor. As torpedoes tore at the ship, he carried its mortally wounded captain to safety and got behind an anti-aircraft gun. Then he helped rescue crewmembers before abandoning ship as the *West Virginia* sank. He would die on Thanksgiving Day 1943 in the sinking of the *Liscome Bay*, still a messman.

Humiliation, abuse, and violence emanated from the towns that surrounded military bases. In early 1942, servicemen from Harlem became embroiled in clashes that killed six blacks at camps Claiborne and Livingston in Louisiana. Riots erupted at camps in California, Mississippi, Texas, Kentucky, and Arkansas. Using the pen name, "A Disgusted Negro Trooper," a serviceman wrote to the *Cleveland Call and Post*: "The conditions for a Negro soldier down here is [sic] unbearable and the morale of the boys is very low! Now right at this moment the woods surrounding the camp are swarming with Louisiana hoagies armed with rifles and shot guns even the little kids have 22 cal. rifles and B & B guns filled with anxiety to shoot a Negro soldier."[44]

Battle supported the war effort with typical gusto. During World War I, he had won a commendation for selling war bonds. Now he led numerous fund-raising drives. With Commissioner Valentine's approval, he also allied with the Urban League and Kenneth Clark, the psychologist whose research would one day be crucial to the US Supreme Court's dismantling of separate but equal in *Brown v. Board of Education*. Together, they prepared two hundred African Americans to take the police exam to fill in for officers who went overseas. To do his own part for public safety, Battle assumed the rank of lieutenant colonel in an auxiliary force called the New York City Police Corps.

La Guardia called regularly on his parole commissioner for special duties. In June 1942, Greece's King George II visited New York City to drum up support for his conquered nation. The mayor asked Battle and Florence to join the city's delegation at a Waldorf Astoria Hotel banquet. Still more stirring, that month, La Guardia assigned Battle to escort to city hall Mrs. Conery Miller, sharecropper mother of Pearl Harbor hero Dorie Miller, when she arrived in New York to be honored at a Harlem rally.

The war built toward its bloody crescendo. Japanese forces drove seventy-two thousand troops on the Bataan death march. Lieutenant Colonel Jimmy Doolittle made the first bombing raids on Japan, and US troops landed on Guadalcanal. The Americans and British invaded North Africa, while the Germans retreated from a winter assault on Moscow. In 1943, the Royal Air Force and the US Eighth Air Force began round-the-clock bombing of Germany.

To Florence and Battle, it seemed only a matter of time before Carroll, draft age at twenty-six, would be called to duty. They took respite in Eddy and Charline's purchase of the cottage in Greenwood Forest Farm. Yvonne, now six, and Tony, now two, would have all the space in the world for play. Florence would have the summer garden she longed for. And, much as on Strivers Row, the Battles would join a community of notables. Yvonne's young playmates included the daughter of legendary bandleader Cab Calloway.[45]

In the spring of 1943, Eleanor Roosevelt planned to again visit Harlem, this time to raise money for Mary McLeod Bethune's Bethune-Cookman College. Battle looked forward to once more speaking with the First Lady. Taking command, he organized the American Women's Voluntary Services, City Patrol, and Boy Scouts into an honor guard, complete with a drum major corps. He had become a familiar face to Mrs. Roosevelt. She congratulated him on his new stature as parole commissioner and then made an indelible impression on his spirit.

This was the day on which he saw the First Lady pour the glass of ice water.

The temperature that May 2 topped out at almost seventy degrees. Four thousand people filled the Golden Gate Ballroom. Religious and civic leaders delivered tributes to Bethune. Roland Hayes, a tenor, performed. Mrs. Roosevelt's address made clear her affection for Bethune, along with her belief in equal rights.[46] The heavyset, sixty-eight-year-old civil rights leader then took the podium. When she appeared to be burdened by the heat, the First Lady brought the glass of water.

"I said: 'This is democracy in action; the wife of the President of the United States pouring a glass of ice water for a Negro woman who's real black—she's black as a black shoe—and handing it to her and she was drinking it,'" Battle would recall almost two decades later.

"I think that Mrs. Roosevelt is the grandest woman living today," he added. "She's the most outstanding woman in the world."

AMERICA STARTED A replay of the Red Summer of 1919.

On May 24, white-on-black rioting broke out after the segregated Alabama Dry Dock and Shipbuilding Company in Mobile, Alabama, promoted twelve blacks among its thirty thousand employees to work as welders. In early June, confrontations between Mexican residents of Los Angeles and servicemen on leave produced more than four days of pitched street battles. In June, in Beaumont, Texas, an eighteen-year-old telephone operator accused a black man of rape. Police shot the man to death. They said he had resisted arrest. Ten days later, a second woman reported that a black man had raped her. Although the woman failed to identify a suspect, as many as four thousand people converged on city hall, dispersed in mobs and ransacked black-owned businesses and homes.

Then came Detroit.

Expanding defense plants drew tens of thousands of blacks to a city physically unprepared for the influx. Competition for housing grew fierce. The federal government chose two sites for residential construction, one for blacks, one for whites. Plans called for locating the Sojourner Truth Homes in an all-white neighborhood. Protesting whites burned a cross in a nearby field. Only the protection of more than twenty-five hundred police officers and National Guardsmen enabled six African American families to take residence. In June 1943, in keeping with FDR's executive order, the Packard Motor Car Company promoted three blacks to work on an assembly line that produced bomber engines. Twenty-five thousand white workers walked off the job, one announcing over a loudspeaker, "I'd rather see Hitler and Hirohito win than work next to a nigger."

On a warm Saturday evening three weeks later, a car accident on Belle Isle, a recreation area in the Detroit River, triggered a dispute. An African American man was said to have insulted a white sailor's girlfriend. Groups of blacks and whites squared off, and the fighting crossed the river into the city. The violence intensified with a false rumor that a white mob had thrown a black mother and children into the river. A second false rumor enraged whites. They took as truth a claim that blacks had raped and murdered a white woman. Racial warfare gripped Detroit for three days. The mayor and governor dithered in bringing police and federal troops to bear. When finally they took action, the violence had killed thirty-four people, including twenty-five blacks, most of them slain by the police.

NEW YORK WAS on edge. Frederick Randolph Moore published front-page photographs of blacks who had been beaten by whites. The *Amsterdam News* blared, "Hell Breaks Loose in Eight Cities," referring to Detroit, Beaumont, and Los Angeles, plus confrontations in Chicago; El Paso, Texas; Inkster, Michigan; Chester, Pennsylvania; and Collins, Mississippi.[47]

La Guardia urged New Yorkers to remain calm. "If any white man provokes or instigates assaults against a Negro group, I will protect the Negro group and prosecute the white man," the mayor pledged.[48]

La Guardia had special concerns because his normally good relationship with New York's black community had become strained. The police had shuttered the Savoy Ballroom, a landmark Harlem nightspot. Many believed the cops had responded to complaints about interracial dancing. Far worse, La Guardia had selected the Metropolitan Life Insurance Company to develop an apartment complex on Manhattan's East Side that is today the bedrock community Stuyvesant Town. Metropolitan Life had a hundred thousand policyholders in Harlem, employed virtually no blacks, and had announced that the housing would be open only to whites.

With anger running high, the NAACP's Walter White traveled to Detroit to investigate the uprising. La Guardia sent Deputy Chief Inspector Edward Butler, who was white, and Battle's old friend Lieutenant Emmanuel Kline, the seventh African American to have joined the force. They reported back that the Detroit police had, in effect, "encouraged the whites and had made the Negroes feel that they had no protection."

La Guardia then summoned leaders including White, Battle, and the Reverend Johnson to Gracie Mansion, the mayoral residence, to draw plans for avoiding a riot and for responding should violence break out. There was agreement that the police should show restraint. Police officers would patrol in pairs and be accompanied by superior officers. No one would fire tear gas except as a last measure. Bars would be closed. Pawnshops that sold guns would be guarded. Police would protect passengers in buses and cars. Battle and White "both warned of the mounting emotional tension over the highly publicized mistreatment of Negro soldiers, and that any manhandling of colored men in uniform might quickly be interpreted as racial if the officers involved were white."

A drumbeat of hostility toward black servicemen picked up. On July 17, the headline of the *Age* front page read "Negro Soldiers in Two States Seize Guns, Use Them in Protest Against Treatment; One Killed, 7 Injured."

Then, Battle's prophecy to La Guardia came true. Drawing on his recollections, Hughes wrote:

On August 1, 1943, a white policeman in Harlem shot a Negro soldier in the back. Within an hour, the second race riot in the history of Harlem was in progress. The shooting happened in the lobby of the Braddock Hotel, just down the street from the stage door of the Apollo Theater on West 126th Street in Harlem. That night a woman and a man got into an argument in the lobby. The desk clerk called a patrolman. The patrolman attempted to restrain the woman and pull her away from the man. A Negro soldier, seeing a white officer maltreating, as he thought, a colored woman, remonstrated with the officer, who resented his interference.

Some say the soldier tried to pull the policeman away from the woman, others say not. Some say the soldier wrested the policeman's nightstick from him, struck him, and then ran. At any rate, the policeman fired as the soldier turned away, and the bullet struck him in the shoulder. Just as in the 1935 riots where the crowd spread a rumor that a colored boy had been beaten to death, and it was not true, so in this case the rumor went over Harlem that a white officer had killed a colored soldier for no good reason—had shot him in the back.

This was not correct either. The soldier did not die. In fact, he was only slightly wounded. But before anyone knew this, mobs had surged into the streets, remembering all the black soldiers who had been shot, beaten, intimidated, and Jim Crowed all during the war up to that time. The mobs remembered, too, the beatings Harlem itself had taken through the long years of the Depression. They recalled more recently the names given Harlem in the newspapers of New York—"*Black belt,*" "*muggers,*" "*dangerous.*" A great many folks evidently thought they might as well become dangerous. So they did.

Crowds surrounded the Braddock Hotel and the Twenty-Eighth Precinct stationhouse. Some threatened to kill the officer who had shot the soldier. La Guardia arrived to confer with Valentine. They flooded Harlem with cops. Valentine issued orders that grew out of La Guardia's Gracie Mansion meeting: officers were to protect property, but they were to use deadly force only in response to mortal danger. White arrived at the stationhouse. La Guardia said they would tour the area in a police car. Fearing terrible repercussions if the mayor were to be injured, White said he would sit beside the window with La Guardia in the middle seat. La Guardia refused the offer. "They know my face better than yours," he told White, "so you sit in the middle seat."

As they drove, White saw that "wild eyed men and women, whose poverty was pathetically obvious in their shabbiness, roamed the streets, screaming imprecations." A brick crashed through a storefront window. A fire broke out.

"Heedless of his own safety, La Guardia jumped from the car and screamed at the crowd before the building," White would recall. "I doubt that in the excitement the Mayor was recognized, but such was the fury with which he lashed out at the marauders that his moral indignation shamed and quieted the crowd, which rapidly dispersed."[49]

Another time with La Guardia, White witnessed a scene that broke his heart. He wrote in a memoir:

> I remember especially a toothless old woman in front of a grocery store who moved about the edge of a crowd which had just smashed a store window. In one hand she clutched two grimy pillow cases which apparently she had snatched from the bed in which she had been sleeping. With the other hand she held the arm of a fourteen- or fifteen-year-old boy, possibly a grandson. The minute an opening appeared in the crowd the old woman, with an agility surprising in one of her age and emaciated appearance, climbed through the broken glass into the store window to fill the pillow cases with canned goods and cereals which lay in scattered disorder. When the bags were filled she turned toward the street and looked toward the police car in which La Guardia and I were sitting. Exultation, vengeance, the supreme satisfaction of having secured food for a few days, lighted her face, and then I looked at the sleepy-eyed child by her side. I felt nausea that an abundant society like America's could so degrade and starve a human being, and I was equally sickened to contemplate the kind of man the boy would become under such conditions.[50]

Shortly after 1 a.m., La Guardia made the first of five radio broadcasts appealing for calm. At 1:30, mayoral aides reached Battle at Greenwood Forest Farms. Racing along the highways, he reached Harlem shortly before 3 a.m. and discovered that "the shops along 125th Street were a shambles."

"Because of my handling of the 1935 riot, I was given carte blanche, to take whatever action I deemed wise," he said, adding, "The police had orders not to shoot, so the mobs paid them little mind. They scattered at a raised nightstick or the approach of a mounted cop only to reform again further down the street."

Finally, Battle issued an unprecedented order directly to the mayor of New York City and to White. "Although the head of the strongest organization in the world for the protection of racial rights, the NAACP," White "was himself so light in complexion that he looked like a white man," Battle told Hughes. "I requested both him and La Guardia to go home. I asked: 'Walter, you and the mayor are both too white to be riding around Harlem on a night like this. Neither of you are an asset to calming things down. The fewer white faces in evidence, the better, until order is restored.' They left."

The mayhem abated at dawn. Detroit's upheaval had extended for thirty hours and spread across the city; Harlem's had lasted twelve hours and had been contained to the community. Thirty-four had died in Detroit; twenty-five at the hands of police. Six had lost their lives in Harlem; four of them shot by cops. Two officers had acted in clear self-defense. One cop had killed two fleeing looters in apparent violation of orders. La Guardia's leadership won wide praise.

Eleanor Roosevelt wrote to La Guardia. She had heard from many about the need for additional African American officers and she had gotten to know Battle as a nearly solitary example of black police leadership. She advised the mayor that, with deeper black ranks "there might not be such instances as the past regrettable one."

La Guardia responded petulantly. He told the First Lady he was beset "by agitators and selfish people or by thoughtless and well-meaning people." He minimized the degree of police brutality and defended the department's efforts to recruit blacks. He followed up the next day, telling Mrs. Roosevelt that Harlem residents had complained that black officers were "too rough," and explaining that the department had 155 African American members, including 6 sergeants, a police surgeon, and a parole commissioner—the retired Battle.

"Commissioner Valentine would take one hundred right now if he could get them," La Guardia wrote, blaming the war for difficulty in recruiting African Americans. Left unsaid were two numbers: First, the department had been adding black officers at the rate of only five a year in the three decades since Battle's appointment. Second, the force should have employed one thousand African Americans if the proportion of blacks in the department equaled the proportion of blacks in the city's population.

A FEW WEEKS LATER, Battle and Florence faced the inevitable. On August 25, 1943, Carroll took leave from the fire department to enlist in the US Army, committed to go where he was called in service of a country at war, the country of the Thirteenth, Fourteenth, and Fifteenth amendments. Battle could not help but remember the little boy who had come home on the handlebars of police officers' bicycles. Florence remembered the thirteen-year-old who had made the honor roll in class 8B-1 of junior high. Everyone knew someone who had gone to duty in the Pacific or Europe. Everyone seemed also to know someone who had fallen in the line of duty. Charline, Eddy, big brother Jesse, and Carroll's wife, Edith, could only hope for the best. The war had already exacted a toll on Jesse. Too old for active duty, he had taken a job in a defense plant and had lost a thumb pulling a man out of a machine in an industrial accident. Battle embraced Carroll and placed his son's fate in the Lord's hands, just as Thomas had done for the son who had left home at the age of sixteen, never again to see his father alive or dead.

AS WITH MOST aspects of life in New York, corruption held sway behind bars. State institutions like Sing Sing confined the most serious offenders. City penitentiaries held inmates convicted of crimes that carried shorter sentences. The primary one housed sixteen hundred men behind quarried stone on Welfare Island in the East River. The jail was ruled by gangsters Joseph Rao and Edward Cleary. The crime bosses lived comfortably in hospital dormitories, Rao favoring silk shirts and expensive cigars, Cleary tending to a pet dog named Screw Hater. They made their livings importing narcotics via carrier pigeons. Shortly after La Guardia became mayor, his correction commissioner staged a naval assault to reclaim the jail. In the ensuing investigation, two former prisoners swore that well-connected inmates had advised purchasing paroles through Battle's nemesis-turned-benefactor,

Jimmy Hines.[51] The parole commission chairman insisted that political influence played no role in any of the board's actions. When La
Guardia named Battle a decade later, the same man was still chairman. Whether or not he had ever been corrupt, cash could enter the
picture as inmates sought to buy release from behind bars. Battle told
Hughes of spurning the occasional dirty deal: "Once in a while I was
offered money to use my influence in releasing prisoners, sometimes
innocently and sometimes with knowingly unlawful intention of
bribery. One Italian mother who scarcely spoke English, desperately
anxious for the release of her son, threw herself on her knees in front
of my desk, weeping and begging me to take a roll of bills she pulled
from her purse if only I could hasten the freedom of her boy. I gently
refused, and explained to her as clearly and simply as I could how
our laws and regulations work."

In a more sinister case, the family of a man convicted of "the in-
decent handling of young girls" used political channels to offer Battle
cash for a favorable ruling on a quick release from prison. "When I
refused this offer, some of the politicians of his district told me in no
uncertain terms that they would see to it that I got nowhere should I
ever attempt to run for political office," Battle told Hughes, adding
that he ignored the threat and kept the man behind bars.

Battle also gave Hughes a nutshell description of how he identified prisoners meriting release. "My function on the parole board,
as I saw it, was to assist in the rehabilitation of those who have, in
varying degrees, outraged society," he said. "This could not be done
justly, I felt, without duly considering those very essential factors
which establish the odds for or against an offender's rehabilitation,
and to find the factors one had to look well into his past life."

When La Guardia appointed Gehrig and then Battle, Executive
Director David Dressler of the state division of parole doubted the
mayor had chosen wisely. He later came to believe that Battle "made
up the real backbone of the Municipal Parole Commission."[52]

THE ARMY SENT Carroll for basic training at Camp Claiborne in Louisiana. Notorious to black Americans, the base was both segregated

and in the heart of Jim Crow South. The indignities of even a New York City firehouse paled in comparison with the hostile caste structure of the nearby town of Alexandria. In 1942, the black press reported that three thousand African American troops had rioted there. While the circumstances and toll were unconfirmed, the *Amsterdam News* front page informed the Battles: "Six Soldiers Reported Killed in Dixie Rioting."

Frightening and outrageous news arrived steadily. When Private James Smart died in the Camp Claiborne hospital, the commander shipped his flag-draped casket home to Union Springs, Alabama. He provided Smart's mother with a first-class railroad ticket, allowing her to accompany her son's body. The trip required changing trains at Monroe, Louisiana. There, a conductor separated mother and son, limiting her to a Jim Crow coach and giving her a receipt for a refund of the difference between the cost of first-class and Jim Crow travel. Despite legal representation by future US Supreme Court Justice Thurgood Marshall, three black Camp Claiborne soldiers were sentenced to hang for the alleged rape of a white woman. When nine sick Camp Claiborne soldiers were transported to a distant hospital, they made an overnight stop in Texas, near a base that was beginning to house German prisoners of war. One of the nine described what happened in a letter to the *Pittsburgh Courier*:

> The only place that would serve us was the lunch room at the station. But we couldn't eat where the white people were eating. To do that would contaminate the very air of the place, so we had to go to the kitchen.
>
> About 11:30 the same morning, about two dozen German prisoners of war came to the lunchroom with two guards. They entered the large room, sat at the table. Their meals were served them. They smoked and had a swell time.
>
> There they sat; eating, talking laughing, smoking. They were ENEMIES of our country, people sworn to destroy all the so-called democratic governments of the world. And there we were. Men sworn to fight, to give our lives for this country, but WE were not good enough to sit in the lunchroom.[53]

Battle did what he could: with twenty-five other Harlem residents, he sent a telegram of protest to President Roosevelt:

> We learn that white soldiers brought back from overseas for recreation and relief from battle are to be given approximately two weeks each at government expense at luxurious hotels and resorts at Lake Placid, Santa Barbara, Hot Springs, Miami Beach, Ashville, and perhaps other pleasure places. But Negro soldiers are to be required to go to the Theresa Hotel in New York's Harlem and Pershing Hotel on Chicago's South Side. Such a plan is a reprehensible act which is an insult to Negroes buried in foreign soil, having died in the belief that they were fighting for democracy.

SIX MONTHS INTO his training, Carroll came home on his only leave— home to his wife, Edith; home to Jesse; home to Charline, Eddy, and their two children; home to Battle and Florence. College-educated, athletically gifted, trained as a firefighter, Carroll had done well among his black comrades. He had already made corporal. The family bid Carroll farewell with a party in the great old townhouse. He returned to Camp Claiborne as a stepping-off point for Europe.[54]

LIFE WAS CHANGING for Wesley as well. After twenty-two years of often heroic service, he requested a transfer from the Hell's Acres of Lower Manhattan to a battalion headquarters closer to his home in the Bronx. He cited in his application to Commissioner Patrick Walsh: "Serious nervous illness of my wife and the fact that all of the children have married and there is no one at home with her at the present time."

"It is a 44 mile round trip from my residence to work," Wesley noted. "Also this is my first and only request for a transfer in close on to 23 years of service." When Walsh gave no break to the new leader of the Vulcans, Wesley turned for help, ever so politely, to an old friend of his father's from the glory days of Grand Central Station— former New York governor and presidential candidate Al Smith.

"Should you be kind enough to bring this to the attention of our very humane and just Commissioner Patrick Walsh, I am sure that he will do it if it is possible," Wesley wrote.

Six months later Wesley renewed his request. Finally, Walsh approved a transfer to an area that had far fewer serious fires and placed Wesley close to his wife of twenty-seven years.[55] The duties were easier, but the department's racial degradations became ever more severe.

IN 1944, WHITE firefighters up through the hierarchy united to stop the department's black ranks, small as they were, from growing. A captain newly assigned to Harlem established Jim Crow beds for his few African American firefighters. Propelled by the insult to the heart of black America, Wesley and the Vulcans planned the then-radical act of picketing. When word reached City Hall, La Guardia ordered the captain transferred. The Vulcans stood down only to see a different captain install Jim Crow beds in a Lower Manhattan firehouse. This time the Vulcans appealed for La Guardia's help in a tellingly unsigned letter. The writer begged the mayor's pardon by stating: "Anonymity is usually associated with a cowardly attack, but it should be obvious that were I to sign my name to this letter, life would be made so intolerable for me that it would be impossible to continue in the Department." A month later, the unnamed writer reported to La Guardia that the captain had ordered a lieutenant in charge of yet another company "to adopt similar 'Jim Crow' tactics."[56]

To Wesley's disappointment, the mayor appeared to take no action. With segregation proliferating, he pushed the Vulcans into a public stand. Years later he would recall that, as a senior battalion chief, he was largely impervious to retaliation, while others faced severe jeopardy. "It took courage for the young colored fireman who was just starting his career. With a family to think of, he had everything to lose should he have been dismissed from the department," Wesley would say.

As a first step, he led a six-man committee to notify Commissioner Walsh that the Vulcans had voted unanimously to seek a meeting with the mayor "regarding certain flagrantly undemocratic practices of racial discrimination in some firehouses." The committee reported that the department would assign no more than three African Americans to a single company in order to maintain segregated beds. Company leaders often posted the names of black firefighters on specific bunks. The committee also reported that the Vulcans had compiled a list of every firehouse with Jim Crow beds, offering three examples as evidence.[57]

When Walsh agreed to meet with the Vulcans, Wesley, accompanied by an NAACP lawyer, opened the discussions. Walsh signaled both cooperation and exasperation, telling Wesley, "I do not know why God made colored people but I guess he knew what he was doing." Meanwhile, white firefighters pressured La Guardia to close his door to the group. Wesley responded by asking a prominent black judge to intercede with the mayor. He wrote: "The fact that (white opponents) so far have been successful in preventing our group from seeing the Mayor has caused the opposition to take greater courage and become more brazen than ever. In fact to such an extent that instead of the condition (Jim Crow beds) remaining static or improving for the better, it has become worse and is right now spreading to other companies in the department."[58]

The firefighters union president, a man named Kane, promised Walsh that union members would pass a resolution permitting any firefighter to select with whom he would rotate a bed when shifts changed. What Kane didn't know was that his delegates included an African American who had passed for white and who had kept the Vulcans informed about union strategy.

The spy revealed that Kane planned to extend the meeting long into the night so that everyone but his loyalists would drift away. Then he would introduce and pass the resolution. Wesley rallied the Vulcans to stay for as long as the meeting lasted and, more important, he enlisted the help of his battalion aide-de-camp, who happened to be Jewish. The aide spread a rumor that the union planned to apply Jim Crow rules to Jews. Jewish firefighters turned out in force. Together, the blacks and Jews not only defeated the union resolution but passed one of their own, which Wesley described as "an emancipation proclamation for we Negroes in the fire department."

The impact was minimal. When La Guardia continued to demur and Walsh failed to order full integration and equal treatment, Wesley enlisted Councilman Benjamin J. Davis—a graduate of Amherst College and Harvard Law School and the only African American member of the municipal legislature—to convene a hearing into the Vulcans' complaints. On December 14, 1944, Wesley led a delegation into a City Hall showdown. With fire department brass seated along one wall and the Vulcans facing them across the chamber, Wesley testified that the department's sixty-seven black firefighters were assigned to twenty-six firehouses. Twenty of the companies had imposed segregated sleeping arrangements, he said. He told of beds screened off and of beds beside the toilets. He told of communal tables that were closed to African Americans and of companies that prohibited African Americans from sharing spare helmets and equipment when necessary. Davis urged the council's City Affairs Committee to launch an investigation to substantiate Wesley's testimony. His white fellow councilmen refused. Instead, they voted to give the fire department time to make reforms, thereby avoiding a politically explosive confrontation and perpetuating a racial structure that many accepted as the natural order.[59]

Still, Wesley counted the very fact of a public hearing as a victory. Soon enough, he faced bitter reality. Ten months later, he outlined worsening abuses for the Reverend Adam Clayton Powell Jr., who had now been elected to Congress. He told Powell: "The Negro firemen of the New York Fire Department are in hopes that some courageous person will help us."[60] In truth, Jim Crow beds and commissaries were only the most visible representation of the department's hostility. More insidiously, commanding officers barred African Americans from driving rigs and serving as hook-and-ladder tillermen. Central administrators excluded blacks from working as building inspectors, turning away even a graduate of the Brooklyn Polytechnic Institute. The medical office marked the files of black firefighters with a "C" and provided segregated services. All too predictably, the brass excluded African Americans from parades.

Progress came in painfully slow increments, in large measure because La Guardia, who spoke from the heart about racial equality, accepted the prejudices of his fellow white citizens as a fact of political life. His biographer Kessner wrote: "Many of the plain New Yorkers whose cause he championed were biased against blacks. They were not prejudiced in the same way as some of the southern bigots who participated in lynch mobs and straight-out violence, but rather in a way that was more insidious. They would deny blacks a job, refuse to live near them, view them as inferior human beings, and deny their children equal opportunities. As mayor, La Guardia worked with such people, understood them, did not think that they were necessarily evil, and sometimes compromised with them."[61]

La Guardia's mayoral successors similarly accommodated the racial animus that prevailed in the firehouses—so much so that more than half a century later, blacks would compose no more than 3 percent of the fire force.

In April 1944, the newspapers carried brief accounts of the death of Casper Holstein at the age of sixty-four. He had been released from prison, had lived in near poverty, and had suffered a stroke. For two years, a man named Alverstone Smothergill had cared for Holstein in Smothergill's apartment. The papers described Smothergill as having once been a beneficiary of Holstein's generosity. A few other grateful beneficiaries paid for a funeral and for a gravesite, which kept Holstein's body from burial in a pauper's grave. Battle was one of the few people who attended the service for a man who had given so much to so many, who had helped propel the fleeting cultural Renaissance, and who had been so easily forgotten so quickly.[62]

THE WAR TOOK Carroll to the beach at Normandy on D-Day and then on the long hard march across France and into Germany in a segregated unit attached to Patton's Third Army. Battle and Florence could only pray they would never get a knock on the door. After being delayed by her duties as a mother, Charline finally graduated from Columbia University's Graduate School of Arts and Sciences with a master's degree in psychology. She enrolled Yvonne and Tony in private schools in Lower Manhattan that offered superior educations, first the Little Red Schoolhouse for kindergarten, then City and Country, whose faculty included music teacher Pete Seeger. Battle began to work with Eddy and Charline to expand the cottage at Greenwood Forest Farm. Carroll came home from the war as a top sergeant of an outfit that had fought in the decisive Battle of the Bulge. He was invited to take a staff job in the fire commissioner's office, but he preferred the excitement of responding to fires in a hook-and-ladder crew.

AT MIDNIGHT ON December 31, 1945, La Guardia's third and final term came to a close. A far different man followed Battle's great mayoral patron into office. William O'Dwyer had arrived in New York as an Irish immigrant boy with twenty-four dollars in his pocket. He had worked as a grocer's clerk, coal shoveler, plasterer's helper, bartender, and police officer during the heyday of Tammany rule. Then he had gone on to become a lawyer and Brooklyn district attorney before realizing his mayoral ambitions, despite a history clouded by apparent favors to organized crime figures.

Still, Battle mixed high admiration for La Guardia with optimism about his successor. He viewed O'Dwyer as a friend from the past. While accounts of O'Dwyer's police career focus on his pounding a beat in Brooklyn, Battle recalled that O'Dwyer "knew me very well, because I helped to break him in" as a patrolman in Harlem.[63] When O'Dwyer named Battle to serve on a commission that would plan the fiftieth anniversary celebration of the consolidation of the cities of Brooklyn and New York into Greater New York, Battle proudly foresaw building a close relationship with yet another mayor.

WESLEY NEARED THE end of his third decade on the fire force. One day in 1949, he sat outside his battalion headquarters in the Bronx. As he would later recall, a chauffeur-driven Cadillac pulled up. A distinguished looking white man stepped out.

"Do you remember me?" the man asked.

When Wesley answered no, the man introduced himself as Dick Dawson, sat beside Wesley on an empty chair, and "cried like a baby." Dawson had been among the firefighters who had conspired to drive Wesley out of the department at the start of his career. He had been among those who had asked for transfers on the ground that they refused to work with a "nigger." He had also been the first man to leave the company when the commissioner's one-year ban on transfers had expired. Dawson told Wesley that he had eventually left the fire department and had grown wealthy as a real estate investor.

"He said he had everything to make him happy but one thing and that it was on his conscience as to how he had treated me those thirty years back. And would I forgive him? That was the only thing that marred his complete happiness. I said, 'Forget about it. I certainly forgive you.'"

"He asked me if there was anything that I needed or that he could do for me and I told him, 'No, thank you.' The man left with tears in his eyes."

AN AIDE TO Mayor O'Dwyer, a black man, made an appointment to see Battle. He showed up with a Democratic elected official, who also was black. Battle knew both men well. He expected nothing untoward. Then his visitors said they were emissaries of a white Tammany Hall district leader who wanted a horseracing bookmaker released from a thirty-six-month sentence. They said Battle "would do all of them a favor. I would not lose anything by it." Warily, Battle agreed to look into the case. After the emissaries left, he determined that the bookie was connected to a notorious gambling ring and ruled out taking "such a despicable case before the board for review." Returning to apply pressure, the elected official was even more explicit.

"This white leader insisted that I do something for this man," Battle wrote. "If I didn't, I would be sorry someday. On the other hand, I would be rewarded."

Well used to the security of mayoral favor, Battle rejected the demand out of hand: "I sent word by this politician to the white leader that this case stinks to high heaven."

Case closed—or so he thought.

IN APRIL 1948, seventy-year-old Bill "Bojangles" Robinson danced in front of an audience that included Milton Berle, Henny Youngman, and Irving Berlin and then collapsed backstage at the Copacabana nightclub. Although he had suffered a heart attack, he refused to stop dancing. Nor did he stop gambling or consuming a gallon of vanilla ice cream daily. After another coronary, Robinson died on November 25, 1949. Battle and a group of the dancer's friends gathered at the Delmonico Hotel, in a room rented by Ed Sullivan, the *New York Daily News* theater writer who had just launched a variety show on the new medium of television, a program that would become one of the most successful ever. Robinson's friends planned a grand sendoff.

The funeral was to be held at Reverend Adam Clayton Powell Jr.'s Abyssinian Baptist Church, but Battle felt the house of worship would be too small to accommodate the masses who would want to pay respects. He arranged for Robinson's body to lie in state in the cavernous 369th Regiment Armory. An estimated fifty thousand people filed by a flower-bedecked bier, Robinson in a blue suit and white shirt, the foot of his casket draped with the American flag.

Three thousand people filled the Abyssinian Church for the funeral. The honorary pallbearers included Bob Hope, Duke Ellington, Louis B. Mayer, Cole Porter, Joe Louis, and Jackie Robinson. At Battle's suggestion, Mayor O'Dwyer excused Harlem's children from school so they could line the route of the funeral procession. In the church vestibule, Battle chatted with O'Dwyer, the Reverend Powell, and Battle's friend the Reverend John H. Johnson. The mayor offered a surprise.

"Sam, I am going to reappoint you to the parole commission when your term expires and you don't have to have anyone come to see me about it," O'Dwyer pledged, relieving Battle of a growing anxiety. His term as commissioner would be finished on January 4, 1950. Remembering all the support he had needed for advancement in the past, Battle was just beginning to strategize about the backing he should bring to bear on O'Dwyer. Now, in the presence of the ministers, Battle thanked O'Dwyer and sat through the funeral with a mix of grief and happiness. He saw more to do in public service, and—who knew?—perhaps he could do more for the race.

In his eulogy, Powell told the congregation: "Bill wasn't a credit to his race, meaning the Negro race, Bill was a credit to the human race. He was not a great Negro dancer, he was the world's greatest dancer. . . . Somewhere, I know not where, but I know it is some-where, Bill says, 'Copacetic!'"[64]

Outside, Battle marched behind the hearse and dozens of flower cars for a full five miles to New York's theater district where "beautiful girls, white and colored, of the theatre appeared with tributes of flowers. A choir sang. And all of Broadway paused to pay tribute to the memory of one of its great ones gone."

Then, at home, recounting his conversation with the mayor, Battle told Florence that all was copacetic.

But he was wrong. O'Dwyer appointed another man. Once more, Battle felt the fool for having placed his trust in a white politician. Once more, he sought an explanation for the betrayal. His mind went back to the parole commission's corrupt currents, to the politicians who had pushed him to release the man who had abused young girls, to the emissaries who had threatened reprisals if he refused to free the gambling ring bookmaker—and he knew that, without La Guardia's protection and with O'Dwyer's connivance, the forces that had once sent him into exile in Canarsie had done him in again.

Out of work for the first time since he had left home at the age of sixteen, and no longer a man of official standing, Battle sought resurrection. The police department had numerous deputy commissioners, as many as seven. After six months on the sidelines, he secured an audience with O'Dwyer. The mayor now promised to make Battle New York City's first black deputy police commissioner.

"I went away happy to our summer home," Battle wrote.[65] Yet, knowing better than to trust O'Dwyer, he confided only in Florence. After an apprehensive month, the announcement was made: rather than naming Battle, O'Dwyer chose his mayoral chauffeur, who was also a police detective. The appointment boosted the detective's $5,150 annual salary to $8,000 and making him eligible for a $6,000-a-year pension—for which he quickly filed. The appointment was nothing more than a going-away gift to a friend, one later rescinded by a court. A police scandal dating to O'Dwyer's days as Brooklyn district attorney was about to chase him from City Hall. President Harry Truman came to the rescue by naming O'Dwyer US ambassador to Mexico.

Vincent Impellitieri took over as mayor. Soon, City Hall let it be known that Impellitieri planned to name an African American deputy commissioner. Battle pressed for the appointment. When he visited Sugar Ray Robinson's training camp with Tony, the boxer gave Battle "the solemn promise that he would recommend and support me for deputy police commissioner to his friend Mayor Impellitieri." It wasn't enough. Impellitieri instead chose Billy Rowe, a writer for the *Pittsburgh Courier* who had been a war correspondent in the South Pacific and had been present on the USS *Missouri* at Japan's formal surrender. In his handwritten notes, Battle called "Billy" a friend, adding, "Anyone would have been glad of the appointment."[66]

At that, the four-decade career that had started in hostile silence, carnival debasement, and isolation under the flag of the United States of America was over. Having refused to play ball, Battle wrote proudly: "I would rather have honesty and character than prestige and wealth. I can walk and ride the streets of this city, hold my head up, look all men in the face."[67]

CHAPTER SIX

FORGOTTEN

SHORTLY BEFORE MIDNIGHT on August 9, 1952, Hughes finishes the final draft of the book they've called *Battle of Harlem*. He and Battle each sign the manuscript. The eighty thousand words go out to publishers. In quick succession, Simon and Schuster, Henry Holt, and John Day decline to take it on. They have good reason. Relying heavily on Battle's own words, Hughes has vividly brought to life Battle's coming of age, his Northern ramblings, his courage in breaking the color line, and the brutality that followed. But as Battle's career progresses on the page, Hughes's finely realized vignettes give way to rambling chapters. In one, titled "Leisure Time," Battle meanders for almost five thousand words through parole board records, membership in the Elks, the racial unfairness of general circulation newspapers, ideas for reducing juvenile delinquency, segregation in Harlem movie theatres, the births of his children, and more. Throughout the last half of the manuscript, people enter and leave the story briefly and without context. Important events are half realized. Then, too, there is hardly a market for a book that, properly told, would chronicle the prevailing racism of the day.

Battle is proud to have started with little and to have risen higher in his life than most white men, regardless of the color of his skin. He remembers being told that if he failed, his failure would be taken as proof of the black man's inferiority. He knows that he performed better than the white men around him, because that was a black man's only shot at succeeding. And he knows that he proved wrong all those who damned the race. He wants that story told. He wants to hold in his hands the autobiography of Samuel Jesse Battle, to see it on a shelf in the library, to give a copy to Tony. He wants to watch the movie that was to be made, and he wants his neighbors and New York and all of America to watch the film. But after three years of grudging labor, Battle is left to swallow a bitter pill and move on.

WITH TIME ON his hands, Battle became even more involved in civic and fraternal organizations like the New York Urban League. The family also opened a liquor store in Harlem, a privilege generally secured by political connections. Happy to leave behind the racism of his workplace, Eddy quit the fabric company to manage the business. Carroll, who had returned to the fire department after the war, helped out, while continuing to serve on a hook-and-ladder company. Battle stopped by the shop regularly to keep things in order. As had happened so often ever since he had gone to work at Grand Central, Chief Williams may have shown Battle the way: his family had earlier established a liquor store in the community.

For several winters Battle took Florence to the Caribbean. In Jamaica, "our names were announced at the airport over the loud speaker: 'Commissioner and Mrs. Samuel J. Battle of New York,'" he remembered. In Haiti, Carl Murphy, editor of the *Afro-American*, Baltimore's black-oriented newspaper, introduced the Battles to the US ambassador. On a third trip, they sailed to the Dominican Republic, Cuba, and then to Miami where "we met segregation and discrimination under the Stars and Stripes."

On June 28, 1955, Battle and Florence "had journeyed along together for fifty years." Two hundred guests celebrated their golden wedding anniversary at a dinner party in a banquet room of the Park-Sheraton Hotel. "My beautiful wife was dressed in a magnificent gold cloth gown," Battle reminisced, adding, "This was easily the most elaborate and happy affair of our lives."

As a gift, Battle took Florence on a cruise to Europe aboard the *Ile de France* ocean liner. They visited London, Paris, Geneva, Florence,

Venice, and Rome. At the Vatican, he secured a certificate signed by Pope Pius XII. They gambled at Cannes. They toured Waterloo. A few months later, Battle and Florence returned to Paris, this time because he represented the Harlem branch of the Young Men's Christian Association at a centennial celebration of the YMCA's world alliance. The eighth-grade dropout was proud to say that he participated in a workshop at the Sorbonne.

From spring through fall, Battle became devoted to the cottage at Greenwood Forest Farms. He sat in the sun on an Adirondack chair, sometimes passing an afternoon with Jackie Robinson. Retired from baseball, Robinson had joined Battle in helping the Urban League, and they would share stories as Tony listened in awe. It was a peaceful time, but Battle also saw the seasons turning. He was diagnosed with diabetes. Never before had he suffered an ailment worse than the flu. In 1948, he weathered the death of his firstborn, Jesse, who had succumbed to a long fight with alcohol at the age of forty-two, as well as the passing of Wesley's father, James Williams, the Chief, at the age of sixty-nine. In 1952, Wesley was injured when the chauffeur of his battalion chief's car collided with another vehicle as they raced to a fire. His injuries forced Wesley to step down after thirty-three years in the fire department for a retirement that would last until his death at the age of eighty-nine, when the *Amsterdam News* would mark his passing with a scant six paragraphs.[1] Battle sat on the dais at a testimonial dinner in honor of Wesley's accomplishments. He described the guests as a who's who of New York's civic society. Eventually, Carroll too began collecting a fire department pension. For a time, he operated his own liquor store and later relaxed into a long retirement, living in the Bahamas and Florida.

Meanwhile, one by one, Battle saw the great figures of old Harlem dying off. He served as an honorary pallbearer at the funeral of W. C. Handy, the jazz great who had been his neighbor on Strivers Row. He was among the mourners at the funeral of Dr. E. P. Roberts, who had delivered Jesse, had attempted to save Florence D'Angeles, and had known that his word as a black physician would count for nothing in Battle's fight to join the police force. The *Amsterdam*

News noted that, in his fifty-eight years as a physician, Roberts had delivered thousands of Harlem's children and the children's children as well. The service was marked by "triumph, beauty and dignity," the paper reported.[2]

Frederick Randolph Moore, who had known more about Harlem and had fought harder for Harlem in the pages of the *Age* than anyone, took to the grave so much that was being forgotten. Among the lost memories were the World War I bravery of Henry Johnson and Battle's cousin Needham Roberts.

Just months after returning from France, Roberts had been honored at Carnegie Hall, where "enthusiasm ran riot" in the audience. He had shared the stage with Teddy Roosevelt, W. E. B. Du Bois, and Irvin S. Cobb, one of the journalists who had interviewed Johnson and Roberts on the day after their epic combat. A Southerner whose father had fought for the Confederacy, Cobb said the valor of black soldiers had changed his perception of African Americans for good. Filled with hope, Roberts heard Cobb declare: "I do not believe the Negro will be denied credit South or North for the big part he has taken in the war. I am sure that in the future a term sometimes spoke in derision, often in jest, n-i-g-g-e-r, will not spell anything but true American."[3]

Twenty years later, with no job and no prospects for one, Roberts would look back bitterly, telling an interviewer, "Those negroes fought in vain." Then, as Battle neared forced retirement, Roberts had placed a noose with a fixed knot over his wife Iola's head, had placed a noose with slip-knot around his own neck, and had hanged them both by kicking a box from beneath their feet.[4]

Johnson's end, too, had been unhappy. Succumbing to poverty and drink, he had died at the age of thirty-two and had been buried in Arlington National Cemetery, his only recognition the French *Croix de Guerre*. More than a half-century later, in 1996, the US military would award him a Purple Heart and would follow up in 2002 with the nation's second-highest commendation, the Distinguished Service Cross. At that time, the military would deny Johnson the top recognition of the Medal of Honor, finding insufficient documentation of his heroism

Battle also saw America's pages turning. The modern civil rights movement was gaining traction. Battle saw the rise of a new generation of African American activists, and they were making unprecedented claims to equal rights.

In 1954, Thurgood Marshall and the NAACP Legal Defense and Education Fund persuaded the US Supreme Court to overturn *Plessy v. Ferguson*, the decision that in 1896, when Battle was thirteen years old, sanctioned separate and purportedly equal treatment of African Americans. The landmark reversal—*Brown v. Board of Education*—established by unanimous declaration of the court's nine justices: "Separate educational facilities are inherently unequal" and thus were unconstitutional.

In 1955, Rosa Parks refused to sit at the back of a bus in Montgomery, Alabama, and was charged with disorderly conduct. Most of the city's fifty thousand African Americans boycotted the bus service and drove revenue down for 381 days. The law mandating segregated transportation was unconstitutional, the US Supreme Court declared. In 1957, nine African American students walked into all-white Little Rock Central High School under the protection of the 101st Airborne, dispatched by President Dwight Eisenhower.

Rejoicing at the milestones, Battle focused anew on the history he made in a day when blacks were even more on their own, when there was no help to be found in the courts, in mass protests, in federal troops, or in the White House. Yet over and again, he had shown the way as a "first." More than ever, he wanted the story told, to have the record reflect his contributions to the betterment of African Americans, to document that he had set the example. He gave a fifteen-thousand-word interview to a researcher from Columbia University's Oral History Project. And he returned with new hope to *Battle of Harlem*. Neither a writer nor an editor, he enlisted an old friend to help revise the manuscript.

George Edmund Haynes had been the first African American to secure a PhD in economics from Columbia University and had co-founded the National Urban League in 1910. While Haynes set out to place the happenings of Battle's life "in the larger national framework into which my New York progress led me," Battle approached Mrs. Roosevelt to ask whether the former First Lady would write a promotional foreword for the work. Of course, she remembered Battle, and, of course, she agreed to his request.

While they spoke, Battle recalled the glass of ice water that Mrs. Roosevelt had brought to blacker-than-night Mary McLeod Bethune in a hot, crowded auditorium. Mrs. Roosevelt responded simply: "But she wanted it. She needed a glass of water."[5]

After reading the manuscript, on May 6, 1960, Mrs. Roosevelt wrote five paragraphs that urged readers to look past the clutter of Hughes's half-hearted efforts to appreciate the sweep and significance of Battle's story:

> This is a record of a man's life and as he tells it you not only see one life but you see the struggles and the victories and the defeats of a whole group of U.S. citizens. What courage it took, what remarkable stamina to be the first Colored policeman in New York City: There were qualities of mind and heart and body that were purely personal but above everything else there was the realization that he was fighting not for himself alone but for his people. That comes out in the pride when each "first" is won.
>
> There are records, of course, here of people met and incidents that occurred that some people may not find very interesting but as a whole story I think there are few people who will not feel not only an interest but a pride in each hard won victory.
>
> I want to recommend this book to those who think that success in life comes purely by luck. In this case it came through hard work and staunchness of purpose, and I surmise that for many people this is the only way success arrives.
>
> At 75 years of age Samuel J. Battle is active and still an interested and good citizen of a democracy. I hope he will continue for many years for his example will do more to help the young people of his race who have to struggle against difficulties than all the words that their teachers and those who try to help them can possibly speak.
>
> Congratulations on a life well lived!

Battle updated the book to record that the fire department then had six hundred black members, including three captains and fourteen lieutenants. He counted twelve hundred African Americans in the police department, including sons of his fellow pioneers.

"They are all my children and some grandchildren for whom I look back with great pride and forward with pleasure," he wrote.[6]

It all came to naught.

Battle and Florence now lived alone in the great old townhouse. Charline and Eddy had bought a home in the suburb of Englewood, New Jersey. The high school there was integrated so that about 10 percent of the student body was black. Gym classes included social dancing. Teachers paired boys and girls only of the same race. Charline, who had risen to a top administrator for New York City's after-school programs, objected. The school board abolished the dance program. "Pretty-born" Yvonne was nonetheless elected homecoming queen. Battle noted proudly that she and Tony had gone on to colleges of the high caliber he had wanted for them. Yvonne was at Bard and Tony was at Bates, each school an elite liberal arts institution.

In 1966, Battle fell ill. The diagnosis this time was leukemia. Although the outlook was fatal, visitors to the townhouse would find him in good spirits. "There is nothing to worry about," he would tell them.

One afternoon, he summoned to his bedside four of his nephews and a grand-nephew, the grandson of Moses P. Cobb and his sister Sophia. His last words to the five young men were: "The torch has been passed."[7]

When he was younger than they were, Battle had seen Booker T. Washington in the flesh. As his life came to a close, he witnessed the majesty of the Reverend Martin Luther King Jr., the inspiration of the March on Washington for Jobs and Freedom, and the by-any-means-necessary fire of Malcolm X. He saw a hard struggle ahead for the race but, ever optimistic, he also expected progress.

"Not just for the Negro's sake, but for the sake of my country I look forward to the day when all of us will do unto others as we would have others do unto us," he had written to close his book.

On August 7, 1966, Samuel Jesse Battle died at the age of eighty-three, a man who had bent the long moral arc as far as he could and then was erased from memory.

APPRECIATIONS

G, always G.

My readers: Bren, Mame, Court, Brent, Pat, Chris, Lauren, Barbara, Vince, and Jim.

My rascals: Jerry, Didi, Mary, Orla, Liam, Bridgey, Arthur, Joe, Agnes, Peter, and a player to be named later.

Mort Zuckerman, enabling publisher; Sam Roberts, New York treasure; Helene Atwan, perceptive editor; Seth Fishman, steadfast agent.

Bry, uncle Bry.

G, forever G.

NOTES

ABBREVIATIONS

AMN—Amsterdam News
BDE—Brooklyn Daily Eagle
BN—Battle's written notes, Langston Hughes Papers, Beinecke Rare Book and
    Manuscript Library, Yale University
CD—Chicago Defender
COH—"The First Black Policeman Remembers," from "The Reminiscences of
    Samuel J. Battle," February 1960, Oral History Collection of Columbia
    University
NYA—New York Age
NYT—New York Times
WWP—Wesley Williams Papers, Schomburg Center for Research in Black
    Culture

CHAPTER ONE: QUEST

1. BN.
2. Paul Laurence Dunbar, *The Sport of the Gods*, 1902, http://www.guten-
berg.org/files/17854/17854-h/17854-h.htm
3. COH.
4. "Negro Policeman Hazed by Silence," *NYT*, August 17, 1911.
5. Alan D. Watson, *A History of New Bern and Craven County* (New Bern,
NC: Tryon Palace Commission, 1987), 58–59, 158–59; Vina Hutchinson,
Images of America: New Bern (Charleston, SC: Arcadia, 2000), 27, 32,
36; Lynn Salsi and Frances Eubanks, *Images of America: Craven County*
(Charleston, SC: Arcadia, 2001), 12, 25, 28.
6. US Bureau of the Census, Tenth Census, 1880, Ancestry.com; Jeffrey J.
Crow, Paul D. Escott, and Flora J. Hatley, *A History of African Americans
in North Carolina* (Raleigh: North Carolina Department of Cultural Resources, 2002), 51.
7. State v. Mann, 13 N.C. 263 (1829).
8. Milton Ready, *The Tar Heel State: A History of North Carolina* (Columbia:
University of South Carolina Press, 2005); Watson, *History of New Bern*,
375, 398–99, 401–2.

9. John W. Cromwell, *The Negro in American History: Men and Women Eminent in the Evolution of the American of African Descent* (Washington, DC: American Negro Academy, 1914), 172.

10. Hatley, *History of African Americans*, 80.

11. Watson, *History of New Bern*, 488.

12. Ibid., 489.

13. Eubanks, *Images of America*, 11, 56; Watson, *History of New Bern*, 559.

14. Gilbert Osofsky, *Harlem: The Making of a Ghetto* (Chicago: Elephant Paperbacks, 1996), 30.

15. Edwin G. Burrows and Mike Wallace, *Gotham: A History of New York City to 1898* (Oxford, UK: Oxford University Press, 1999), 1050.

16. Ibid., 1073.

17. Idell E. Zeisloft, *The New Metropolis; 1600—Memorable Events of Three Centuries—1900; from the Island of Mana-hat-tan to Greater New York at the Close of the Nineteenth Century* (New York: Appleton and Company, 1899), 104, 109.

18. Letter from Robert Hunter, June 23, 1712, at http://people.hofstra.edu/alan _j_singer/Gateway%20Slavery%20Guide%20PDF%20Files/3.%20British %20Colony,%201664-1783/6.%20Documents/1712-1719.%20Slave %20revolt.pdf

19. US Bureau of the Census, Eighth Census, 1860.

20. US Bureau of the Census, Twelfth Census, 1900.

21. Ray Stannard Baker, *Following the Color Line* (New York: Harper Torchbooks, 1964), 132.

22. Zeisloft, *New Metropolis*, 124.

23. COH.

24. COH.

25. BN.

26. "West Side Race Riot," *New York Tribune*, August 16, 1900.

27. "The Riot in Akron," *NYT*, August 24, 1900.

28. Garry L. Reeder, "The History of Blacks at Yale University," *Journal of Blacks in Higher Education*, January 31, 2000, 125.

29. Edmund Morris, *Theodore Rex* (New York: Random House, 2001), 54.

30. "Yale Commemorates Her Bicentennial," *NYT*, October 24, 1901.

31. Timothy Thomas Fortune, "A Boy's Life in Reconstruction," *Norfolk New Journal and Guide*, August 13, 1927.

32. Emma Lou Thornbrough, *T. Thomas Fortune: Militant Journalist* (Chicago: University of Chicago Press, 1972), 3–34.

33. David Levering Lewis, *W. E. B. Du Bois: Biography of a Race* (New York: Owl Books, 1994), 38.

34. Thornbrough, *T. Thomas Fortune*, 44, 105–11, 124–25, 137–286.

35. US Bureau of the Census, Eighth Census, 1860.

36. "Brooklyn's Colored Policeman," *BDE*, March 8, 1891.

37. "On the Force," *BDE*, March 5, 1891; "Colored Policeman," *BDE*, March 6, 1891.

38. "Overton's First Tour of Duty," *BDE*, March 7, 1891.

39. "Colors Clash," *BDE*, March 27, 1891.

40. "Hired to Whip Overton," *BDE*, April 19, 1891; "Think It False," *BDE*, April 20, 1891.

41. "Stand by Him," *BDE*, March 30, 1891; "Let Off Light," *BDE*, April 7, 1891.

42. "Eighteen New Policemen," *BDE*, July 9, 1982.

43. "The Color Line," *BDE*, April 25, 1892; "Still Another," *BDE*, May 14, 1892.

44. Ibid.

45. "Maybe Overton Has a Good Case," *BDE*, June 12, 1892; "Patrolman Overton Fined," *BDE*, June 14, 1892.

46. "Points About Policemen," *BDE*, August 14, 1892.

47. "Overton Will Resign," *BDE*, November 18, 1892.

48. "Colored Patrolman Hadley Dismissed," *BDE*, November 29, 1892.

49. "Another Colored Policeman," *BDE*, December 8, 1892; "Points About Policemen," *BDE*, December 11, 1892.

50. COH.

51. Borough of Brooklyn Death Certificate, No. 18138 of 1901, New York City Municipal Reference Library.

52. "$3-Million Police Station Dedicated at 123d and 8th," *NYT*, October 30, 1975.

53. Jervis Anderson, *This Was Harlem: A Cultural Portrait, 1900–1950* (New York: Farrar, Straus and Giroux, 1987), 25–26.

54. "New York's Rich Negroes," *New York Sun*, January 18, 1903.

55. "John W. Connors, Founder Organized Colored Baseball in New York, Is Dead," *NYA*, July 17, 1926.

56. Perry Bradford, *Born with the Blues* (New York: Oak Publications, 1965), 169.

57. "The Southland Troubadour," *NYA*, October 23, 1948.

58. Theda Skocpol, Ariane Liazon, and Marshall Ganz, *What a Mighty Power We Can Be: African American Fraternal Groups and the Struggle for Racial Equality* (Princeton, NJ: Princeton University Press, 2006).

59. "Negro Policeman Now a Regular Cop," *New York Sun*, January 18, 1912.

60. Mary White Ovington, *Half a Man: The Status of the Negro in New York* (New York: Longmans, Green, 1911), 148.

61. US Bureau of the Census, Twelfth Census, 1900.

62. Wesley Williams, *The Seven Generations That I (Wesley Williams) Have Witnessed; Up from Slavery: Four Generations of the Williams Family Span*

the Modern History of the Republic, from Pre-War Slavery Days to the Present, WWP.

63. "Bowery Derelicts Pay Thorley Honor," *NYT*, November 21, 1923.

64. Abram Hill, "Chief James H. Williams," WPA research paper, Schomburg Center for Research in Black Culture; Eric Arnesen, ed., *The Encyclopedia of U.S. Labor and Working-Class History, Volume 1* (New York: Routledge, 2007), 665.

65. "57 Years a New York Doctor," *AMN*, October 13, 1951.

66. Mary White Ovington, *The Walls Came Tumbling Down* (New York: Harcourt, Brace, 1947), 40.

67. New York City certificate of marriage, Borough of Manhattan, No. 13951 of 1905, New York City Municipal Reference Library.

68. Ovington, *Half a Man*, 40–41.

69. "After Brutal Policemen," *NYA*, July 27, 1905; "Guilty Police Shall Not Escape," *NYA*, August 3, 1905.

70. "Become Police and Firemen," *NYA*, December 28, 1905.

71. Ernst Christopher Meyer, "Infant Mortality in New York City: A Study of the Results Accomplished by Infant Life-Saving Agencies, 1885–1920," International Health Board, 124; Ovington, *Half a Man*, 53.

72. New York State Census, 1905.

73. "White Landlords Make Objection to Church," *NYA*, June 11, 1914.

74. "Beautiful Homes for Colored People," *NYA*, October 25, 1906; Ovington, *Half a Man*, 47.

75. "Negroes Filling Up 99th Street Block," *NYT*, August 14, 1905.

76. Register of New York City, Section 7, Liber 127, 365–68; Liber 128, 145–50; Liber 151, 134–46; Liber 152, 297–301; Liber 159, 7–15.

77. State of New York Certificate and Record of Death, No. 24535, 1908, New York City Municipal Reference Library.

78. Wilbur Young, "Equity Congress," WPA research paper, Schomburg Center for Research in Black Culture.

79. Geoffrey C. Ward, *Unforgivable Blackness: The Rise and Fall of Jack Johnson* (New York: Vintage, 2004), 14–15.

80. "Crowds See Johnson," *Washington Post*, March 30, 1909; "J. Johnson Hits Great White Way," *Chicago Daily Tribune*, March 30, 1909; Ward, *Unforgivable Blackness*, 143.

81. "Negro Police for New York," *NYA*, August 5, 1909.

82. "The Trouble in Harlem," *NYA*, August 5, 1909.

83. "Subject of Negro Police," *NYA*, August 19, 1909; "New York Negro Policemen," *NYA*, August 19, 1909.

84. "Will Not Take Examination," *NYA*, September 2, 1909.

85. Cornelius W. Willemse, *A Cop Remembers* (New York: E. P. Dutton, 1933), 147–49.

86. Reverdy C. Ransom, *The Pilgrimage of Harriet Ransom's Son* (Nashville: Sunday School Union, 1949), 215.

87. "Send Johnson $20,000," *NYA*, June 9, 1910.

88. Bradford, *Born with the Blues*, 171.

89. Ibid.

90. "Whites and Blacks in Many Riotous Battles," *New York Tribune*, July 5, 1910; "Eight Killed in Fight Riots," *NYT*, July 5, 1910; "Eleven Killed in Many Race Riots," *Chicago Daily Tribune*, July 5, 1910.

91. "Johnson in New York," *Washington Post*, July 12, 1910.

92. "Johnson's Arrival a Negro Gala Day," *NYT*, July 12, 1910.

93. Benton Pride, *Wesley Williams: A Credit to His Race*, WWP.

94. Thomas Roy Peyton, MD, *Quest for Dignity: An Autobiography of Negro Doctor* (Los Angeles: Warren E. Lewis, 1950), 3–4.

95. COH.

96. "New York City Has a Colored Police Officer," *NYA*, June 29, 1911.

97. Charles Anderson to Booker T. Washington, July 5, 1911, Booker T. Washington Papers, Library of Congress; "Commissioner Waldo," *NYA*, June, 1, 1911.

98. Ibid.

CHAPTER TWO: STRUGGLE

1. Langston Hughes to Maxim Lieber, December 30, 1935, Langston Hughes Papers, Beinecke Rare Book and Manuscript Library, Yale University.

2. *Harlem Home News*, July 28, 1911, and August 25, 1911.

3. "First Negro Named for City's Police," *NYT*, June 29, 1911.

4. COH.

5. BN.

6. "The Negro as a Policeman," *NYT*, June 30, 1911.

7. COH.

8. "Negro Policeman Hazed by Silence," *NYT*, August 17, 1911.

9. COH.

10. "Negro Policeman Now a Regular Cop," *New York Sun*, January 8, 1912.

11. COH.

12. BN.

13. Wilbur Young, "Equity Congress," WPA research paper, Schomburg Center for Research in Black Culture.

14. "Crowd Threatens to Lynch Negro," *NYT*, October 18, 1911.

15. US Bureau of the Census, Twelfth Census, 1900.

16. Robert Holmes's World War I draft registration card, National Archives and Records Administration, Ancestry.com.

17. Rev. Frederick Asbury Cullen, *From Barefoot Town to Jerusalem* (privately printed, n.d.), 56.

18. "Identify Two Suspects in Police Killing," *New York Daily News*, April 23, 1934.

19. BN.

20. "To Test Legality of Covenant," *NYA*, February 13, 1913.

21. "Enthuse over Negro Regiment," *NYA*, June 12, 1913.

22. Peter N. Nelson, *A More Unbending Battle: The Harlem Hellfighters' Struggle for Freedom in WWI and Equality at Home* (New York: BasicCivitas, 2009), 10–13.

23. Mary White Ovington, *Half a Man: The Status of the Negro in New York* (New York: Longmans, Green, 1911), 85.

24. New York State Department of Labor, *Annual Report of the Industrial Commission for the Twelve Months Ended September 30, 1915*, 114.

25. Clifford M. Holland, "'Blowout' Difficulties in Tunneling Under East River, New York City," *Railway Review*, December 30, 1916.

26. "Subway Saga," *NYT*, November 8, 1964.

27. "General Miles to Negroes, Talks of War and the Future of the Black Race," *NYT*, August 3, 1914.

28. W. E. B. Du Bois, "Mr. Trotter and Mr. Wilson," *Crisis*, January 1915, 119–20.

29. W. E. B. Du Bois, "Colored Men and Women Lynched Without Trial," *Crisis*, January 1915, 145; "The Lynching Industry," *Crisis*, February 1916, 198.

30. Benton Pride, *Wesley Williams: A Credit to His Race*, WWP.

31. Wesley Williams photograph collection, Schomburg Center for Research in Black Culture, Photographs and Prints Division.

32. State of New York Certificate and Record of Marriage, New York City Department of Health, No. 3480, 1915, New York City Municipal Reference Library.

33. "Bad Faith Charged by Street Car Men," *NYT*, August 15, 1916.

34. "Car Strikers Raid Stops Bronx Lines," *NYT*, July 27, 1916; "State and City Prepare to Meet Great Car Strike," *NYT*, August 2, 1916; "Death and Disruption Have Marked Transit Strikes in this City," *NYT*, December 39, 1965.

35. Tony Gould, *A Summer Plague: Polio and Its Survivors* (New Haven, CT: Yale University Press, 1995); Andrea Ryken, *Polio in Twentieth Century America: A "Children's Disease" in a Child-Centered Culture*, April 8, 2008, Undergraduate Library Research Award, Paper 3, http://digitalcommons.lmu.edu/ulra/awards/2008/3.

36. "Identify Two Suspects in Police Killing," *New York Daily News*, April 23, 1934.

37. W. E. B. Du Bois, "The Waco Horror," *Crisis*, July 19, 1916.

38. "Negro Troops of N.Y. N. G.," *NYA*, June 29, 1916.

39. Nelson, *A More Unbending Battle*, 5–7; Gail Buckley, *American Patriots: The Story of Blacks in the Military from the Revolution to Desert Storm* (New York: Random House, 2001), 190.

40. Napoleon B. Marshall, *The Providential Armistice: A Volunteer's Story* (Washington, DC: Liberty League, 1930), 12.

41. Nelson, *A More Unbending Battle*, 1–2; "The Fifteenth," *NYA*, October 5, 1916; Wilbur Young, "Negroes of New York: Equity Congress," WPA research paper, Schomburg Center for Research in Black Culture.

42. James Weldon Johnson, *Black Manhattan: Account of the Development of Harlem* (orig., 1930; New York: Da Capo Press, 1991), 231.

43. Nelson, *A More Unbending Battle*, 10–13.

44. *Brief Adventures of the First American Soldier Decorated in the World War, as Told by Neadom Roberts*, 1933 (Richmond, VA: Collection of the American Civil War Center at Historic Tredegar).

45. Arthur W. Little, *From Harlem to the Rhine: The Story of New York's Colored Volunteers* (New York: Covici Friede, 1936), 9–13.

46. Marcus Garvey, "The Conspiracy of the East St. Louis Riot," speech, July 8, 1917, *The Marcus Garvey and Universal Negro Improvement Association Papers* (volume I, 1826–August 1919) (Berkeley and Los Angeles: University of California Press, 1983), 217.

47. Harper Barnes, *Never Been a Time: The 1917 Race Riot That Sparked the Civil Rights Movement* (New York: Walker & Company, 2008), 123–68.

48. "Negro Guardsmen in San Juan Riot," *NYT*, July 4, 1917.

49. "Hayward Begins Inquiry into Riot," *NYT*, July 5, 1917.

50. "Negro Policeman Slain by Burglar," *NYT*, August 7, 1917; Patrolman Killed in Battle with Negro Burglar," *New York Tribune*, August 7, 1917; New York City Department of Health Death Certificates No. 7291 and 26338 of 1918 for Henry Oliver Holmes and Ella Homes, New York City Municipal Reference Library.

51. Little, *From Harlem to the Rhine*, 357.

52. Ibid., 46–47.

53. "First Negro Troops in Spartanburg," *NYT*, August 31, 1917.

54. Little, *From Harlem to the Rhine*, 54–55.

55. Ibid., 57, 67–68.

56. Ibid., 75–76.

57. "Two N.Y. Negroes Whip 24 Germans, Win War Crosses," *New York Tribune*, May 20, 1918.

58. Buckley, *American Patriots*, 200.

59. Chad L. Williams, *Torchbearers of Democracy: African American Soldiers in the World War I Era* (Chapel Hill: University of North Carolina Press, 2010), 118–19.

60. Recommendation for the Medal of Honor, Sergeant Henry Johnson, submitted by US Senator Charles E. Schumer, May 15, 2011.

61. Bill Harris, *The Hellfighters of Harlem: African American Soldiers Who Fought for the Right to Fight for Their Country* (New York: Carroll & Graf, 2002), 39.

62. "City Firemen Hail Once-Scorned Chief," *NYT*, October 29, 1976.

63. Marshall, *Providential Armistice*, 11, 12.

64. "Fifth Av. Cheers Negro Veterans," *NYT*, February 18, 1919.

65. World War I army service card, Henry Johnson, New York State Archives.

66. W. E. B. Du Bois, "Returning Soldiers," *Crisis*, May 1919, 14.

67. "Negro Killed in Harlem Race Row," *NYT*, September 16, 1919.

CHAPTER THREE: BETRAYED

1. Langston Hughes to Arna Bontemps, December 27, 1950, Langston Hughes Papers, Beinecke Rare Book and Manuscript Library, Yale University.

2. Arnold Rampersad, *The Life of Langston Hughes, Volume II, 1941–1967: I Dream a World* (Oxford, UK: Oxford University Press, 2002), 187.

3. Cornelius W. Willemse, *Behind the Green Lights* (New York: Alfred A. Knopf, 1931), 51.

4. "The Old Toms Prison Under Criticism Again," *NYT*, June 30, 1929.

5. Willemse, *Behind the Green Lights*, 30.

6. "Fire College Instruction: Handbook of Instruction for Fire Lieutenants and Fire Captains," advertisement, *Fire Department Motor Apparatus: Description and Equipment of Every Type of Motor Apparatus in the New York Fire Department* (New York: Civil Service Chronicle, 1916).

7. "City Firemen Hail Once-Scorned Chief," *NYT*, October 29, 1976.

8. Wesley Williams photograph collection, Schomburg Center for Research in Black Culture, Photographs and Prints Division.

9. M. R. Werner, *Tammany Hall* (New York: Greenwood Press, 1932), 188.

10. Richard Zacks, *Island of Vice: Theodore Roosevelt's Doomed Quest to Clean Up Sin-Loving New York* (New York: Doubleday, 2012), 23–27.

11. Werner, *Tammany Hall*, 466.

12. Zacks, *Island of Vice*, 41.

13. Franklin Matthews, "Wide Open New York," *Harper's Weekly*, October 22, 1898.

14. "Police Praised As Sergeants Dine," *NYT*, March 8, 1907; "Police Gifts for McAdoo," *NYT*, January 24, 1906; "Police Lieutenants Entertain Taft," *NYT*, February 23, 1910; "No Cheers for Bingham," *NYT*, February 9, 1909.

15. "Whitman Watches Hylan; He Could Be Removed," *NYT*, January 25, 1918; "Devery Funeral Tuesday," *NYT*, June 22, 1919; "Devery's Mourners the Lowly and High," *NYT*, June 25, 1919.

16. Werner, *Tammany Hall*, 557; "$12,000 For Enright in 'Fictitious' Stock Deal with A. A. Ryan," *NYT*, September 21, 1921; "Bank Records Show Enright Deposited $100,421 in 4 Years," *NYT*, October 18, 1921.

17. Annual Report of the Department of Health of the City of New York, 1921; E. P. Cook, MD, "Bronchopneumonia in Early Childhood—Its Treatment," *Journal of California and Western Medicine* (March 1930): 170; Department of Health, Certificate of Death, No. 5743 of 1920, New York City Municipal Reference Library.

18. US Bureau of the Census, Thirteenth Census, 1910; Fourteenth Census, 1920.

19. James Weldon Johnson, *Black Manhattan: Account of the Development of Harlem* (orig., 1930; New York: Da Capo Press, 1991), 165–66.

20. "The Reminiscences of Benjamin McLaurin," 1960, Oral History Collection of Columbia University.

21. Eslanda Goode Robeson, *Paul Robeson, Negro* (New York: Harper & Brothers, 1930), 70, http://archive.org/stream/paulrobesonnegroo11552mbp#page /n93/mode/2up.

22. "The Reminiscences of George S. Schuyler," 1962, Oral History Collection of Columbia University.

23. Anderson, *This Was Harlem*, 130.

24. "Murdered Man a Bigamist," *AMN*, December 6, 1922; "Items of Social Interest," *AMN*, December 6, 1922, and December 20, 1922.

25. "The Reminiscences of George S. Schuyler."

26. "The Future Harlem," *NYA*, January 10, 1920.

27. Arnold Rampersad, *The Life of Langston Hughes, Volume I, 1902–1941: I, Too Sing America* (Oxford, UK: Oxford University Press, 2002), 10; Langston Hughes, *The Big Sea* (New York: Hill and Wang, 1993), 40.

28. Rampersad, *The Life of Langston Hughes I*, 6.

29. Hughes, *Big Sea*, 34.

30. Langston Hughes, "The Fascination of Cities, *Crisis*, January 1926, 140.

31. Hughes, *Big Sea*, 81.

32. "Making a Joke of Prohibition in New York City," *NYT*, May 2, 1920.

33. Daniel Okrent, *Last Call: The Rise and Fall of Prohibition* (New York: Scribner, 2010), 207–8.

34. "Indict Arnold Rothstein," *NYT*, June 7, 1919; "Inspector Henry Is Freed by Court," *NYT*, June 23, 1921.

35. "Faithful Unto Death," *Evening Telegram* (NY), February 23, 1916; "Enright Promotes Ten to Be Captains," *New York Sun*, April 27, 1919; "Changes Surprise Police," *NYT*, June 26, 1919; "Samuel G. Belton, Police Aide, Dead," *NYT*, February 11, 1958.

36. "Capitol Theatre to Open Friday," *NYT*, October 21, 1919; "Capitol Theatre Opens to Throng," *NYT*, October 25, 1919.

37. "Bandits Get 10,000 in Capitol Theatre Holdup During Play," *NYT*, December 19, 1921.

38. "Employee One of 3 Seized in Capitol Theatre Hold-Up," *New York Tribune*, December 22, 1921.

39. David Suisman, "Co-workers in the Kingdom of Culture: Black Swan Records and the Political Economy of African American Music," *Journal of American History* 90, no. 4 (March 2004).

40. "Dempsey and Wills Agreement Signed," *NYT*, July 19, 1922.

41. Robert C. Hayden and Jacqueline Harris, *Nine Black American Doctors* (Reading, MA: Addison-Wesley, 1976), 48; Robert C. Hayden, *"Mr. Harlem Hospital": Dr. Louis T. Wright, a Biography* (Littleton, MA: Tapestry Press, 2003), 19, 65; P. Preston Reynolds, MD, "Dr. Louis T. Wright and the NAACP: Pioneers in Hospital Racial Integration," *American Journal of Public Health* (June 2000): 883–92.

42. "Memories of New Bern: The Great Fire of New Bern of 1922," Joseph Patterson speech transcript, New Bern–Craven County Public Library website, http://newbern.cpclib.org/research/memories/pdf/Fire.pdf; Peter B. Sandbeck, excerpts from *Beaufort's African-American History and Architecture, Beaufort, North Carolina History* website, http://beaufortartist .blogspot.com/p/african-americans-in-beaufort-1995.html.

43. "Negro Policeman Shot by a Hold-up Suspect," *NYT*, December 20, 1921.

44. "Boddy Dies in Chair for Police Murder," *NYT*, September 1, 1922; "Boddy Guilty, Grins at Death Verdict," *NYT*, January 1, 1922.

45. "Policeman Killed By Crazed Negro to Avenge Boddy," *NYT*, January 20, 1922.

46. "Negro Shoots Down Another Policeman," *NYT*, May 9, 1922.

47. "Negro Thug Killed in Fight at Station," *NYT*, June 28, 1922.

48. "Many Cases Indicate Epidemic of Brutality as Practices by Members of Police Force," *NYA*, July 15, 1922; "Additional Developments in the Matter of Police Brutality Indicate Need of Change," *NYA*, July 22, 1922; "Eyewitness Tells the Story of Beating Herbert Dent to Death," *NYA*, November 11, 1922; "Crowds of Negroes at Boddy Funeral," *NYT*, September 5, 1922.

49. "Charges Enright Misused Police Welfare Fund," *NYT*, January 31, 1926; "Enright Sails for Brazil," *NYT*, November 23, 1934; "Charges Enright Misused Police Welfare Fund," *NYT*, January 31, 1926.

50. Martin A. Gosch and Richard Hammer, *The Last Testament of Lucky Luciano* (Boston: Little, Brown, 1975), 58; James Lardner and Thomas Reppetto, *NYPD: A City and Its Police* (New York: Henry Holt, 2000), 200; "Enright Must Show His Liquor Records," *NYT*, September 14, 1923.

51. David Ewen, *A Journey to Greatness: The Life and Music of George Gershwin* (New York: Henry Holt, 1956), 41; Stanley Crouch, "About Jelly Roll Morton," Nonesuch Records website, 1997, http://www.nonesuch.com /artists/jelly-roll-morton.

52. "Fear Sweeney Will Confess," *NYT*, February 20, 1913; "Sweeney Ready to Bare Vice Graft," *New York Tribune*, February 20, 1913.

53. "Too Many Saloons in Harlem," *NYA*, October 1, 1914.

54. "Resort Keepers Released in Bail After Vice Raid," *New York Tribune*, January 11, 1917; "Wilkins Gives Up Cabaret in New York," *NYA*, October 4, 1917.

55. Bricktop with James Haskins, *Bricktop* (New York: Atheneum, 1983), 34.

56. "Detectives Who Raided Barron Wilkin's Cabaret Pinch 23," *CD*, March 11, 1922.

57. Bricktop with Haskins, *Bricktop*, 75–78; Stanley Dance, *The World of Swing: An Oral History of Big Band Jazz* (New York: Charles Scribner's Sons, 1974), 52; Edward Kennedy Ellington, *Music Is My Mistress* (Garden City, NY: Doubleday, 1973), 64; Konrad Bercovici, *Around the World in New York* (New York: Century, 1924), 237.

58. "Punished, He Says, for Police Raid," *NYT*, September 26, 1923.

59. COH.

60. Ibid.

61. Ibid.

62. "Officials Witness Bouts at Pioneer," *NYT*, December 13, 1923.

63. Arnold de Mille, "The Shooting of Barron Wilkins," WPA research paper, Schomburg Center for Research in Black Culture; "Baron Wilkins Murdered," *CD*, May 31, 1924; "Barron Wilkins, Negro Cabaret 'King' Is Slain," *New York Herald*, May 24, 1924.

64. "Cabaret Owner Shot by Gambler," *NYA*, May 31, 1924; "Barron Wilkins Murdered," *CD*, May 31, 1924; "Old Timer Recalls History of Barron," *CD*, May 31, 1924.

65. "Barron Wilkins Murdered," *CD*, May 31, 1924; "Thousands Attend Wilkins' Funeral," *NYA*, May 31, 1924; "Barron Wilkins Funeral," *CD*, June 7, 1924.

66. "NY's Only Colored Fireman Saves Six from Burning Building," *NYA*, October 25, 1924.

67. COH.

68. BN.

69. Wesley Williams to the *New York Age*, August 8, 1925, WWP.

70. *AMN*, August 12, 1925.

71. "The Negro and the Finest," *AMN*, September 9, 1925.

72. Henry F. Pringle, "Jimmy Walker," *American Mercury*, November 1926, 272.

73. Langston Hughes, "Youth," *Survey Graphic*, March 1925, 663.

74. Charles Spurgeon Johnson, "An Opportunity for Negro Writers," *Opportunity*, September 1924, 258.

75. Hughes, *Big Sea*, 245; Langston Hughes, "The Negro and the Racial Mountain," *Nation*, June 23, 1926, 694.

76. Rampersad, *The Life of Langston Hughes I*, 141.

77. James Weldon Johnson to Carl Van Vechten, March 6, 1927, James Weldon Johnson Collection of Negro Arts and Letters, Beinecke Rare Book and Manuscript Library, Yale University.

78. "Manhattan Lodge of Elks Tenders Testimonial Dinner to Sgt. Battle," *AMN*, August 4, 1926.

79. BN.

CHAPTER FOUR: COMMAND

1. Rev. Frederick Asbury Cullen, *From Barefoot Town to Jerusalem* (privately printed, n.d.), 102.

2. Sugar Ray Robinson with Dave Anderson, *Sugar Ray* (New York: Da Capo Press, 1994), 35–37.

3. Charles S. Johnson, "Black Workers and the City," *Survey Graphic*, March 1925, 641–42.

4. US Bureau of the Census, Fourteenth Census, 1920; Fifteenth Census, 1930; Charles S. Johnson, "Black Workers and the City," *Survey Graphic*, March 1925, 643; T. J. Woofter Jr., *Negro Problems in Cities* (Garden City, NY: Doubleday, Doran & Company, 1928), 79; New York Urban League, "Twenty-Four Hundred Negro Families in Harlem: An Interpretation of the Living Conditions of Small Wage Earners," 16 (1927 typescript at Schomburg Center for Research in Black Culture); Winifred B. Nathan, *Health Conditions in North Harlem, 1923–1927* (New York, 1932), 19, 31; "Thousands of Worshippers Take Part in Dedication of Mother Zion's New and Magnificent House of Worship," *NYA*, September 26, 1925.

5. James Weldon Johnson, "The Making of Harlem," *Survey Graphic*, March 1925.

6. "Sergeant Battle Returns from Vacation," *AMN*, September 28, 1927.

7. "Modern Ideas Followed in Building New School," *NYT*, March 1, 1903.

8. Affidavit of Leroy Leeks, People of the State of New York v. Leroy Leeks, Court of General Sessions of the County of New York, Index No. 50235 of 1927, New York City Municipal Reference Library.

9. "Freed of Murder as Accuser Recant," *NYT*, October 21, 1927; "Innocent Man Near Death Chair," *AMN*, October 26, 1927.

10. Constance Valis Hill, *Tap Dancing America: A Cultural History* (Oxford, UK: Oxford University Press, 2010), 63, 67.

11. "New York, We're Here!," *AMN*, August 22, 1927.

12. James H. Williams to Patrick Cardinal Hayes, September 9, 1927, WWP; Wesley Williams to Robert F. Wagner, November 17, 1962, WWP.

13. "Wesley Williams Wins Promotion," *AMN*, September 21, 1927.

14. "Side Lights on Society," *AMN*, May 9, 1928.

15. "John Brown Pilgrims Plan for Placid Trip," *Lake Placid (NY) News*, April 27, 1928; "John Brown and Abraham Lincoln," *Lake Placid News*, May 18, 1928; Ned P. Rauch, "Lake Placid Club: The Beginnings," 5, in *The Lake Placid Club, 1890 to 2002*, Lee Manchester, ed. (Jay, NY: Makebelieve Publishing, 2008), http://www.slideshare.net/LeeManchester/the-lake-placid-club-1890-2002.

16. "An Ordinary Shawl with an Extraordinary Story," blog post, *Ohio History*, February 20, 2014, http://ohiohistory.wordpress.com/2014/02/20/an-ordinary-shawl-with-an-extraordinary-story/.

17. Sadie Hall, "Casper Holstein," WPA research paper, Schomburg Center for Research in Black Culture; "Light Went Out on $150," *NYT*, July 18, 1905; Shane White, Stephen Garton, Stephen Robertson, and Graham White, *Playing the Numbers: Gambling in Harlem between the Wars* (Cambridge, MA: Harvard University Press, 2010), 151.

18. J. Saunders Redding, "Playing the Numbers," *North American Review* (December 1934): 533.

19. Winthrop D. Lane, "Ambushed in the City: The Grim Side of Harlem," *Survey Graphic*, March 1925.

20. BN.

21. BN.

22. White et al., *Playing the Numbers*, 154; Hall, "Casper Holstein."

23. "Negro, Back Home, Lauds Kidnappers," *NYT*, September 25, 1928.

24. "Congressman Pritchard of North Carolina, Republican, Refuses Office Next [*sic*] Negro," *NYA*, April 13, 1929.

25. "Identify Two Suspects in Police Killing," *New York Daily News*, April 23, 1934.

26. BN.

27. Cheryl Lynn Greenberg, *Or Does It Explode: Black Harlem in the Great Depression* (New York: Oxford University Press, 1991), 42.

28. James Weldon Johnson, *Black Manhattan: Account of the Development of Harlem* (orig., 1930; New York: Da Capo Press, 1991), 169, 284.

29. Langston Hughes, *The Big Sea* (New York: Hill and Wang, 1993), 245–47.

30. Greenberg, *Or Does It Explode*, 44–45; Nancy Cunard, *Essays on Race and Empire* (Peterborough, Ontario: Broadview Press, 2002), 95–96.

31. "Christmas Cheer Brought to Thousands of Harlem Poor by Generous Civic Organizations," *NYA*, January 2, 1932.

32. "New York Panorama: A Comprehensive View of the Metropolis, Presented in a Series of Articles by the Federal Writer's Project of the Works Progress Administration in New York City," *Portrait of Harlem* (New York: Random House, 1938),142.

33. Mayor's Commission on Conditions in Harlem, *The Negro in Harlem: A Report on Social and Economic Conditions Responsible for the Outbreak of March 19, 1935*, 53, 68–69, 73, 87–88, La Guardia Papers, New York City Municipal Reference Library.

34. BN; US Bureau of the Census, Fifteenth Census, 1930: "Society," *AMN*, January 22, 1930; "Battles Give Annual Party," *AMN*, March 26, 1930; Charline Battle Hunter College Transcript; California Passenger and Crew List, No. 2712, 1932; "Mrs. Enrique Cachemaille Confined to Sanitarium with Nervous Breakdown," *NYA*, June 3, 1933.

35. "Crowley Battle in 1931 Recalled," *NYT*, February 21, 1955; "Coll Is Shot Dead in a Phone Booth by Rival Gunmen," *NYT*, February 8, 1932; "2 Policeman, 3 Thugs and Child Slain in Battle During 12-Mile Hold-Up Chase," *NYT*, August 22, 1931.

36. "Police Radio Helps Trap Two in Forgery," *NYT*, February 25, 1932.

37. "Major Crime Here Down 17% Last Year," *NYT*, March 20, 1933.

38. "Lieut. Wesley Williams, Only Negro Officer in New York Fire Fighting Forces, Wins Praise for Bravery," *NYA*, April 7, 1928; "Lieut. Wesley Williams Is Hero in Allen Street Fire; Had Narrow Escape," *NYA*, June 29, 1929; undated, unattributed newspaper photograph, WWP; "8 Firemen Trapped in Blazing Building," *NYT*, November 18, 1933.

39. Samuel Battle to Wesley Williams, September 6, 1933, WWP.

40. "Society," *AMN*, July 5, 1933; "Ass'n Reveals Tourney Prizes," *AMN*, July 26, 1933; "Ramses of N.Y.U. Sponsors Frolic," *AMN*, April 28, 1934.

41. Randall Kennedy, "Racial Passing," *Ohio State Law Journal* 62, no. 1145 (2001), http://moritzlaw.osu.edu/students/groups/oslj/files/2012/03/62.3.kennedy.pdf.

42. US Bureau of the Census, Fifteenth Census, 1930.

43. White et al., *Playing the Numbers*, 178–79; "Negroes No Longer Control Harlem Numbers Business as Kings Work for Bronx Beer Racketeer," *NYA*, August 13, 1932; "Two Put on Stand," *NYT*, August 18, 1938.

44. "Numbers Banker Slain," *NYA*, March 11, 1933.

45. J. Richard (Dixie) Davis, "Things I Couldn't Tell Till Now," *Collier's*, July 29, 1939, 20.

46. "Committee Chosen to Present Harlem's Needs to Mayor," *NYA*, April 7, 1934.

47. Thomas Kessner, *Fiorello H. La Guardia and the Making of Modern New York* (New York: McGraw-Hill, 1989), 70.

48. "Rid City of Gangs, Is Order to Police," *NYT*, January 12, 1934.

49. "City and State Officials Speak at NAACP Celebration," *NYA*, March 24, 1934; "La Guardia Says He'd Be Glad to Help De Priest," *Afro-American* (Baltimore), March 24, 1934.

50. "Identify Two Suspects in Police Killing," *New York Daily News*, April 23, 1934; "Murder of 3 Cops Admitted by Felon Dying of Wounds," *New York Daily News*, May 3, 1940.

51. "Miss Charline Battle Takes Vows and Changes Her Name," *AMN*, June 16, 1934.

52. Walter White, *A Man Called White: The Autobiography of Walter White* (Atlanta: University of Georgia Press, 1995), 3–4, 11.

53. John H. Johnson, *Fact Not Fiction in Harlem* (Glen Cove, NY: Northern Type Printing, 1980), 50; "Blumstein's Store to Hire Negro Clerks," *NYA*, August 4, 1934.

54. "Summer College Students Offer to Picket Discriminating Store; League Preparing for Parade," *NYA*, July 21, 1934.

CHAPTER FIVE: RESPECT

1. Arnold Rampersad, *The Life of Langston Hughes, Volume I, 1902–1941: I, Too Sing America* (Oxford, UK: Oxford University Press, 2002), 13.
2. "Harlem Greets Negro Lieutenant," *NYT*, January 9, 1935.
3. "Negro Fireman Battle Discrimination," *AMN*, October 13, 1934.
4. Oswald Garrison Villard, "Walking Through Race Prejudice," *Nation*, January 30, 1935, 119.
5. "Rid City of Crooks, La Guardia Orders," *NYT*, April 30, 1934; Lowell M. Limpus, *Honest Cop: Lewis J. Valentine* (New York: E. P. Dutton, 1939), 178; Thomas Kessner, *Fiorello H. La Guardia and the Making of Modern New York* (New York: McGraw-Hill, 1989), 358.
6. "One-Man-Raid Battles Does a Carrie Nation," *AMN*, May 12, 1934.
7. Mayor's Commission on Conditions in Harlem, *The Negro in Harlem*, 100–106; "Mayor Orders Investigation of Harlem Riot," *Afro-American*, March 24, 1934; Kessner, *Fiorello H. La Guardia*, 373.
8. Mayor's Commission on Conditions in Harlem, *The Negro in Harlem: A Report on Social and Economic Conditions Responsible for the Outbreak of March 19, 1935*, 1–2, La Guardia Papers, New York City Municipal Reference Library.
9. Arthur Garfield Hays, *City Lawyer: The Autobiography of a Law Practice* (New York: Simon and Schuster, 1942), 281–82.
10. "Police Are Hissed at Harlem Hearing," *NYT*, May 5, 1935.
11. "Hays Chides Police at Harlem Inquiry," *NYT*, May 19, 1935.
12. Mayor's Commission on Conditions in Harlem, *The Negro in Harlem*, 102, 107.
13. Alain Locke, *Harlem: Dark Weather Vane*, La Guardia Papers, New York City Municipal Reference Library.
14. COH.
15. "Holstein Seized in a Police Raid," *NYT*, December 24, 1935.
16. COH.
17. Ibid.
18. US Bureau of the Census, Sixteenth Census, 1940.
19. "Battle to Mark 25 Years as Cop with Youthful Outlook," *AMN*, June 27, 1936.
20. "Negro Celebrates 25 Years on the Force," *NYT*, June 29, 1936.
21. Clay Moyle, *Sam Langford: Boxing's Greatest Uncrowned Champion* (Seattle: Bennett & Hastings, 2006), 372.
22. Ernest Hemingway, "Million Dollar Fight: A New York Letter," *Esquire*, December 1935, 35.
23. Langston Hughes, *I Wonder as I Wander: An Autobiographical Journey* (New York: Hill and Wang, 1956), 315.
24. William J. Baker, *Jesse Owens: An American Life* (New York: Free Press, 1986), 123.

25. Ibid., 127; "Harlemites Hiss Olympic Parade," *CD*, September 12, 1936.

26. "Olympic Stars Get Welcome of City," *NYT*, September 4, 1936.

27. "Sportopics: The Mighty Has Fallen," *AMN*, September 26, 1936.

28. "Prominent in Week's News," *AMN*, January, 29, 1938.

29. "History of Bethune-Cookman University," B-CU website, http://www .bethune.cookman.edu/about_BCU/history/index.html.

30. Blanche Wiesen Cook, *Eleanor Roosevelt, Volume 2: The Defining Years, 1933–1938* (New York: Viking, 1999), 161.

31. COH.

32. Dorothy Height, *Open Wide the Freedom Gates: A Memoir* (New York: Public Affairs, 2003), 82–83.

33. BOH.

34. "Fire Fighters Organize Club in Department," *AMN*, September 20, 1941.

35. "Indicts Man in Holt Slaying," *AMN*, February 24, 1940; "Mayor at Funeral of Slain Policeman," *NYT*, February 17, 1940.

36. Sondra Kathryn Wilson, ed., *In Search of Democracy: The NAACP Writings of James Weldon Johnson, Walter White, and Roy Wilkins (1920–1977)* (Oxford, UK: Oxford University Press, 1999), 172–73.

37. Football Records of the New York Yankees, 1940–1941, http://www .luckyshow.org/football/NYYanks3.htm.

38. "Hundred Guests at Matron's Surprise Celebration," *AMN*, April 1, 1939.

39. "On Parole Board," *NYT*, August 21, 1941.

40. Dominic J. Capeci, *The Harlem Riot of 1943* (Philadelphia: Temple University Press, 1977), 59.

41. Buckley, *American Patriots*, 270.

42. David F. Schmitz, *Henry L. Stimson: The First Wise Man* (Wilmington, DE: SR Books, 2001), 146.

43. Walter White, *A Man Called White: The Autobiography of Walter White* (Atlanta: University of Georgia Press, 1995), 189–92.

44. "A Disgusted Negro Trooper," to *Cleveland Call & Post*, August 16, 1944, in Phillip McGuire, ed., *Taps for a Jim Crow Army: Letters from Black Soldiers in World War II* (Lexington: University Press of Kentucky, 1983), 196.

45. "By Way of Mention," *NYA*, July 24, 1943.

46. "First Lady Praises Mrs. Mary Bethune," *NYT*, May 3, 1943; "Harlem Turned Out Sunday in Honor of Noted Educator and Leader," *AMN*, May 8, 1943; "Mrs. Roosevelt Assails Bigotry in Harlem Talk," *New York Herald Tribune*, May 3, 1943.

47. "Hell Breaks Loose in Eight Cities," *AMN*, June 26, 1943.

48. Capeci, *The Harlem Riot of 1943*, 82.

49. White, *A Man Called White*, 236–38.

50. Ibid., 3–4.

51. "The Reminiscences of David Dressler," 1972, Oral History Collection of Columbia University; "Welfare Island Raid Bares Gangster Rule Over Prison," *NYT*, January 25, 1934; "Affidavits Name Hines Parole Czar," *NYT*, January 31, 1934.

52. "The Reminiscences of David Dressler," 1972, Oral History Collection of Columbia University.

53. "Six Soldiers Reported Killed in Dixie Rioting," *AMN*, January 17, 1942; "Jim Crowed as She Escorts Body of Her Soldier Son," *Cleveland Call & Post*, July 18, 1942; "German Prisoners Ate In Station Dining Room in Texas, While Negro Soldiers Were Forced to Accept 'Kitchen Hand-Outs,' Army Veteran Writes Courier," *Pittsburgh Courier*, April 8, 1944.

54. "By Way of Mention," *NYA*, February 5, 1944.

55. New York City Fire Department Transfer Request, July 25, 1941, WWP; Wesley Williams to Alfred E. Smith, August 18, 1941, WWP; New York City Fire Department Transfer Request, January 10, 1942, WWP.

56. Anonymous to Fiorello La Guardia, August 9, 1944, WWP; Anonymous to Fiorello La Guardia, September 18, 1944, WWP.

57. Wesley Williams and others to Patrick J. Walsh, October 14, 1944, WWP.

58. Wesley Williams and others to Hubert T. Delany, November 16, 1944, WWP.

59. "Fire Commissioner to Investigate Jim Crow Charges of Firemen," *NYA*, December 16, 1944.

60. Wesley Williams to Adam Powell Jr., October 20, 1945, WWP.

61. Kessner, *Fiorello H. La Guardia*, 527.

62. "Casper Holstein Dies, Fabulous Harlem Figure," *New York Herald Tribune*, April 9, 1944; "Former 'Policy King' in Harlem Dies Broke," *NYT*, April 9, 1944; Casper Holstein, "One-Time Numbers King, Dies Broke," *Afro-American* (Baltimore), April 15, 1944.

63. COH.

64. Jim Haskins and N. R. Mitgang, *Mr. Bojangles: The Biography of Bill Robinson* (New York: Welcome Rain Publishers, 2000), 21–24, 296–97.

65. BN.

66. BN.

67. BN.

CHAPTER SIX: FORGOTTEN

1. "New York's First Black Fire Chief Dies at 89," *AMN*, July 7, 1984.

2. "Dr. E. P. Roberts Buried After 58 Years as Medic," *AMN*, January 17, 1953.

3. "War Correspondent Lauds Negro Soldier Fighting in France," *NYA*, November 9, 1918.

4. "Needham Roberts, Who Bagged 24 Germans in the War, Waxes Bitter Over the Way the Whites Have Treated Us," *Pittsburgh Courier*, November 26, 1938; "New Facts Brought to Light in Roberts Double Suicide," *NYA*, April 30, 1949.

5. COH.

6. BN.

7. John H. Johnson, *Fact Not Fiction in Harlem* (Glen Cove, NY: Northern Type Printing, 1980), 96; Charles Cobb, grandson of Moses P. Cobb, interview with author.

INDEX

Abyssinian Baptist Church, 181, 230, 281

Acuna, Chile, 213

Adams, Big Frank, 179

African American Methodist Episcopal (AME) Zion Church ("Freedom Church"): baptism of Carroll at, 107; Anne Battle in, 7; Thomas Battle in, 10; christening of Charline at, 94; dedication of new building for, 193; Jesse Owens at, 250; Reverdy Ransom of, 63–64; Paul Robeson at, 190; thirty-first wedding anniversary at, 246; Alexander Walters of, 41; wedding of Charline at, 227–29

Afro-American Council, 41–42

Afro-American Realty Company, 56

Agard, Harry F., 158–60

Aikens, Thomas, 238

Alabama Dry Dock and Shipbuilding Company, 265

Amalgamated Association of Street and Electric Railway and Motor Coach Employees, 107–8

AME Zion Church. See African American Methodist Episcopal (AME) Zion Church ("Freedom Church")

Amsterdam News (newspaper), 152–53, 183, 193, 196, 199, 212, 238, 246, 250, 266, 273, 286

Anderson, Charles, 72, 74, 75, 177, 181

Andreini, Norman Gelio, 37

Astoria Café, 172

"Atlanta Compromise," 26–27

Avery, Charles, 39, 52, 82

Bacharach Giants, 176

Baer, Max, 247

Baltimore, Charles, 118–19

Baltimore Police Department, 253–54

Battle, Anne Vashti Delamar, 5–7, 12, 15–16, 22–23, 166, 188, 193, 208

Battle, Carroll Henry: birth of, 106–7; education and childhood of, 194, 217; in fire department, 258–59, 285; marriage of, 246; military service by, 264, 271, 272–73, 274, 278–79; retirement of, 286

Battle, Charline Elizabeth. See Cherot, Charline Elizabeth Battle

Battle, Edith, 245, 258

Battle, Florence Carrington: courtship of, 43; at Elks testimonial dinner, 188; fiftieth wedding anniversary of, 285; at Greenwood Forest Farms, 264; as hostess, 212, 217; and Langston Hughes, 135; marriage of, 47–48; surprise birthday party for, 259; thirty-first wedding anniversary of, 246; travels by, 285–86; twenty-eighth wedding anniversary of, 217; twenty-fifth wedding anniversary of, 212

Battle, Florence D'Angeles, 57–58, 94

Battle, James, 13

Battle, Jesse Earl, 51, 57, 194, 211, 271, 286

Battle, John Edward, 6, 24, 233

Battle, Mary Elizabeth. See Oden, Mary Elizabeth Battle

Battle, Nancy, 15, 23, 37

Battle, Samuel: adolescent years, 13–15; arrival in New York, 15–19, 21–23; attempt to entrap, 87; banishment to Canarsie, 177–78, 182–84; birthday parties, 207, 212; and black regiment in World War I, 109–11, 121, 127, 128; childhood of, 7–9; completion of book by, 284–85; courting by, 42–43; death of, 290; death threats to, 87; dream of New York, 4–5; early years as police officer, 88–89, 91–94; and Equity Congress, 89–91, 109–10; fighting by, 5, 8–9; as Harlem police officer, 95–97; as houseboy, 37; and Langston Hughes, 2–4; and integration of New York Fire Department,